T0365935

FREEDOM
FROM THE
ROMAN CATHOLIC
CHURCH

FREEDOM

FROM THE

ROMAN CATHOLIC

CHURCH

MICHAEL JENISON

ARCHWAY
PUBLISHING

Archway Publishing books may be ordered through booksellers or by contacting:

Archway Publishing
1663 Liberty Drive
Bloomington, IN 47403
www.archwaypublishing.com
844-669-3957

Scripture are taken from the Holy Bible, King James Version (Authorized Version). First published in 1611. Quoted from the KJV Classic Reference Bible, Copyright © 1983 by The Zondervan Corporation.

ISBN: 978-1-6657-4271-9 (sc)
ISBN: 978-1-6657-4272-6 (e)

Library of Congress Control Number: 2023907407

Print information available on the last page.

Archway Publishing rev. date: 05/04/2023

CONTENTS

FROM THE AUTHOR WITH LOVE

I have traveled the world in search of answers. The Bible ruined me at a young age because I took it literally. I believed I would be punished for lust and sex. With this book guilt will be removed for premarital sex, masturbation, and lust. Our bodies don't lie to us and the whole world is horny but the whole world believes the Bible is against sex. The polytheistic religions have important gods in our bodies and in the stars. There is a greater connection to God through polytheism than Christianity.

The lies of the Bible we will escape with this book. I have crafted it in love and want to be loved for bringing this sexual freedom to my country and the world. Traveling the world gave me the chance to see the faces of those poisoned by the anti-sex doctrines of the church. We could be restored to God, and we could have integrity to tell the truth. Believing pre-marital sex is a sin has messed up the whole world.

Being born into a lie and dying in that lie is too much for me. The absolute block on physical love causes us to make love like hypocrites and lead a dry life. If America were lubricated with the philosophies of the Gnostic Jesus, we would be better. They celebrated with a love feast and now we cannot have pre-marital sex.

The Bible does not say the things we think it does. It is hard for people to read the Bible and keep it in context. I suggest the Bible is the words of man not God. There are too many mistakes and the violence, racism, and hatred toward women is all in there. The Bible curses us when we believe the curse. If it weren't for Adam, we would not have Jesus or need for him.

What we understand about the Bible now is minimal. We just know its stories. Once we compare monotheism with polytheism, we see the whole picture. In America we are too narrow in our beliefs and compared to my friends in Europe we lack curiosity. The fact that we are all prisoners to our own bodies doesn't occur to us. We think pre-marital sex is a sin and we do it anyway.

The whole world is crooked before God thanks to Christianity. This book deals with the forbidden books. The pagan temples and gothic cathedrals of Europe make sense and tie the whole story together. If nobody lied to us about sex, we would still be in the garden. People would have sex again. Fertility gods and the Gnostic orgy shows us how far we have fallen from grace.

We believe Jesus said to look and lust is adultery, and the Roman Catholic Church has enforced its anti-sex beliefs on us. Now with this book we can be free of the edited Bible. What did God really say about sex? And how did they change the Bible to hide Baal? All these things and more await you my dear reader. We have an everlasting freedom once we come to grip with all these Bible lies that make us think God is mad at sex.

The church has used the punishment for sex for evil. Women are subjected to slavery and a double standard. Once we know the difference between what we believe the Bible says and what it does say we are free. Know the whole story before you judge yourself and others.

We sit in America waiting for the return of Jesus who we assume will be mad at us for having pre-marital sex. We put hookers in jail, and we believe he was married to one. We teach God killed Onan for masturbating and lust is adultery. Most Americans are hypocrites when it comes to Christianity. In Italy people understand me better since they have so much Bible art.

The idea of art being an idol is a poison the church uses to kill the gods. You say the god was pagan or an idol and the superstitions of Jehovah take over. Since we have believed we were free from the ten commandments for 2,000 years and still enforce them on people creates this evil, punitive, criminal God we believe from our Bible stories. We do not know the Torah has 613 commandments and we figuratively say Christ died in vain to put us under the law again. The first commandment is no god before me and the second is no idols. This defines the God we know, and he is jealous and angry for us worshiping idols.

If we read the myth of the idols that would be one thing, but we judge on appearance only. We have only a superficial understanding. The gods and goddesses that wait behind the Bible for us are the idols. The Bible is just a bunch of sexist and racist stories to make us all white men. The Egyptian is a problem since Jehovah kills them at the Red Sea. We lose all the wisdom, and the gods the Bible was based on. We think it is enough to just read the Bible to know who Jesus is.

From the orgy to the orgasm, I am on top of the world with the keys to freedom. The trick is that the Bible is edited for sex, and I studied this in Europe and America until I figured out that the Bible is changed to cover sex. Therefore, there could be an adult Bible that is not as finicky about sex. We carry the burden of Jesus and the upside down cross. The symbols to the Bible are obliterated and we assume it is enough to read the story and keep the commandments.

Now more than ever we need a spiritual overhaul. The 2,000-year-old religion banned sex and now we have an escape. Go back to Gnosis and polytheism and our true history will expose the many lies and deceptions of the Bible we think God wrote. A book plagiarized and re written hundreds of times is no longer true. Time has run out with 2012 A.D., and we are done with the book of Revelations. It won't repeat anymore.

Many gnostic and polytheistic people hold the answers to interesting history. We have it now at the tip of our fingers. The freedom to have sex and masturbate without guilt from God. These false teachings of the church are enforced even in our culture and America must appear as the world's biggest hypocrite. This judgment from Revelations puts us in a hell we cannot escape but it is also a hell on earth. We are not having sex often, yet the Virgin Mary made love at fourteen. We teach she was a virgin, and you need to be a virgin to please the Demon Jesus in the Bible. He kills people for masturbating and puts them in hell for lying about it according to the altered Bible.

Since we know these things are not true, we must consider the advancements we have made since Jesus. We have Old Testament parallels, alphabets, temples, pyramids, and ancient literature to bring the Bible up to date.

I have been to pilgrimages around the world, and I feel I have a special relationship to the Virgin Mary since I went to Tepeyac in 2002 and wrote my book about her Nine Days to Healing a Spiritual Pilgrimage. These Mary's speak at their places of pilgrimage and the stories are incredible. I toured eleven countries in Europe for eleven months: fifty-four cities in 2000. I published The Lords of the Poison in 2007 with the photographs of the Atlantis that Plato wrote about, and I reveal astonishing things that this book covers as well.

I want us to know God in America but not the God of the altered Bible. We wonder why we have so many problems with racism when God in the Bible is a racist and a murderer. The lies are right in the names of the Patriarchs: Abraham, Isaac, and Jacob (Father, Laughter, Heel Catcher). Jacob is a deceiver and there is a pattern the Bible uses to cover up its own lies. It surely is the hand of men, and it always has the best interest of the white male in mind but not the woman.

This book deals with racism and even slavery. We are prisoners of Noah's ark but can we take it back further to see that no ark story in the world contains slavery (Ham) but the Bible does. Religion is so superficial, and people are so misled that we enter life and exit life believing a lie. They thought they could motivate us to good behavior and the mission failed.

Now with this jumbled up book of lies we settle for less. The history, gods, literature, and faith of the Native American is lost to Christ. He holds the idols that makes all gods idols. With polytheism we kill the devil and bring back the gods. It is fun to connect the gods of different cultures and see what they have in common. We find out God is older than the Bible, but we take the Bible too literally and don't advance ourselves with its symbolism. This causes the basic story that Americans know: Adam and Eve, the ten commandments, and the cross.

They give you the medicine when you are not sick. It is all for money and the Roman Catholic Church does many things Jesus said not to do. It is as if we have never studied Jesus in America and we rely on the simple three step story. The ignorance of Elijah, Jewish books like the Talmud, Zohar, Qabalah, and the Apocrypha mess up our understanding. They took the good books out of the Bible, but some people still use them.

CHAPTER 1

MASTURBATION

S elf-love or gratification is prohibited!
In 1994 I studied Sexual Variations in college. There were over 700 students in the class and four teachers who pass the microphone around to discuss the topic of the day. We sit around and watch porno. There was a day for everything, and they were interesting. The best was Masturbation Day.

One of the teachers, the tall one, walked with the microphone to the stage in front of the big class. A bunch of students chanted: "King...." And they call him the "king of masturbation" one student yelled out "The god of masturbation!"

The teacher took the stage while the class chanted. He explained the 60's to us and the length parents would go to stop their children from masturbating. American companies sold masturbation detectors and gloves for the girls. They took children to the insane asylum to let them see crazy people in cages masturbating. They told them they went crazy and blind from masturbating.

When the King said the myth about hair growing on your hands everybody including the women looked at their hands. American Ivy League doctors in the 60's believed masturbation caused blindness and hair on the hands.

The main story I got out of this class was the story of the masturbator in the Bible. Onan and Er were illegitimate children of Judah and the Canaanite Shua. Er marries Tamar in the Bible (Genesis

38:6), Er did evil in the eyes of the Lord and the Lord killed him. According to law Onan must impregnate Tamar. "And Onan knew that the seed should not be his; and it came to pass, when he went into his brother's wife, that he spilled it on the ground, lest that he should give seed to his brother. And the thing which he did was evil in the eyes of the Lord: wherefore he slew him also (Genesis 38:9-10)."

The teacher said there is an error in the Bible and explained how the church changed certain words to have sex evil. Notice in Genesis how Judah and others have sex with women before they marry them (Genesis 34:2) and Jehovah did not kill them. Are we supposed to believe that God whacks you for whacking off? Onan knew the inheritance would not be his, so he pulled out of Tamar. This stealing is the bad part, and we don't even know why Er was killed. Do we believe God did not kill persons for all these sexual sins? And then supposedly strikes down poor Onan for jacking off. HIs hand was not involved, and he only pulled out. Now in the dictionary is the word onanism or masturbation.

I would prefer God kill thieves that try and steal my inheritance instead of a bunch of masturbators. Our freedom from the Roman Catholic Church starts with Onan. A lie that tells us we sin against our own bodies by having sex with ourselves. This guilt and shame go back to the church, but the procreation only theory is Egyptian. That is why we believe sex is for making babies only.

Descended angels, and gods, become "fallen angels" with the story of The Sons of the Gods (Elohim) looking at the daughters of men and having sex with them. This may have produced the heroes and giants that roamed the pages of the Philistine encounter with Samson who had his eyes put out like the sacrifice of Jesus for the fallen angels.

Everything in the Bible makes a circle on the map but if you read it straight through it gives one the impression that Jehovah takes arrogance in bombing Sodom and Gomorra., He killed all but Noah with wife, his three kids and their wives that supposedly repopulated the world. The anger in the book of Genesis starts in the garden where Adam and Eve are naked. This gives you the impression the serpent is almost phallic and the tree in the middle of the garden is symbolic. There are so many holy trees, trees of life, and other symbols in the pagan religions. We have the only Bible that is good according to us Christians. The pastor of a Christian church does not study the other monotheistic cultures and claims Pagans and Gentiles are bad or worth less in the eyes of Jehovah.

The masturbation thing goes on forever if we do not get illuminated. In the chapter before Onan *She chem* has sex with Dinah, Jacob's daughter. Jehovah does not kill him or punish him:

"And when *She chem,* the son of Amor the Hivite, prince of the country saw her, he took her, and lay with her, and defiled her.

And his soul clung unto Dinah, the daughter of Jacob, and he loved the damsel, and spoke kindly unto the damsel.

And *She chem* spoke unto his father, Hamor, saying, "Get me this damsel for my wife. (Genesis 34:2-4)."

Her brothers freak out, but Jacob plays dirty tricks on them. All the lying, stealing, and evil can be done without punishment when Jacob and Moses are killing and denying the existence of the Elohim (gods) to promote selfish arrogant Jehovah. Then we believe Onan and Er are doing evil in the eyes of the Lord. Check the dictionary for onanism and remember there is an "error" in the Bible. The lie is of the Roman Catholic Church who edited the Bible for piety and like to call the Bible the Word of God.

If this, lie of spilling the seed on the ground to steal the inheritance from his brother is a measure of the hate that our father has for us; I must ask what the devil does? What if your own earthly father killed you for masturbating? Now think of God angry at you. *She chem* found love with Dinah the Heel Catchers daughter. Since they are making a baby supposedly it is, okay?

It is hard to believe Onan dies for spilling his seed and Er for no reason. All the evil that has happened in the Torah up to this point is okay, but God intervenes personally to kill Onan and Er. The Catholic Church has changed words to give them a different meaning. They have always been against sex but to tell somebody they will die for masturbation and go to hell for pre-marital sex is evil. Elohim is good but Jehovah is the servant of Moses. Jehovah kills everybody that gets in his way, and we say Jesus is his only begotten son.

The eventual killing of someone who sinned is one thing. God executing Onan and Er personally seems very mean. The Bible is evil against the Harlot, and we lose the basic love teachings of Jesus. The very fact that we say Jacob is good after what he has done is amazing. The prostitute took money or a goat for sex. In America, we say it is okay to have sex with someone you are not married to as long as it is free. No money exchanged between consenting adults.

It seems the only moral of the Bible Americans relate to is sex. They lie and steal all the time and do horrible things. If sex is an issue everybody acts like it is the main thing. A man gets busted for a blow job and it stops America from doing any other business. If we went after liars and thieves in America, we would be busy all day, but a minor sexual item comes to make us jealous, and we respond with the death penalty for jacking off.

CHAPTER 2

FORNICATION

The word fornication means 'idolatry' in the Bible, and we use it to mean "pre-marital sex." Here is an example of Dinah, Jacob's daughter having premarital sex.

"And Dinah, the daughter of Leah, whom she bore unto Jacob, went out to see the daughters of the land.

And when *She chem*, the son of Hamor the Hivite, prince of the country, saw her, he took her, and lay with her, and defiled her.

And his soul clung unto Dinah, the daughter of Jacob, and he loved the damsel, and spoke kindly unto the damsel.

And *She chem* spoke unto his father, Hamor, saying, Get me this damsel for my wife."

(Genesis 34:1-4)

Jacob approves if the son of prince Hamor the Hivite will become circumcised:

"And they said unto them, we cannot do this thing, to give our sister to one that is uncircumcised; for that were a reproach unto us:

But in this we will consent unto you: if you be as we be, that every male of you be circumcised:

Then we will give our daughters unto you, and we will take your daughters to us, and we will dwell with you, and we will become one people.

But if ye will not hearken unto us, to be circumcised; then will we take our daughter and we will be gone (Genesis 34:14-17)."

Prince Hamor and his son were pleased with this since *She chem* loved Dinah. *She chem* was considered the most honorable in his house. His pre-marital sex with Dinah ended in marriage while today we believe fornicators burn in hell. How strict we are compared to Moses. In only four chapters of Genesis, we arrive at the story of Onan and Er. They are killed by the Lord not by man. Usually, man kills man but for Israel Jehovah is against all their enemies. We imagine the Jewish Patriarchs to be in the New Jerusalem waiting for us.

Jehovah kills masturbators personally is not true. Onan was breaking the husband law to impregnate Tamar; Er's wife. Since he pulled out and spilled on the ground, he is not using his hand. He was having sex and pulled out, but the Roman Catholic Church has put an error in the Bible just as they changed descending angels into fallen ones. For what sin? Lust with the eyes! Thank you, Samson our Savior and Jesus, to the Giants. People missed this one and I got it right away (see Judges 13-16).

Another change is in the book of Job. The Bohemoth or Hippo has a dick like a long cedar tree (40:17). It was changed to his tail is like cedar. This changing of the Bible does not seem to bother anyone. All religions are false except for Christianity, and we are to abstain from Idols. This makes all false but Christianity and even though we are not under the law, Christian's judge by it and they do not know it very well.

My mission statement could be: Unveil the Elohim and not just the Jewish ones. Lilith is okay but Ishtar is bad? The Bible demolishes the goddess. The rib, Jezebel in the dung, and the wicked woman in the box going to Babylon in a Pagan Polytheistic spaceship or something, the woman is transformed in the Bible. She comes from a rib not a glorious vagina. This is so obvious that a man is controlling a woman, yet we ascribe it to the Father, Son, and Holy Spirit.

The whole Bible is fucked up and the Gnostic truth is you are born with Jesus. He is inside of you already but since America is not knowledgeable about Gnosis, we suffer every day. The original disciples had a Love Feast - Orgy! Now we believe God punishes masturbation with the death penalty and we lie about the interpretation of the word fornication. It never meant pre-marital sex.

If whores like Tamar are to be burned alive for playing the Harlot and Jezebel is thrown into the dung, why don't we do a museum for the Bible women who sacrificed their lives. The prophet Elijah ran from Jezebel, but Jehu had her killed.

Since the Bible doesn't tell us her face was like porcelain and she was beautiful we imagine Jezebel to be a monster. She has had sex for money, and she is Queen of Israel. This is hard to believe a queen would take money for sex. The Phoenician woman is unique to all women of the world! I understand they are the only culture that did not look down on taking money for sex. The word "only" is quite powerful when you think of all the cultures of the world. One after another poor food whore is doing it for free. Add money to that sex we take you to jail for fornication. America has tons of money to entrap John's with hot low priced cop hookers. Who could resist $40 but now $100,000 or more for a year in jail. They make it to where you can't get a job since one must register as a sex offender.

This severe punishment comes from a Christian country that taught me in church pre-marital sex was a sin. A sin called 'fornication' which puts you in hell is forgiven if it is free. America says get it free and we won't put you in jail. Even though you may burn in hell. If you pay for it that blow job may cost, you time in jail.

One would hope that I am right about pre-marital sex and masturbation or else we are in trouble. Jehovah killed Onan for spilling his seed. We interpret the severe death penalty for spilling seed and thanks to the Roman Catholic Church masturbation. Men in the Bible have many wives and in order to not "defile" a woman they stay at home. Men can do it and women cannot. God has no wife they say. Or is it us the bride of Christ waiting like virgins for their husbands.

Knowing this story of Onan set me free from The Roman Catholic Churches lies about sex. There is an error in the Bible called Onan and Er. That is too severe a punishment. If your earthly father reads the Bible and punishes you for masturbation how horrible would that be.

Parents trying to prevent their children from jacking off. They will go to any extreme since we believe lies about the Bible and therefore God.

This fake Jesus that we worship is no different than the pagan gods that preceded him. Dionysus, Krishna, and others come out when the "Three Wise Men (The belt of Orion)" lines up with Sirius on Christmas. Happy Easter could be happy Ishtar (Babylon). All the constellations we need to know about are in the book of Job. Orion is the Duat (home of the gods to the Egyptians) and is involved with the Scorpio (Israel).

The idea of God not having a wife and being very angry is seen in the book of Genesis. The expulsion from the garden shows Jehovah is a harsh Lord. Then the flood, Sodom, and the enemies of Israel feel the wrath of Jehovah. The Catholic Church has changed his teachings while the Gnostics respect the Jewish Law. In America it seems we just sin and say sorry. There is no law it is all based on belief.

The word fornication is not one of the ten commandments. There are 613 commandments in the Torah, but we have heard of ten. Not once in the Torah does it say thou shalt not fornicate. The rest of the Old Testament Jehovah says Israel is fornicating when they worship other gods or idols. Can you have premarital sex with an idol? No, you can't so it does not mean pre-marital sex and here we are 2000 years after Jesus asking ourselves if we will go to heaven.

In the Gospels Jesus deals with the prostitutes and adulteresses. He says for him without sin to cast the first stone and forgives them. He also according to legend was married to a prostitute. In America for it to be legal it would have to be a porn star. They have pre-marital sex for money. What about Henry the fifty-year-old Christian virgin waiting for his wife? He is suffering for Jesus, but Jesus did not say sex was bad. Then the Torah does not say fornication or pre-marital sex. St. Paul is a celibate and so are we until we get married. The Greeks said: St Paul is Jupiter and Barnabas is Mercury. Jesus is the bright morning star Venus or the feathery serpent Quetzalcoatl.

The Virgin Mary is a virgin, note the virgin in her name, so she cannot have sex with the gods.

Virgo has Bethlehem in the stars and the Sun God was Jesus. They have us blocked every day. Ra the Sun God kills the Serpent daily. How many days have these serpents added up in Christianity. They scare you with sex, and hell and you obey and support them. They don't contribute much with their puny book of miracles.

Every American woman who enters a church will be taught the Bible says pre-marital sex is a sin. The sin that keeps you from heaven and from God. There is a separation between lust and you. We will always be guilty of lust unless we poke our eyes out.

Imagine if we did not believe this teaching for all these years. We would have incredible art and people would not drink the sexual poison of the church. Now we are fallen from grace. We look to Moses but not to Jesus. We think Moses said the word fornication and we are wrong about so many things.

The Gnostics had a love feast or orgy and Irenaeus the church father called them Satanists for the orgy. Later Alchemy grew out of Gnosticism and what we believe as history is the myth of Jesus the Gnostic Solar God who went around with the planets like Jesus goes around with his disciples. The orgy was obviously pre-marital sex, but it is not God but man teachings that Satanists have orgies.

Imagine what the orgy would have been like. The Gnostic Gospels of Jesus and his smiling artwork that shows the joy of liberation from the cross. We don't smile anymore but we gave the orgy of Jesus to Satan. The wife of Jesus goes to jail and the porn star makes another movie. The legalization of prostitution would help us make up for lost time. The church having all this control over us and the government to giving us a free will. The American women are ruined but other countries have prostitutes.

With a prostitute everything is possible, and you don't have to tell anybody. All these clergy that fucks the children would have a choice. They most likely have a frigid cold wife that is afraid to look or lust. With a beautiful whore we could lure the child molesters away from our children. After bars is when we would go to a whorehouse. Everybody has a job and men can do it to. Ugly men can go with beautiful women.

"Know ye not that the unrighteous shall not inherit the kingdom of God? Be not deceived: neither fornicators, nor idolaters, nor adulterers, nor effeminate, nor abusers of themselves with mankind,

Nor thieves, nor covetous, nor drunkards, nor revilers, nor extortioners, shall inherit the kingdom of God (1 Corinthians 6:9-10)."

These scriptures create for the Christian a new law of Moses. We are not under the law of Moses anymore but the law of celibate Paul. Anything on the list almost sounds to the modern mind like the sex, drugs, and rock and roll are the sins. What about being "effeminate" is bad to the modern mind? This and the rest of the Bible is one big law. St. Paul even tells people he is celibate, but they don't have to be. I love this freedom and understanding from St. Paul himself. He says it is better to marry than to burn but if people embraced celibacy, it was a beautiful thing.

He serves God like a wife and has time to complete his mission as the Jupiter of the New Testament. He laid down the laws as articulate as possible, but we are still fallen from grace and ignorant of the pagan and polytheistic saviors that came to this planet. The sexy man in the Bible is Noah in Genesis chapter nine. He is drunk, nude, and angry at Ham (Africa) for looking at him nude. Probably more happened and some say the story of Ham and Noah is the story of Seth and Horus. Some say Ham emasculated Noah and even sodomized him.

If looking is all that happened that would be the worst. Consider Noah's sin:

"And Noah began to be a farmer; and he planted a vineyard.

And he drunk of the wine and became drunk; and he was uncovered within his tent.

And Ham, the father of Canaan, saw the nakedness of his father and told his two brothers outside.

And Shem and Japheth took a garment, and laid it upon both their shoulders, and went backward, and covered the nakedness of their father; and their faces were backward, and they saw not their father's nakedness.

And Noah awoke from his wine and knew what his younger son had done unto him.

And he said, cursed be Canaan; a servant of servants shall he be unto his brethren.

And he said, Blessed be the Lord God of Shem; and Canaan shall be his servant.

(Genesis 9:20-27)."

I have struggled with these verses since I was fifteen years old. I was a teenage black belt and got saved. I studied the Bible everyday with my karate discipline. I got saved at fifteen and went to the church. They taught us the usual. Premarital sex was a sin, no masturbation, and no lustful behavior. When I would go to the library to figure out all the lies, they were telling me it was too late. I was hooked and on a mission.

Every country I travel to has a good bookstore. I check those verses I call the Noah Nine. I also check to see if they say Rome is the Babylon of the church. The story of Noah is horrible if the son of Africa is cursed into playing this role in our history. Hamites fuck their fathers and cut off their dicks! The father turns a continent into a slave, and we still believe in Noah to this day.

Since it does not say Ham butt fucked Noah, we take it as it is written. Jehovah is already so mad he is destroying his creations. Just like Abraham's father Terah and the idols. Let's say Noah is only mad because of "looking" and they had some shame about parental nudity. This anger is in the words: "Cursed be Canaan." A land they wanted to conquer anyway. The next book is Exodus but Moses, the author of the Torah according to Jesus, is a slave of the slaves. HIs story of Joseph is like Jesus and the Exodus is a lot a wizardry.

CHAPTER 3

SEX AND THE LAW

T he volcano on Santorini blew in 1500 B.C and caused the flood the
Bible speaks about and the plagues of the Nile (see my spiritual
travel book The Lords of the Poison on Lulu). This starts the false
Bible that is a hybrid of other sources. Cave walls, tablets, and now
books record the gods of Sumerian, Babylonian, Phoenician, Greek,
and Romans. They connect through Venus and Venus is clogged up
by men. Jesus cannot seem to come together with Mary Magdalene
as husband and wife. We would use it as the wisdom that shows us
the true picture.

"But I say unto you that whosever looks on a woman to lust after
her hath committed adultery with her already in his heart (Matthew
5:28)."

This verse needs to be interpreted in context; but the idea of lust
being as bad as adultery is not true. A look verses the action. What
is worse? What if the Pharisees judged Jesus for hanging out with
prostitutes? Jesus may have said of the Pharisees "If you look at a
woman, they think you are sleeping with them." This internal law
of Spirit is what wars against the flesh. Interesting the Bible always
talks about adultery and spiritual adultery but not rape. Not much
protection for children or women but the woman as a possession is
supposed to be the rib virgin.

Now women have more freedom but what stops us from getting
laid is the belief that fornication is pre-marital sex. They are calling

adulterers whores but never does the Bible spell it out. Pre-marital sex is a sin that fucks all of us up. We are not getting married as young as the Virgin Mary.

Now people are missing experiences and waiting for the right one. I would like to explore as many women as I can before I die. Many men are like me but with prostitution illegal we must get it for free or go to jail. American women want dinner before sex and feel entitled to it. The prostitute is a temporary marriage since money was involved.

Look at how complicated things are for us in America. You start off being taught the three big lies of the Roman Catholic Church: 1. Masturbation is a sin 2. Pre-marital sex is fornication 3. To look and lust is the same as adultery. These three keep us in line and in the margins of the Bible are our sexual body parts. The Hippo lays in slumber waiting for his tail and penis to be switched back. Moses has a foot for a phallus and a phallus for a foot. Abraham touches your thighs, but it is really your balls. The Queen of Sheba has wine in her vulva but that was changed to navel.

The Egyptian Book of the Dead taught me about the forty-two gods in the body. The phallus is Osiris, the neck in Isis, the feet are the feet of Ptah, the chest is the Mighty One of Terror, and the buttocks are the guardians to the eye of Horus. These are the ones I remember, and the number forty-two comes up in sacred literature.

I studied Egypt, Babylon, and Sumerians and found out how powerful the gods are. Also in Babylon, Ishtar "Parts her hair and the waters recede after the flood. The gods cried and looked like bloated fish." The gods felt bad for humanity, and it is Phoenician Baal who sits on the Flood Dragon. Science says Santorini's Volcano caused the flood that the Bible speaks of. This explosion also caused the plagues of the Nile we attribute to Moses.

Moses is not the problem if you follow the law. The stories are bad, and he created a criminal and punitive God that supports the sins of Abraham, Isaac, and Jacob (heel catcher or deceiver). I would not be killing masturbators in the book of Genesis. Noah is a children's story believed by adults. Ham is Africa and the Bible tries to disguise the sons of Ham...Egypt, Ethiopia, Libya and the whole hot continent is in slavery. Guess what? Noah is not the true builder of the ark. King Zuisudra the Sumerian built it, and many countries have the flood story but only one includes Ham as slave.

How does Jesus treat the Canaanite girl? In Greek she is called puppy and in English dog. The crumbs under the table come from ancient racism. People who could not get along went to war. The day Horus and the night Setesh war daily and Ra kills the serpent daily. The constellations have stopped telling their stories. Gods are forbidden and the father of Jesus leads the Elohim. People think Jesus wrote the Old Testament. Moses, Elijah, and Jesus are the transfiguration our Lord showed St. Peter.

Look at what Jesus shows St. John (The Disciple Jesus Loved); the truth it is revealed in a parable. The two of them sit at the river and Jesus says I will appear to you across the river. John sees a little girl across the river and says: "Lord are you by the little girl?" Jesus says to the beloved disciple: **"I am in the little girl."**

We were already saved, and Jesus is already in us. All matter is evil, and the smiling Jesus is the symbol of his joy leaving the material world. I have never seen a smiling Jesus in all my travels.

The flood stories go back to **Gilgamesh.** The world's first poetry is Sumerian; 1500 years older than Homer is Gilgamesh and Enkidu in the **Enuma Elish**. I think Esau is a copy of Enkidu and the Bible has many thresholds were history and myth come together. Outside the Bible are constellations, legends, gods, serpents, and everything we need to make a myth about **Gnostic Solar Jesus.** Get rid of the fake history we believe in today.

Sexually the church has power over the entire world. My world was messed up as well seeing I have refused to settle down with many women. I have been a slut and a player, and I loved it more than marriage. In America this is taken away from me. Europe is sex all the time and the people are more mature. In America it is very hard for me knowing I could go to jail for having pre-marital sex with a hooker. I go to hell for fornicating according to the Bible babes. And finally, if I jack off Jehovah might kill me. Our expectation should be that American men are horny but too cheap to pay a prostitute.

Jail, hell, disease, unwanted pregnancy, and emotional turmoil are all a part of the sex package in America. The president that makes prostitution legal can say he gave every American a job. Why does the blow job go for free when someone will pay you? Look at Tijuana, Prague, Budapest, Barcelona, Lisbon, Amsterdam, Antwerp, Brussels, and all over Germany for safe prostitution. When are we going to be treated like adults in America? Do you see problems in those countries? They don't have fighting time only fucking time.

Here is me in Christian America with adults that think Noah is true. They don't mind the slavery on the son of Africa. The sin of Noah is he was nude and drunk when his son saw him and got cursed with the old slavery bull shit. Anybody can figure out this story that they want the Canaanites to be slaves. Zuisudra or Unatapsin is the real story, and it has no child father nudity. This is sick and disgusting, and flood stories are a dime a dozen. Many cultures have them, but the Bible does not go to Egypt anymore. They stole the moon in the round house of Joseph and more need be written. Joseph was like Jesus in many ways, and some say Bob Marley was Joseph.

CHAPTER 4

PAGAN SAVIORS

The only good sexual book in the Bible is the Song of Songs.
Jesus and Mary Magdalene should have a similar book. Heaven
touches Earth in the Song of Songs. She is black and he is white. He is
the wisest man in the world with 700 wives. Do you think Solomon
had pre-marital sex? He is not shown much in the art of Italy. His
father made war against giants and Solomon inherited the spiritual
Salem of Melchizedek peacefully. People do not understand the books
of Solomon: Job, Ecclesiastes, Proverbs, and the Song of Songs also
known as the Song of Solomon. It is used at Lebanese weddings and
the character of Solomon is rare in America.

Proverbs five teaches against adultery yet nobody reads it.
Thou shalt not murder also has a warning and reasons to respect
the 613 commandments. If we were not under the sexual curse of
the Roman Catholic Church, we would see fertility gods appear
everywhere. All through history they come and save us from one
thing or another.

The pagan saviors come at Christmas through virgin birth and
the belt of Orion. It becomes the three wise men in the Bible and lines
up with Sirius. Jesus imitates the sun on his journey, but the sun (Ra)
already had a son Osiris. Ra stays in the constellation of the Southern
Cross for three days. It is as if he resurrects and I have seen the story
of Jesus in the constellations and the hybrid Bible.

It tells you to know God one way and one way only. All non-Jewish gods are false, and all religions are false but Christianity. Since Jesus is already inside of us why all this trouble with the law and the angry God that enforces it. Death penalty to everyone and Jesus means "Jehovah Saves" and Christ means "Anointed." If he was El Jesus or Elohim Jesus or even Jehovah Jesus it would not sound like Jesus Christ is the only God in the universe. The excuse for all others being fake or polytheistic or pagan makes one think **the King of Constantine was Mars** and we still do not line up the planets or let Venus save history.

Baal means 'Master" and he is the son of El who resides in the pantheon with Anat, Kothar (creator of the gods), Yom (the serpent that swallows Baal), Pidray (the dew), Mot (the moon and god of infertility) and Lotan (Leviathan). Baal resurrects like Jesus, Horus, and Osiris and all the pagan saviors that follow the three wise men and the star Sirius. We find the dust was the home of the gods all along. The scorpion Jacob Israel struck the ankle and now we find Abraham, Isaac, and Jacob (heel catcher deceiver) in Lecce. Achilles and the other polytheist who have climbed ladders to see Bethlehem in Virgo (The Virgin) are there.

The constellations on the *Tilma* of **Guadalupe** tell the whole story and places Revelations 12 at 1531 A.D. December 9 at 10:20am in the morning. Juan Diego would be the child of revelation 12 but the Bible scholars have not found a sign of life in our land. It is all in Israel and Rome is still considered Babylon, yet they don't know Gilgamesh 2/3 god and 1/3 man or Hercules 1/2 god and 1/2 man. We have divinity in us, and Jesus doesn't enter us he is in us. The Gnostic Gospels are not read in church, and they have the puny gospels and the Old Testament they like to lie about. We are from Adam, and he is so far-fetched I cannot believe his myth became history along with the others like it. Myth has become history and as an adult I see the Bible differently.

I see heaven and hell. Jesus saves us from hell, so I believe in him. The youth pastor said God wanted me to be "On fire for the Lord Jesus Christ." Next thing I know I quit karate for church and my grades went down. They would make promises in the name of God. We will have nice cars and beautiful wives. Experience taught me these things are not so. I should have pursued a career instead of writing about my experiences with God.

CHAPTER 5

SEXUAL FREEDOM

The virginity and the guilt and shame over sex messes with me to this day. Don't others want to feel the freedom I found when I understood Onan and Er. God can't be mad at me, and I picture Zeus throwing a lightning bolt at a masturbator. We would all be dead, and none have died of it since Onan. The problem is this, our Christian Culture has put a wedge between all that breathes and God. God is against sex and Jesus is to. This is what we think yet we still have sex. This is a limping relationship that involves saying you are sorry after sex. **With this sex book the whole world is free from the curses of the Bible.**

The evolution of pure ideas and anti sex logic is based on ignorance. This was not a way to displease or please the Elohim. Egypt had a procreation only theory that the Christians adopted. Babies only, no pleasure is the measure we must go against. What would it be like if everyone received this teaching and learned the errors in the Bible are sexist?

We would reunite with God, and we would not be hypocrites, saying pre-marital sex is wrong and then doing it anyway. Is pre-marital sex ever punished on television? Children all over the world are exposed to an ugly message. God is a joke, and we don't fear hell. Then again are all these people on television going to hell? Your favorite actor was not a virgin in real life before he was married but we expect him to be.

This keeps us guilty all the time. If we lust, we sin and if one of the two is a virgin one sinned. They used to have sex at a young age when you would be virgin anyway. This pressure is on us, and the missed orgy of the Gnostic Jesus is such a secret tucked away in the past. It makes one think pre-marital sex is not a sin when one thinks of the original disciples worshiping Jesus as a Hot Solar Deity at the Love Feast.

Now we cannot even masturbate in private, or Jehovah might intervene. The words of the Torah are twisted by the Roman Catholic Church.

The church will probably never paint the Gnostic Orgy. What was it like to worship Jesus as a solar deity connected to the constellations? Yet the Gnostic Gospels are not a part of the canon since they make Jesus look like a man. At first, he was a man and then Constantine changed him. We are the victims waiting for an update and now I am here to give it to you.

We think ill of God and believe Jesus was against sex. We should be reading the Qabalah, Talmud, and the Zohar to understand the Old Testament, not a Bible Commentary only. Stories from the Torah debated by two Rabbis is helpful. What happened to the Jew, Irenaeus? He is Satan as well but this time there is no orgy. The church uses the word Satan (Adversary) rather loosely.

Ra kills the serpent every day when the Sun rises. Horus harpoons Seth and the night goes away. All these dead serpents, 365 a year, are adding up. We don't celebrate the Sun yet because the cross doesn't have a circle around it. Put Jesus in the Roundhouse of Joseph and look at the similarities. The book of Genesis is the beginning and the end. The brothers bow to him, and he goes into a pit and rises. Pharaoh would be like God and Joseph his son. Next book in the Bible, Exodus, curses the Nile. We all go along with Noah and Moses because they are white and represent slavery which Christians embrace. Everybody wants Moses so they can be part of the book.

CHAPTER 6

BAAL AND THE WORD

I am a polytheist and I believe in Baal and his pantheon. It is important to understand Baal. Jehu, Elijah and Jezebel are new to those who say Baal (and others) is the devil. Baal is like a pure god without the law and the lies. Just back up from Abraham, Isaac, and Jacob and the pure god El and his son Baal are the father son combination seen in the story of Saul trying to pin David to a wall with a spear. The spear missed him but in Baal's myth it says: "El, laughing in his heart and chuckling in his liver picked up a spear and chased Baal out of the cave. Every time he hit Baal; Baal became immortal."

Also see Mt. Zaphon where the twin rivers meet. El is surrounded by his pantheon and Baal prays for his friend on Earth: "My friend wants to have children. Why should he not have them? All his friends have them." After Baal intercedes for his friend Anat his consort prays: "Build me a house for Baal or I will fill your grey beard with blood and crack your skull." El says, "Yes my daughter, Baal shall have a house." El does not get mad at Anat when she threatens him with war. He is a nice kind God. Baal and Anat have parallels with Osiris and Isis. The female raises the male from the dead.

This pantheon is the older Old Testament. We trace God back to the book of Genesis and the history is compact. The Bible singles out only Baal and not his pantheon. It is obvious the Bible is full of lies. Things do not match history. If Osiris is Baal and Isis is Anat we have the connection through the Egyptian Book of The Dead. It seems Anat (Venus) lines up with the gods.

The reason we are sinners is because of Eve. She is not going to lay on you and bring you back to life. Isis gave her power to Osiris and the goddess has lost this power with Mary Magdalene. She searches for Christ in the cave but if she brought him back to life the woman would be restored to goddess.

The woman has been torn down from the rib of Adam, the dung death of Jezebel, and the wicked woman in the box for Ishtar. The gods are all over the Bible, but we assume they are bad and label them pagan. Dagan in the book of Judges is worshiped by the Philistines (Giants) and he and El are considered the father of Baal. If we saw the whole pantheon working, we would see Jehovah as a part of it. In a Babylonian myth I read Jehovah comes through the window to announce the birth of a new god.

This is like the sun or the solar myth of the eternal Jesus coming through the window. All these beliefs follow the moon and the sun. In the Mayan Popul Vuh (The Book of The Community) the moon and sun are heroes that travel to Xibalba. The book is sacred and lines up with the Sun and Moon (The Hero Twins).

Other tests in Hades or Hell are won by Greek Hero Hercules. He was half man and half god. He is a son of Zeus (Jupiter, Marduk, and Baal). All fertility gods have Virgo (The House of Bread) to restore them, but Mary Magdalene is a whore who used to be his wife. St. Peter, our first Pope crucified upside down as a political criminal, stole from Mary Magdalene the ministry she would have inherited from Jesus.

I can feel the guilt the first Pope felt for stealing from a woman two thousand years ago. Today it is as if the women do not exist. They believe in the three sexual sins this book brings freedom from. Everybody needs a fertility goddess to become a Word. The words of God are in the Bible but the Word of God (John1;1) is us. They are gods that became flesh, and our souls sit with the lamb on the throne of God in heaven. We are supposed to be the word of God and the

Bible the words of God. We attribute Onan to God (Elohim) instead of a little mistake Jehovah made. The power of Moses is the second commandment which knocks out all religions. I will think Buddha is bad since his idol is different from Jesus. To keep the story of Noah consistent we keep Egypt at a distance.

Since Egypt is the cradle of civilization, we find gods that correspond to Greek and Roman gods. This is a big trail of idols and books that the Christian could read and find out Phoenician Baal is Babylonian Marduk (Bel Marduk). Baal leaves a trail on Earth. The stars and circle around the cross protect us from believing our ancestors lies.

The zodiac is everything and angels turn into gods. The sick poison of Christianity is that it claims to be the only true religion. We must scoff and the Buddha and the Hindu. If Christ came back (soon) all these books on the Millennial Prophecies would be read. They are full of gods and our history.

Does one really want to trade in the gods for Abraham, Isaac, and Jacob? We only have a white Jewish God to choose from. All others are the devil. In America we are very lazy about study. People think there is a hell, yet they do not read about it. The Jesus we worship denies the horny Gnostics, so he won't look like a man. Everybody is a Satanist that has an orgy (Irenaeus).

St. Paul says we all know an idol is nothing but don't stumble your brother. The Roman Catholic Church has every right to make artwork and tell the Bible story. You don't need an idol or support if you read the legend. Michael the Arc Angel will strike Satan and kill him. Ra does this every day, but we do not celebrate until we get to heaven.

In heaven they don't have sex either, but Sons of the Elohim had sex with earthlings and produced Nephilim (Giants). Thus "fallen angel" they sinned with their eyes like Samson. They were heroes and men of renown. In Christianity they seem to keep the devil alive and there is no hero to kill the devil. I don't see Jesus depicted killing the devil in Europe and in America we are not even looking forward to the death of the devil by St. Michael.

If we take Satan back to the garden of Eden to become the serpent with no wings, we find sex. The original sin is shame of nudity and disobedience to the Elohim. Moses uses the volcano on Santorini to do his dirty work and then gives his God the credit. Destruction, punishment, and hatred pour out from our criminal, and punitive God.

Today we have our own father images. The amount of people in prison in America is big. My father died when I was nine, so I was vulnerable when I was fifteen and born again. A new heavenly father that asks for behavior that was relevant three thousand years ago. Jesus put the whole picture together like a cross. Love God with your heart, mind, and soul and love your neighbor as yourself. This takes care of the vertical relation first and then the horizontal position second. No more law or prophets are needed just love and according to John, the Gnostic disciple, God is love.

The jail factor is the lawless Christianity that judges' others by the law of Moses but not themselves. They claim the Holy Spirit teaches knowledge and they do not know there are 613 commandments, not just ten. This amongst many errors in the Bible show it is the pen of man. They had intention of selling guilt with God on the cross. Eve did it once for us all and we all sin; but once again there is no hero.

Revelations has the seven headed dragon that the heroes of the myth have dealt with on their journey. Phoenician Baal kills Lotan (Leviathan) and Hercules beheads the Hydra. In the creation story the Spirit of the Elohim hovers above the Deep, which could be Sumerian Apsu or Tiamat. It seems we are dealing with evil Neptune. Volcanos erupting, gods of the sea stir up chaos, and these natural phenomena were associated with the evil god of Moses. To this day we give him the credit for all the dead Egyptians at the bottom of the Red Sea. They tried to stop their slaves from leaving and Jehovah gathers them together for final execution. Just like Samson and the Philistines were all gathered under one roof. Jehu and the ministers of Baal is the same thing.

Since our father in heaven is a racist, slave owner, liar, deceiver, heel catcher we turn out this way. Had we read the myth of Jesus the

Sun God we would have our zodiac back. To not look up at the stars is a shame. To see the perfectly proportioned belt of Orion and to think of how never in America has somebody shared a myth about a constellation. Orion is the Duat - home of the Gods- in Egypt and the three wise men in the Bible.

The woman is the missing key obtaining this Lordship. Ours are blocked out so we call Mary the Virgin Mary, and the words "Virgin" is enough. The church in order to control us changed the myth of Jesus to history. Now we all squeeze through stiff sentences of Moses and pretend the Bible accounts for more than the twelve tribes.

When the Virgin Mary of Guadalupe appeared in the stars, she took certain constellations with her. The story of Revelations 12 is in her starry mantel. This connects us to every calendar. Juan Diego sees the Virgin and he sees his wife, Maria Lucia. He took peyote at the temple of Tonantzin. She appeared to him as his dead fourteen-year-old wife. Now we see the Aztec connection to the stars is time.

The unplugging of monotheism only and the opening of a choice that suits the individual is better. Gnosticism became Alchemy and had we followed the Gnostic Jesus it would be sacred to us. With Catholic churches we have the Mason's deciding where to lay each brick. We could study the churches and their pagan roots.

The many churches, cathedrals, and temples in Italy represent doom. Michael the Arc Angel kills the devil at the end of the world, and this allows the devil time to gain converts impersonating Jesus the Sun God. Imagine the art in Italy if we were Gnostic. I imagine a smiling Jesus, solar power, and orgy; along with the Gnostic teaching that all matter is evil, and the universe was created by Aeon's (Lesser Spirits) and separation from matter is why Jesus smiles.

This means death is a good thing, but the Gnostic have no concept of sin, only knowledge. Gnosis means knowledge and America does not respect the original Jesus enough to have a church for those of us who do not believe pre-marital sex is a sin. Knowledge is the higher power. Even though the Gnostics had no concept of sin they respect the Jewish law, unlike the Americans who call all religions but their non historic Jesus, Satan. Hindu, Buddha, and all the East would be helpful like Job who showed us more than Jacob's Ladder in his book. Orion and the Bears are in there and Jehovah appearing in a whirlwind like Seth to test Job. Jehovah and Satan made a deal or did God and Jehovah make a deal?

Remember that you have Baal backwards. He makes love to his seven wives (The Pleiades) and it rains. What if we told our children when it rains Baal is making love to his wives? El, Baal's Father, according to one tradition and Dagan according to another we call El God in English but not the Canaanite one that Moses poisoned us against. I see more interaction in the stories with El and Baal. The father son combo that could replace Abraham and exalt El Elyon, God Most High.

All one must do is say Baal Jesus or Master Jesus! We see a Phoenician that was written about before the Torah gave birth to the Jehovah Elohim. Phoenician El has Anat to intercede for us and she is a powerful Venus. She saves Baal and is the star of the show. She talks to El (God) and he answers her kindly. I would much rather have learned the myth of Baal to Jesus who put me in hell for not believing in him.

It seems like it would work to scare somebody with the flames (Daniel) if they don't bow to the idol of Mary and Jesus (Isis and Horus). Open the star gates and let a flood of illumination show us the other forms of Christ...Quetzalcoatl, Baal, Horus, Bacchus. Turn the word pagan into polytheistic and the hurt goes away. Elohim is plural of El so we have divine beings and angels around Jehovah. He seems to lead the gods and tells people they are angels and fallen angels.

If you pull the thread of sex out of the Bible and correct it the Bible goes back to its original. No fierce celibate God to threaten us with hell. The psychology of the unknown keeps us on our toes. What if it is true, we go to hell for not believing? Then the miracles of Jesus to help and heal our blindness comes into play. We don't separate the authors of the Bible; we just say God said. This makes Jesus the author of the confusion and the evil in the Old Testament. We have hybrid Bible, but we don't study it to know this stuff.

The Old Testament is very foggy and everything we need to know happened in the book of Genesis. Later Jehovah verse Ra the Sun God and the Bible beat the Book of the Dead. If we read the Old Testament more, we would see the branch of God growing in the Bible to the fertility gods of the forbidden countries.

We should love the gods the way they love us. Build temples to Baal and study the Phoenician alphabet for its twenty-two characters from the ox to the tau. It is all Phoenician and parallels the Old Testament. Brainwashing is the reason we don't know this. We are sure our leaders are telling the truth when they are a good speaker. What brings back history? Sumerians, Babylon, Phoenicia, Greece, Rome, Assyria, and Egypt are countries with the love Goddess.

If we understood the deities that are inside of us it is interesting to see the phallus in the Book of the Dead. The place of the soul or Ka connects to Ra…the Ka sits at the right hand of Ra like the lamb on the throne sits next to God. The lamb is supposed to be Jesus, but he has replaced us. Would not we want that seat with God? To be right next to him?

We are the Word, and our soul is the lamb on the throne. They are selling us our salvation! According to the Gnostic we were already saved but we need knowledge. The four gospels are all we accept of Jesus. The Gnostic is not read in church, so we have very little knowledge of Jesus. We think the Old Testament will fill it in and prove the Bible to be of God. What about all the plagiarism and copying from the old cave walls? The fertility gods run free and the reason you do not known about them is you think they are idols. Yet Jesus is an idol and St. Paul set us free from the commandments.

CHAPTER 7

SEX IS SIN?

The basics of the Christian religion is to know Adam and Eve, the commandments, and the cross. We are sinners and we need to be baptized for it. All these customs are in other religions, but we should not consider them enemies. They happened before the Torah was written and the view the Bible gives on history is hardly accurate. Where is Alexander the Great in the Bible or Cyrus the Persian? They are all missing so Jehovah keeps track of history with Abraham, Isaac, and Jacob.

Two or three eunuchs throw Jezebel out of the window. Why does the Bible not know if it were two or three of them? Jacob is the third in a performance by the patriarchs and we must wrestle with his demon. The hatred for women in the Bible is sick. They are slaves! Inanna or Ishtar would liberate them from the false male sided history. Lilith is as far as you can go with the Jewish, but she is Adam's first wife, and she is Venus.

If you love sex, you will treasure this teaching. While America is behind the three sexual sins of the Roman Catholic Church, we also have no prostitution. The virgins of Mary's day were about fourteen. They know an older unmarried man is expected to not even have a prostitute or jack off. We will explode like this but imagine the world without the three sexual lies of the church. We would all have a job as a prostitute, and we are having pre-marital sex anyway.

The beauty of knowing others is something I feel inside of me.

I do not want to be with one lover only for the rest of my life. It is not natural. If I could do every woman, I wanted to it would be a heaven on earth. Now we are only supposed to do married sex to make children but what if we went wild and legalized prostitution. They would be the sexy nurses for the horny and it seems to me Jesus hung out with them for a reason.

Do you ever think they might have mentioned premarital sex was a sin in the Gospels? The adulterous and the hookers came to Jesus, but nobody said: "I am not married, and I had sex." We take it so strict we ruin each other's lives. From the Gnostic orgy to getting killed for jacking off is extreme. One is so free and curious. The other is impossible and it is punished by the death penalty. Do you want to pass on this fake Jehovah of the Roman Catholic Church on to our children?

Through the story of Onan, I felt God's love. He did not kill him for masturbation but for not doing his duty. Those that want to feel God's judgment look at how he feels about stealing. Now look at the Roman Catholic one, from the changed Bible who kills for masturbating. This is so mean and has bad karma. Even Jesus himself is mean, introducing hell to those who don't believe. He cannot stand on his own two feet since we don't study the Gospels much and most Americans have never heard of "Gnosis."

Er is killed and the reason given was: "He did evil in the eyes of the Lord." Why doesn't God come down and kill more often? In the New Testament he did it to Ananias and Safiras for stealing. Now Christians lie and steal all the time and they are usually tight with their money if it is not for the church. We could be something else. Something better, with temples of Baal and Gnostic churches. Learn the Old Testament like the Gnostics and don't trust anybody from the church. They do not have your best interest in mind and this Jesus love was stronger in the early church. In America people don't seem to like each other and they always look horny. This is not the time to believe in the Roman Catholic Jehovah who kills Onan and Er while letting the unmarried have sex. The sex turned into love and hate but it is still being rewarded. Having sex is okay but masturbation is punishable by death. You would have to kill everybody!

We are putting ourselves through a living hell. Not to mention horny men may rape you and sexually frustrated people might kill you. In 1996 I was in Amsterdam for three days and I asked a Dutch Man about prostitution. He said, "We don't want our women raped." I love how he said it and I wish America loved its women enough to have their free will back. They cared about their country and any man in the world can go with an assortment of prostitutes or sex workers that represents many countries around the world.

One can have sex all over Europe in brothels and the sexy beautiful women have set prices. They do not look at you if you are ugly and say keep your money. Sometimes they like you better, but the marriage is for money and the money last for a half hour. It is honest and it is like getting down to business.

On one tour of Europe in 2001 I traveled to fifty-four different cities doing research on brothels. With enough money a man can have more prostitutes in a week that the average America does in a lifetime. That is so sad the ugly fat American cannot be loved for his money. He is supposed to get it for free and then ask Jesus for forgiveness for premarital sex. The lies men tell women are numerous and women believe the same lie from many men. I have seen many old and ugly men get worshiped by whores and that is the only physical love they are going to get. In America they like massage, in LA they are everywhere, and I think what if they were hookers? A different woman every day of the week, and don't worry porno kid be the porn star and wear a condom.

To not see the women of other counties like this is a dream and one time I had a vision that I went to heaven with a beautiful model from Budapest. She is the most beautiful woman I have ever seen, and I made love to her. She took me to heaven with her face and I saw gods like men on couches watching me. This goddess turned into light, and I see her face and her light every day.

Every American would have their lust fulfilled by a real person and the teaching of Onan shall one day be corrected. Could you hate your own son or daughter so much you kill me? This is what the Catholic Church wants to scare us with. The big evil God eating sinners in hell has a devil named Satan for his friend and his tail winds back unto the Canaanite Myth. El is drunk and this horned guy with a pointed tail threw him into the underworld. The joke of modern religion is every story is out of date and you cannot understand the Bible without a book about the Bible.

If men and women start to exchange money the women could get in on some fantasy sex, they cannot have with their husbands. Since we are all having pre-marital sex, we are all guilty, but we do not care or worry much about hell. We teach our children the lies of the church and they don't even know there is more than one creation story.

Jesus means in Hebrew "Jehovah Saves" so we are attached to Jehovah more than the Elohim and people think this does not mess us up. The only history we know is false and nobody can get them in the lie. This scares me that a historian cannot tell the Christian to study Gilgamesh, 1500 years older than Homer, and read about two friends instead the ugly Bible crap where the heroes fuck people over but it okay since they were pagans.

The Bible is racist, and we are used to hearing the Bible's names for Africa and Phoenicia. A very important note to those who think the Egyptian Magic is killed by Moses. Never go back there, do not trade, and do not marry foreign wives is all in the logic. Solomon did those three and he is not as popular as his father David. We lack the wisdom of Solomon and the knowledge of the Gnostics.

Solomon wrote the wisdom books but since he is sexual and has 700 wives, we do not talk about him. It is hard to trick your followers to not have pre-marital sex when a righteous man wrote the **Song of Songs.** The **Kebra Negast** shares his bedside manner. The best advice a father gave his sons is the Proverbs. Every subject in life has wisdom. Solomon says in Ecclesiastes: "Enjoy life while you are young, before the caperberry bush is no longer stirred and the grasshopper drags himself along." What kind of advice is that to the Christian in America who is a virgin. Enjoy sex while you can before it is too late.

Wise old men can give advice in retrospect, and I listen to them. They give me advice on life and tell me what they learned on their journey. I have traveled and enjoyed myself in Europe four different times. I see amazing people and history. I am going to brothels and churches where I see Mary Magdalene. She does not look like the hookers outside her churches in Italy.

Solomon may have had a grasshopper, but Canaanite El had a member longer than the seas. This suits me perfectly since I travel and see women as Venus. It says in the praise to El: "Blessed are you El, your member is longer than the seas." Think of this compared to the grasshoppers in the land of Canaan. "We seem like grasshoppers compared to them." What if everything in Canaan had a healthy exaggeration? Things where bigger for the giants and other Nephilim that roamed Canaan in the days of Anat. Baal has a full-on pantheon and it is not polluted. Osiris and the gods in the body could be suited to Baal and Anat. The way we know the Old Testament; Baal and Osiris would associate with the soul or Ka.

These battles between Baal and his dead brother Mot, the moon, are interesting. Mot juts out his tongue and hits the stars. Baal descends with his axe. Also, Yom the serpent swallows Baal and all these gods sit at a divine assembly in Mt Zaphon. Remember all this stuff is older than the Bible.

Jesus according to the Gnostic is inside of us like Krishna. We feel warm thinking about our savior who was already inside of us. Jesus brought an awakening, but the church sells us our soul and salvation. Osiris would be the heart and the phallus while Jesus would be Ka without the penis. They have made Jesus so nonsexual that we assume he died a virgin. First Mary Magdalene was his wife and then they changed her to a whore. If we found the manuscripts for anything between Jesus and Mary Magdalene it would be like the Song of Songs. What we would learn and apply manifests itself with understanding our own sacred sexual language. Follow the Song of Songs and remember her navel is really her vulva.

The love songs to all the goddesses have heroes that have stepped beyond what Christianity has to offer. No sex until marriage and this is the only moral they seem to have. Nobody gets mad about lies and stealing but the God who kills masturbators will get you for adultery. Don't you realize all sex is bad in Christianity and we are forced to wait until an older age to have sex?

We are on a bee line to hell as it sits now. The three big ones and our misinterpretation led us to ask forgiveness but not change. The law is kept through faith, and one would have to know the law to follow it. We are so ignorant of our own religion, and nobody seems to care about the original Jesus. They just trust the church and obey them in chastity and hell.

The scope of this book is not just to get us all laid more by removing the curse of ignorance.

We are restored to God, the God that loves us, who sent Jesus and many others. We receive it by the story of the church, and therefore we don't read Gilgamesh or have any interest in the different pyramids. What happens in the world is seen in the Mayan Calendar, but the Bible is a stale book. It will repeat itself forever or until judgement day where we are judged by our works. They tell you to believe in Jesus and start donating 10% of your income. They are rich because of this.

We sit with the angry God who fucked us up sexually. White Moses and white Noah the biggest racists in history have their myth made history by the church to control us. We don't not know what Jesus was like or if it was okay. What if he was having sex with the prostitutes or had many wives? The Virgin America risks their religion every time they lust after God's beautiful creation. We are not orgy free we are guilty of thinking about sex, and we are afraid of expressing ourselves.

The curse has been on us since Eve. Whatever they wanted to say, they made up, and they gave it to us. Don't jack off or I will kill you is the loving God of the Roman Catholic Church. To the Jews it means one thing but to the Catholic and the Protestant it means Onan died for onanism. With a Bible in one hand and a dictionary in the other I resist the church with all my might.

People are having pre-marital sex all over the world; and all over the world it is a sin. To pay for it will put you in jail in America. The point is this, we are having sex already, but we think God is mad. And one is partially embarrassed and would not suggest sex to a stranger. To a sex worker you give her the marriage act, your money, and your body. 24 hours a day, 7 days a week we could have sex with as many women as we could afford. When the money runs out leave the whore house and everybody has a job; and the price would be good.

This makes up for lost time and for me, and personally I feel hoodwinked by the church. When I was born again at fifteen, they told me to be a virgin and pray for a wife. I wanted a model, smart, sexy, generous, and spiritual. Everybody was married so it made sense that I would get my model girlfriend and marry her. This church tries to set up people of the opposite sex.

This church messed up my mind so bad I put a pistol in my mouth in 1998 when I came back from Italy to live with my mom. God was dead and the church was just a business. I learned of the lies of the church too late in life; and lost my model girlfriend. I was a virgin for a year when I dated her. She was quite a find; the church was glad I lost her. At least I would not fornicate. I lost my virginity at twenty-one and I resisted the women in modeling. I had become a model myself and had many opportunities to break with God and sleep with them. I humped boobs and butt cracks to get off and eventually I developed a fetish with the ass.

Not having a woman did nothing for me. God never brought me my wife. Everybody else is married so I was staying virgin for nothing. I missed out on beautiful women and learned to live with blue balls. What they stole from me and how they stole it makes me want to kill myself. I have tried too many times with a pistol and then in 2013 I got bi-polar medication and I calmed down.

When I drink and see the women, I am so happy until I realize I can't have them. In a brothel or gentlemen club one may have a choice of fifty women. Amsterdam and Antwerp are big and so is Tijuana and all of Spain. You see them and do them and there does not have to be any talking or long dates. You get the one you want and there are many to choose from.

A rich guy and a poor guy go to the same brothel. The poor guy says to the rich guy, "I'm too poor to date women in America so I come here after saving up a lot of money." The rich guy says how many do you do in a night?" The poor guy says, "Eight" The rich guy responds to him, "I am richer than you, but I cannot do that in America. They will never go for it, and you would have to feed those food whores in between each fuck. It would be too much jealousy."

The poor guy never felt richer. He can do more in another country than America. Every fantasy can be brought to life for money. Once your money is gone you go home.

The rich guy in America is going to learn dating gets expensive. Once a couple is attached, they might go out every day. This amount of money would allow the rich guy to fuck enough women to kill him. We waste our money every day trying to find a person born into the three lies of the Roman Catholic Church and still be ready for sex. If we did not have them, we would be like the Gnostic with no concept of sin but need for knowledge. Adults doing this is fine. Jesus involved makes the love happen or should I say the Eros happen. By the way, Eros is the oldest of the gods, making it look like we were horny from the beginning. Who can carry this enormous cross of guilt and shame? We cannot even relieve ourselves jacking off. The American prostitute will put you in prison. Adultery has all the ramifications Solomon wrote about in Proverbs five. If we read the Proverb five, we would not commit adultery. It is too bad the serpent in the garden of Eden was changed from Sophia to Satan.

CHAPTER 8

VIRGINS AND GODS

My experience with women is very frustrating. Especially after living in Italy and traveling Europe I found America to be a country of insane people. Watching people's aftermath of pre-marital sex on television I learn. Understanding they have done it and nothing bad happens. Now a minister with an NIV Bible comes out and tells you about fornication. He holds all the years, comprised one upon another, of ignorance of Revelations and Fornications. They are worshiping idols not having premarital sex with idols. They are like a married woman (Jehovah/Israel) being called a whore. People got married young back then and this was not as cruel as modern America and Christian television spreading the confusing message. On one hand it is okay if it is free. But you will burn in hell! No fornicator, adulterous, abuser of themselves with mankind…will enter the Kingdom of God.

The fire of hell does not scare us. We go about our actions and daily routines hoping all religions are false expect for Christianity (The White Man's Religion). If our actions count in The Book of The Dead, we do a negative confession to Osiris; and the ten commandments are in

The Book of the Dead but instead of saying Thou shalt not The Book of the Dead says, "I have not."

There are forty-two gods in the tunnel leading to Osiris. You say to each one of them, you have not trespassed, or stolen but twenty-one is sexual "I have not committed sodomy." That makes it hard for many of us to get to the end the of tunnel. When Nebuchadnezzar died, he did a Negative Confession where you recite your negative confession to forty-two gods. This number comes up in the Bible when Elisha summons two, she bears to maul the forty-two youths that made fun of him for being bald.

In Babylon the virgins lose their virginity on an altar with an incredible lover. A handsome friend of the king with the horns of a stag on his head gives the virgin a small amount of money in a purse. He goes through the forty-two gods in her body-your eyes are like Hathor above Nut or the Sun above the Water. He lays her down on the universe and makes love to the goddess Ishtar. **The king helped women find their purse was between their legs all the time.** In America it is full of restaurant receipts for the American woman who does not have a free will like the Italian woman (Thanks to the Pope); they are smart to not take money because they will go to jail. Take the food but retirement will be a poor life without the "*figa*" -Italian for pussy.

In Italy in 1996-1998 I met so many prostitutes from Brazil. They leave Brazil for Italy. A land of handsome generous men with big dicks that pay $35 for sucky fucky. In Naples one made $3000 a day just doing blow jobs. All of them bought their mothers in Brazil houses with their pussy. A little Gnostic Alchemy with an Italian man and a Brazilian woman making friction that the American woman who unlike the Italian is not protected by the Pope. Americans do not have free will over their body or their money. I highly doubt an American woman is going to be generous enough to buy a house for mom. She would spend it on herself and a lot of clothing.

We look so stupid dating for dinners and dicks…. the women eat $30 of food and is ready for sex. She could have told him $200 around the world and I'll buy you lunch. In Naples, Rome, and Milan there are hookers everywhere. They go around and line up at clubs, beach brothels, and of course hundreds of men, *Viados*, transexual prostitute, Via=street Dos=two and women hookers on their side of the road. I worked as a bouncer at a different club every night. A line of men and women stop the cars, and we talk to all of them since the traffic stops for them. It is organized and everyone is $35. Well worth it I hear, and they go crazy for the exaggerated women.

America, with your online escorts is a confusing message. You will go to hell for fornicating according to you. But you have John's in jail for sleeping with the wife of Christ? I took money you took food. Can't buy a house with food you poor American!

The weight of the sexual sins on us is great. If we made love not war the whole world would change. Women have suffered enough but the good news is Mother Earth is alive and so is the goddess. All of history starts with Gilgamesh and Ishtar but we jump ahead of time and the Bible is not as old as we think.

In Bologna, Italy there is a church older than the Bible. I stayed there for three days with my friends. They took me to see the churches and we started at St. Maria de Servi. The carpet was red like a brothel and one can put money in the machines in front of the art. Turn the lights on in hell. At the end of the hallway, I see Jesus with five puppies around him. To my left is the Virgin Mary with seven swords piercing her heart. Then a thief on the cross, and then a blue devil from the Divine Comedy eating sinners. Then another thief and Jesus with the puppies stood out to me since in English Bibles it says, "Dogs" to those who eat under the table.

I picked up a flyer near the Jesus and it said: "If you call Abraham a friend, a little angel will sit on your shoulder. - The Virgin Mary." **I chose the Virgin Mary for my angel, and she has spoken to me in Montserrat, Tepeyac, Quito, and Bologna.** This Jesus calling the girl a dog is the way Canaanites are thought of. The twelve tribes get into heaven first and then the Gentiles. I picked Mary since she is Queen of the Angels but when we see the whole battle it seems to be sex.

The word virgin or Virgo is placed on Venus and extinguishes the sexual flame. What would the world be if we did not believe in the three sexual sins of the Roman Catholic Church? For me Bologna caused me nightmares, but I kept the message of the Virgin Mary and published it in 2007 with Lulu (The Lords of The Poison). I knew Abraham meant Father and my father died when I was nine. The whole world is under a father that never existed, and we are punished by the twisting of the words. It is my choice to be tied up like Isaac, but I am like Ezekiel in Babylon when I go to Rome. I am talking to God in my bi-polar way and Ezekiel hears the words "Son of Man" or "Earthling" from the man on the throne.

At this vision enters the gods and the gospels and I believe the man on the throne is Cyrus the Persian. Ezekiel tied himself up to symbolize captivity and he is like big Isaac. Isaac means 'laugher' but nobody laughed. **The Greeks sacrifice laugher to Venus.** Ezekiel is tied up to symbolize Isaac in Babylon. This is a rich cultural bridge and part of Ezekiel's comic street theatre. The fact Greeks even have a Venus to channel positive creativity, joy, and laugher is fantastic. The American's do not relate much to the Virgin Mary even though she appears in Revelations 12. The idea of virginity has always been central to the church.

This has messed up our lives since the church father called the Gnostics "Satanists" for the love feast. They threw out the baby with the bathwater and got rid of Jesus. The strong solar deity and his planets (disciples) are gone and the art they could have left us. Smiling Jesus, separation from matter, and the love feast. We are being controlled sexually and told what to do and we all believe the same thing. Without this book all my hard work goes to nothing, and the world continues to revolve teaching the myth of Jesus the Sun God as history.

CHAPTER 9

SEX AND THE JEZEBELS

E ven Noah's ark instead of the original Sumerian one is believed by adults and children. Probably the child molesters use the story of Ham and Noah to get drunk and nude. This is not a part of the true ark story or the worlds many floods' stories. The Bible curses Egypt and gives Jehovah the credit. If I were to do a Bible quiz in America many would fail. It seems they will believe anything, but they won't study.

For me I like the Phoenician alphabet, twenty-two letters, start with an ox, symbol of father, and ends with the Tau in the shape of a cross. It tells me a story of the father going to the cross. The Phoenicians worshiped El and Baal along with the pantheon. I believe it was discovered at Nineveh in the 50s. The Bible story of Elijah and Baal shows the Bible is hardly true. The symbolism in the story of Elijah, Elisha, and Jehu is like passing a judgment on the Queen. It takes so much to get her, but the Bible calls her a whore. Jezebel in Hebrew means chastity and since Jezebel is thrown by her two or three Eunuchs into the dung; proverbially the chastity of Israel was thrown in the dung while she was Queen of Israel.

This is a great story for demonstrating the hatred toward women in the Bible. Men with grasshoppers are jealous of men with members longer than the seas. They are hiding their women and treating them like cattle. To apply this hatred on the modern American woman will make her feel her father is mad at her. And what bugs me the most is how the only sin is sex. People get away with murder, but God forbid they have sex.

Jezebel was a beautiful Phoenician Queen that married Ahab the King of Israel. She built an idol of Baal and Elijah left heaven to snuff her out. Jezebel got Namath's Vineyard for her husband, and this was the sin that God comes down with special agent Elijah. Jehu is the final confrontation in the tower. She says to him from the tower, "You Omri, murderer of your Master." Omri saw the enemy coming and burned himself down in his own palace. She is also calling him emasculated but closer examination of the word master, Baal. You murderer of your own God.

Jezebel has everything on Jehu the mad chariot driver. Her God is cooler and original with a big happy family. Her alphabet is older than the Greek and Hebrew. I understand that Phoenician culture was the only one that did not see it as bad to take money for sex. When it rains Baal has sex with his seven wives and his sons hump like buffalo and each has the face of their Father.

Once I got rid of Abraham (Father) by making him a friend, I got the father of Melchizedek; El Elyon who is older than Jehovah and Abraham, Isaac, and Jacob. **Free of the thieves I follow Canaanite poetry and Baal.** His wife Anat is perfect for me sexually and the fact that she threatens El with war and he concedes to her and loves her. Jehovah kills masturbators while El is the real name for God and Elohim (Gods)/Judges in the New Testament. We are using plural Elohim for singular God. "Lord God" is Jehovah Elohim.

Jehovah leads the Elohim, Gods turned into angels. This is how we understand Jesus today. He is above the angels on the throne waiting for us in the New Jerusalem. If Dagan, Jupiter, Baal, Mercury, and all the idols popped up that would be gods. We are instructed to be Jewish, but Jezebel still has a Phoenician ring of a female Jesus. The Messiah would clean her at the end, but we jail the wife of Christ.

The chariot of fire will dart across the sky. Jesus will return in judgment wearing goggles. Masturbators run, watch out children of fornication, and the least of these will then be him. How do we treat the least of these? Even pagans love their family, but Jesus said: "Love your enemy as yourself." This is the true judgment? Jesus would create friends out of enemies. There would be peace and we could appreciate each other. All those dammed for pre-marital sex are forgiven.

CHAPTER 10

THE IDOLS AND THE GODS

Since most Americans are not a virgin for very long, we seem very horny and frustrated. If the woman was not poisoned towards us things might go differently. We would have prostitutes and orgy to feast on in the life. The alternative is a boring America where the people believe sex is a sin against God and they do it anyway. No warning on the television that the people having pre-marital sex are going to hell. But this is what we believe.

To keep us chaste they create a mean, evil, and punitive God. Nobody cares if you lie and steal but if you slept with somebody you are evil. Making love is punishable by hell and whacking off with death. When you look at a woman you might as well sleep with her. From the Gnostic orgy to the death penalty and hell might be a little weird. A lie that we support and pay for. They have brought us so little. Yet we give our free will to the government and our chastity to Jesus.

The power of sex and love is incredibly motivating. Temples to the pagan gods and goddesses in America is my vision. Even a temple for Mammon. Learn and study about money. The curse of the second commandment must be removed. Paul says, "We all know an idol is nothing." We have the idols of Jesus and Mary because we aren't under the law we are under grace. The problem is all the art is white and they are not gods. We need books and countries like Italy where I can walk from the statue of Hercules killing Nexus to a church. Both seem real and I feel attached to Zeus and Jupiter after living in Italy. Follow

Venus to your crown and you can be like winged mercury, feathery serpents, Buddhas and more outside the door to Moses. If an idol is sin and we are justified by honoring this ancient commandment, what about the legends of the idols?

I would never know Baal prayed by looking at his image or reading the Bible. The fact the Bible does not acknowledge Anat, or the pantheon is huge. Baal looks like he is taken out by Elijah. The God of thunder and God of the storm could not make it rain fire, but Elijah could; one time. That quick victory over Baal was nothing if we believe in his myth which is older than our God. The Bible is so confusing and seems dead. I never hear somebody quote it on television or solve problems with the words of Jesus.

Anat is my favorite goddess sexually and she is my dominatrix. To yell at El for-Baal's temple to be built is the closest one can be to God. He does not get mad when she threatens him with war. All the goddesses need their lovers to live but we technically consider Anat, Ishtar, and Venus to be idols, fallen angels or Satanists. The church (Father Irenaeus) called the Gnostics Satanists and then built up pagan and polytheistic gods to be fallen angels. The story of Jehovah pulling along the angels is really the gods (Elohim) which would now be better translated angels.

The gods axe the devils and the angels come out at the end of time scenario. They darken the sun and open the pit of hell. We wait for the end of the world to see the return of Jesus. Ra, the Sun God, kills the serpent daily. After the church has all your money, they say they will pay you back in heaven. Satan gets bigger as the gods are against us and we do not acknowledge the Elohim. Jehovah and his mean son Jesus put us in hell for not believing in them.

It is interesting America fears Jehovah but not Alexander the Great. We are so blind racist everything not Jewish is bad; but we don't study the Talmud. All the information the Old Testament has to offer. Funny stories about Rabbi's doing prostitutes. Different schools of thought debating what kind of complement to give a daughter of Israel.

Lebanon (Phoenicia) has Baal in their history unless they learn the trick of the idol is to read the book. Would I say Buddha is an idol? Now there are some legends of Abraham's father, Terah, he had an idol shop. He did not pay attention to little Abraham, so Abraham got mad and burned down his father's idol shop. This is foreshadowing putting the gods in hell. The fallen angels fell for what reason? Sex! The Gnostics are Satanist according to Irenaeus for what reason? Sex!

The only moral I find American's to have is they do not have much sex. When I am in Paris, Barcelona, Budapest, Prague, Lisbon, and Berlin I have a lot of sex for some reason and then I go back to America, and everybody wants a fake marriage and dating to get money out of me and then they are often frigid and hold back. They need a lot of alcohol and want commitment for a one-night stand. It takes so long to get a woman I just give up and wait for my next trip to Europe.

The time in America is to save money but If I go out, I am not going to meet anybody. You can go have beers in Carlsbad but Tijuana and the Tijuana John (amazon.com) are waiting. Escape America while you can and don't get married too young. You already believe the Bible says you go to hell for it, but you do it anyway. Probably no Gnostic Jesus orgy; with people reading the Gnostic gospels and the gospels "Loaves and fish" (fertility). Probably not going to happen but you can meet people online, take them to dinner, and see if they will have sex with you. Or go to TJ and do eight in a row for less money and less talk.

Horny American men are trying to get their whore to the restaurant so they can pay them for sex. What if a woman told me $200 dinner on the beach for a blow job? I can't go to jail since we are allowed to have sex for free only. How smart, but funny why the American woman doesn't not have the same passion for her man as the sexy Latina? Because he is a penis with a job. Women will try to marry somebody more attractive than them, but they do not want to give it up for free.

The beauty of money is it gives you a language with which to bargain with. What if it was legal, in the USA, to be a sex worker. I give my body to her, and she pays me. We would all be so rich, and that expensive dinner money could be turned into a vacation home. If I said, "Do you hook?" To a woman she can say yes or no and if it is no, I walk away. Instead of saying, "Can I have your phone number so I can call you sometime." And then planning dinner with her to pay her what men have always paid.

The prostitutes in jail can go with the pedophile and rapists to protect us. We will get laid all the time because of the money. Use your imagination and think about how awesome a red-light district in USA would be. We are adults paying each other with food. You cannot have our free will or our bodies. I decide not you! And who are you anyway saying to take the Mary Magdalene of America and put her in jail? Don't you fear the son of Jehovah? Or did you read what he did in the gospels with women?

The ignorance is so bad in America. Nobody knows anything and we are being punished for taking God's name in vain. When you say kill him for God and you will go to heaven is taking God's name in vain. The teaching goes to the grandchildren and the children of the lie that God punishes. Don't lie in his name.

We think in America it is okay to have pre-marital sex under certain conditions. What our parents taught us was no good unless they said to take money for sex. Why be so cheap when it is such a good deal. When I worked in New Orleans my boss told me if they legalized prostitution every woman would do it. The French Quarter is very sexy and has certain clubs that I have been to that I will never forget. The customers of our bar were so hot I wanted to fuck every woman on **Bourbon Street**.

It would be heaven on earth in America if we get rid of Irenaeus and go back to being Gnostic. There is nothing left to read since everything is forbidden. If we were Gnostic, we would take pride in the fact Alchemy came out of Gnosticism. A real force of the solar Jesus with all his stars telling his story without the hybrid Bible, art would be incredible, and I will get a tattoo of a smiling Jesus head to remember to smile at death and go into the loving arms of his father and not the idol of a father you never heard of. Escape Father Abraham with me and don't wait until Jacob wrestles the angel or the truth will live forever and all the famous people in the Old Testament go to the New Jerusalem.

The worst understanding of the idol is that they are all bad. Look at Baal, he looks like the Tin Woodsman in the Wizard of Oz, but read his myth and see where he fits in. The Bible puts Bel in front of things to look devilish. Bel Marduk of Babylon is Baal. Osiris and Baal share some stories. It appears this Thunder God made it rain except when Elijah stopped up the heavens and called fire down on the wet altar. Jehu kills the minsters of Baal and turns the Temple of Baal into a urinal.

Flush the Urinal of Baal and fill the pew with Jehu! What were the 400 ministers of Baal doing when Jehu told his men, "If you leave even one of them alive, I will kill you." They attack but were the minsters of Baal having sex? Was it a Gnostic orgy? Were they studying planets and lining them up for their departure? The possibilities are endless but, in my book, The Mangolishis Popul Vuh (available on lulu) I compare the Old Testament to the **Popul Vuh** (Mayan Book of the Community.). They have the **400 Drinking Boys** killed in an orgy in the Popul Vuh and when the roof caved in on them at an orgy, they became Motz (The Pleiades).

The same number at the orgy and the 400 Drinking Boys of the Popul Vuh could be Motz or drop the z and you get Mot. Mot is Baal's dead brother, the moon, and he is the god of infertility. Baal and Mot fight and Anat brings Baal back from the dead when it rains. Mot or Motz the names are almost the same. With the Popul Vuh the Sun and Moon are the heroes. A native American can relate to Hercules but not Jesus.

Jesus is the white man's religion that Rome made famous. It ended a long time ago. The Bible teaches Jesus, like many gods say, "I'll be back." They want to scare you with the Jesus and hell, but he does not have the keys we do. I want my power back from the mighty

Christ and new copy of the Book of The Dead. To know Osiris, Isis, Thoth, Seth, and Nephty is to know the entrance to **The Boat of a Million Years**. Osiris judges you buy your deeds and not by faith. The Christian religion is very lazy, and they don't seem to have much experience. They like to touch little kids while telling us no fornicator will inherit the Kingdom of God.

An American is proud of their virginity but they do not have experience. Traveling has let me taste delicious pussy in every country I go to. Then I met an American woman on vacation who believed pre-marital sex was a sin. She was boring and wanted me to buy her things. She never suggests sex, but she has marriage in her eyes. Her God won't let her spread her legs or have a good time. She can't know me, and she has no free will. I don't find the interior attractive at all. What I am getting is not a good deal. I want sex only!

People in American bars are all horny and if there was a nearby Gentlemen's Club, they would be so happy. **Sex is the fountain of youth,** and the women share their beauty and youth with their John's. It is the only way young and old make love and both like it. Some of the unattractive men in the brothels get a lot of attention. A man with no legs can use his dick on something besides his hand.

We sit around with this curse of Adam and Eve on us and there are no gods. The Aztec, Maya, and Inca all have Quetzalcoatl the feathered serpent under different names. His city, **Teotihuacan,** has the Ave of the Dead lined up with the Pleiades (Motz in the Popul Vuh), The Pyramid of the Sun and Moon alongside the Temple of Quetzalcoatl and House of the Jaguars are all waiting 2012A.D. The end of the Aztec and Mayan calendar has passed but I wrote about and predicted the starry dates and holy calendar about 2012 A.D. in 2005 when I published **Nine Days to Healing a Spiritual Pilgrimage**. I figured out Revelations 12 in the constellations of the **Tilma of Guadalupe.**

These updates to the Bible and its original sources don't interest the monotheist who always want to tell his story the same way. The gods don't interest the American's and if the gods come back and they find out they were turned into fallen angles and nobody believes in them, will they be mad? I would explain to the space alien that America believes pre-marital sex is a sin, but they do it anyway. They say it is punishable in hell, but they put pre-marital sex on television for their children to learn from the idol.

We have screwed our self for Christianity, and we believe the Bible has the only words God ever spoke. Every god, saint, and angel is sin somehow. We are above the Bible! The Bible is a story told one way, but it is very tricky to understand. Men wrote it and men can write another one. If we connected with the feathery serpent the whole continent would be ours. **Jesus would have come back to his city Teotihuacan a hundred years after his death.** That is soon! 2000 years is not soon. We have done little research on the gods that resemble Jesus. We don't use the stars or constellations, even in the book of Job.

Even an American who does not believe in God will say the Bible is written by men. The books of Enoch would have allowed us to follow the tales of giants, angels, and fallen angles. They have names and could have temples with bookstores. They could be built by masons and alchemist who know the true story.

This graveyard of excuses is Moses and the idol. Is Zeus an idol? The New Testament forgives idolatry if you do not stumble someone else. So, what is the problem? Laziness! You don't have to worship a stick of wood, but you can read his book and see where the Bible was copied. Find the goddess and become a Judge like Samson who stayed with the prostitute until midnight. HIs name in Hebrew means "Sunshine" and Delilah means "She That Weakens." This is like the story of Ra and Isis, she was so beautiful she bit him like a serpent, and he became as weak as any other man.

The story of Samson and Delilah is in the land of Giants. Samson is a killing machine and uses a jawbone of an ass to kill 1,000 Giants. He is from the tribe of Dan (Dawn). Sunshine from the tribe of the Dawn meets She That Weakens. The Philistines gouge out Samson's eyes. What did the fallen angel's sin with? Their eyes, they saw the beautiful women and left heaven to have sex with them. The children of the daughters of men and the fallen angels are the Nephilim or Giants. Some say they descended in fire rockets, but the church has to say they sinned when they lusted after the mothers of the Giants. How interesting it would be in America to visit the art of Enoch if we created the parts of the Bible that were taken out. Giants and their legends and stuff about the world we should know anyway.

The whole Bible goes on, and how much does the average American study the Old Testament? The minsters of television don't say this stuff, but they believe there are dead Egyptians at the bottom of the Red Sea. Jehovah is like Mars, and I wonder why Adam was created out of Red Earth. He fights for Israel! Does miracles to destroy their enemies. Gathers all his hatred toward the Gentile and spreads it worldwide. We do not even know the difference.

If you tell an American that the Bible has been changed and edited for piety, they won't care. If they believed in their God, they would scream. What part of God's word did they change and how did they alter it? Everything sexual is hidden in the margins of my Scofield Bible. The phallus of Moses, the balls of Abraham, and the belly button of Sheba is her pussy. My gods Baal and El are fertile and have exaggerated body parts. "Blessed are you oh El. Your member is longer than the seas." The battle between Mot (the moon) and Baal is interesting that Mot opens his mouth to receive Baal and this tongue licks the stars.

Baal and El switch places in priority just like Jesus and Jehovah. We should like the Old Testament better. It has more information, history, prophecies, and even law which the Gnostic's respected, even though they did not believe in stories like Noah. They took the law out and the father of racism, Noah, is not even true. The sons of Ham are slaves, and this is Egypt, Ethiopia, and Libya to start; pretty much Africa is a slave by one puny verse of nude drunk Noah. And we are led to believe that Ham had sex with Noah and castrated him like Seth and Horus.

The Sumerians with Ziusudra don't have this gross story but we also consider them idol worshipers. It is okay to bow down to a book but if I dance in front of the statue, I must avoid lust. Lazy American pie can look at a picture on the internet with a caption and they think a picture is worth 1,000 words. They don't read books and they are ignorant of their own history and the fake Bible history written to make Daniel tell the future instead of history.

The fact is we don't have very much sex in America compared to Europe. The American woman is entitled. No matter how ugly and poor she wants money or food. She can't enjoy sex without dinner and dancing. She doesn't see a man as sexy, but she is after her free lunch. The devil invented marriage and laughs at us. We can only have sex with one person our entire life and the church must okay it.

The freedom we need is in us, but Jesus is sold to us as if he enters us when we are saved. The Gnostic and Roman Catholic are very different, but the knowledge of the Gnostics makes sense and is a better way of thinking. As is now we have the four Gospels and that is it. No extra Biblical Jesus or Gnostic gospel to expand our knowledge of Christ. The four Gospels end like the art in Italy, bloody. This makes us feel guilty, but the resurrection is common, and Osiris is the first resurrection.

Once again, just like the four Gospels, we are limited and the stuff in the Gospels is not quoted very often. I think we have no idea the amount of important literature is in the Bible or the prophecy of the end of times. Wars happen and the book of Revelations repeats itself. It is also a small book and gives us a vague sense of the afterlife. We cannot keep track of the devils the Christian faith has invented; they gave Satan a great army and all the books in the world.

We don't really worship Jesus or do what he said. We worship the Bible. Michael cannot kill the devil until the end of times. We wait for God's jealous hatred to fill the world with fire, and it is going to be like the days of Noah. Maybe this time the ark will be a spaceship.

If we look at the totems of the evangelist: Bull, Lion, Man, and Eagle we see the Babylonian deity Marduk is the Bull under the throne in Ezekiel's vision. Bel Marduk is Baal and Marduk is the twelfth planet. The Elohim are aliens but we only like the Jewish one. The whole mess is racists, and we allow these men of the past to shape our future.

Any shift to Rome, Greece, Persia, or Babylon is to our advantage. Let's see what Nebuchadnezzar says about Ezekiel. The way it is now we are completely out of context. We know the story of God killing his enemies and then he dies on a cross. Jupiter where are you? The gods are going to become idols and the Gentiles fornicators and masturbators. We are addicted to the color white: Noah, Abraham, Moses, Elijah, and Jesus are always white and never smiling at me.

The tree of life in the book of Daniel shows Nebuchadnezzar's fiery head to be the sun. This is where Bel, the god that aligns the constellations, can connect to any holy book with the Sun and Moon. America put a man on the moon, but we don't know the gods, or the names associated with the moon. The idea of worshiping the sun and moon sounds good to me. It sounds like we could catch up with history.

CHAPTER 11

PAGAN PERSPECTIVES

Hun Hunahpu (One Blower) is the moon in the Popul Vuh. The sun and moon go to Xibalba and fight the demons. They use blowguns and they even hide in them. They use their blowguns to cross rivers of corruption. They go through the various rooms and pass all the tests of the Lords of Xibalba.

I would love for America to replace its national Holy Book with the Popul Vuh. Maybe it could be read on Saturdays by fiery evangelists that could tell the story of the sun and moon in hell passing all the tests the devil could muster up. The sun and moon, Xbalanche and Hunahpu, could be replaced by any name for the sun and moon in other cultures and animate the gods following the sun and moon to Xibalba.

Xbalanche and Hunahpu are called the Hero Twins; I wrote about them in the Mangolishis Popul Vuh (lulu.com). They teach moral Mayan lessons that would be good for the American children. The sun and moon are your friend wherever you go. I see my Mangolishis moon and think of Horus and Jesus. Both walk on water, turn water to wine, born on Christmas, virgin birth, and resurrection from the dead.

The sun and moon never lie they just change their names. We are worried about the jealous God of the Bible putting us in hell and we fight the devil with just one book. The three monotheistic religions don't share. And since they all believe in Noah: rub and dub dub three men in tub. No orgy of the original Gnostic Jesus and his teachings? Do you hear the Book of Thomas is church? Irenaeus dubbed the early followers of Jesus, Satanists for having an orgy. Now we know Satan has the orgy. Where is he: Speak of the Devil and he raises his horns?

The devil's long horns rise into every religion thanks to the Christians. We believe the whole world is wrong, but the Bible is true. The only begotten son is a plagiarized Horus. The difference is one letter in son and sun. The circle unites us to the stars where these Bible stories come from. The way we say every ancient religion is pagan and their gods are false is not good. The things done in the Bible are not that rare if we look at polytheistic literature.

To feel good about saying the countries worship devils reminds me of my young days in church. Everything was bad and God was watching. We had so many rules and the cult drug us down to give our money and our bodies to crime. They asked me to lie on stage one time. They wanted me to say they healed my broken foot. They wanted me to act like it was a miracle.

The lies they told us can happen to anyone who believes the lie. I would stay virgin while others fucked my girlfriend, and I was not prepared for sex by the church. Why my country must be Christian is absurd. Looking through a book of world religions would you choose Christianity? We can fix the problems with books like this. Somebody must expose these lies and they are not easy to find.

The Bible was not written by God, but we force it down each other's throat without reading it. The ugly white saviors have no pyramid to speak of. Enoch may be the closest, but he has been pulled out of the Bible to hide the fallen angels. We are already saved and do not need Jesus. You think he is the bridge of faith to heaven and the rest of the people go to burn for eternity. This is to cruel to even imagine. God is worse than the devil, but Jehovah leads the Elohim. He turns them into angles but, these gods are more powerful than Jehovah and some of them are women.

This small, skinny, plagiarized Bible has sixty-six books left and I think sixty-four removed. I have read and loved the **Pseudepigraph** in Milan. I bought the two expensive books at the bookstore for $150. I went to my apartment in Piazza Jerusalem and read them in three weeks. The Testament of Job reveals the secrets of Satan and God. Satan knocks on Job's door. He appears to his wife in the marketplace and buys her hair off her since she was poor.

All these extra books including the **Apocrypha** are missing. We read the Bible so little and most people in America don't even know what the Torah is. We listen to and believe in lies all day long. The missing book of Wisdom from the Apocrypha is Solomons. After reading his wisdom literature in the Bible why would you want to continue.? If it is not inspired, it is taken out. It would be good for people to read this stuff and it would make us more moral. With Jesus you just worry about the three sins of the church and nothing else. People lie and steal all the time and it is hard to trust your friends.

We are worried about God killing us for jacking off and take the flawed Bible to the pedestal. The only book we believe God wrote. What about Allah? Why don't the Christian preachers teach why the Bible is true and all others are Satanist? Even the original followers of the Solar Jesus are called Satanist. The church cares not that you are ignorant they just want your money. Believe in Jesus and give the church your tithe. They get at least 10% of our income and don't pay taxes. They get rich off telling lies about a savior that is a copy of Horus. It is as if history means nothing to the Christian they are just off to lie and steal. All the poor Americans giving their money to the church should invest in themselves and learn how to pray before and after you read to Bible.

It is still an instrument to get to God and we understand God through the Bible to be a racist. Israel (Jacob) is loved, and Esau is hated. Esau is probably a copy of Enkidu from the Enuma Elish. Then Jacob (Scorpio) stings his children and later promises the entrance to the New Jerusalem. All of us are Esau being hated by God and eating the scraps that fall of the floor. The wisdom and gods of the Native American could help us and it is not polluted.

Spain burned some important Indian Information, but we still have the Popul Vuh. Nobody reads it and nobody cares. We don't read the books about the idols, but we are like Father Abraham who burned down his father's idol shop. Christians put the gods in hell, so they won't have to hear their flood stories, crucified saviors, and avatars of the Gnostic Jesus. Think of Jesus independently from the Bible. He has four books and all other books about him are sin. This is the dragon talking and he lives in the city of seven hills.

The dragons of mythology are slain by heroes and St. George killed a dragon. Saints, gods both male and female, and people interact with the forces of darkness in their own way. In Egypt it is Seth (night) and Horus (day) battling back and forth. Polytheism and Unitarianism connect, like Bel, the stars and the constellations. We can't go on teaching all these sacred books are false. Jesus is too big! He took women away from me, made me tithe, and told me if I follow him, I would be rich and famous with a beautiful wife.

I wrote books and went on pilgrimages to study God closer. I found the Pagan Temple of Osiris in Bologna; Italy and the search was over. A church older than the Bible they say. A plaque on the door says: "This Used to Be the Pagan Temple to Osiris. Now it is the property of the Roman Catholic Church." I had a vision that this plaque fell off the church and into my hands. When I look at the plaque in my hands it was the Book of The Dead. I knew the name Osiris from my Bible notes when it says: "I saw them putting the Branch to their nose."

The Branch is Jesus, Osiris, Baal, Tamuzzi, and Dumuzzi and I knew they were putting to their nose to smell it since the idol or branch was probably in somebody's ass. Kind of makes you think of Ham and Noah. After reading the Book of The Dead I realized what I knew already. Osiris is the phallus, and the plumbing has to do with our soul. This older teaching from an older church is in a city where they celebrate the Black Virgin, Isis and 666 archways she walks through.

To remember this old temple in Bologna is to remember we have a savior in our pants that is probably associated in our brains with the serpent in The Garden of Eden. The church does not want you to know that you are already saved. They tell you one thing after another to keep you going. It is just a business, and do you think the church will help you if you are poor? They want free labor and dollar bills. But the lie remains the same. The Jesus of the church never existed, and all the three monotheistic religions come from Egypt. Egypt is the cradle of civilization and I even think Baal is Osiris and Anat is Isis. They have the same story, and the Phoenicians travel and exchange their women and goods wherever they go.

To think that **Phoenician, El and Baal** live at the **Twin Rivers, Mt. Zaphon** is incredible. We are stuck on the mountain with murderous Moses. He kills an Egyptian and buries him in the sand. Many say Moses was Egyptian and he is a copy of Sargon's birth story. He comes down from the mountain to see the Bull Calf when it was the Age of the Ram that he was ushering in. He breaks the commandments and tells them to kill each other. Moses does not take responsibly. He was their teacher, and they built the wrong animal for the age that had passed. Most people think Moses was mad that they built an idol. That was not the problem at all. They still blow the ram's horn to remember the age.

All the evil of Abraham, Isaac, and Jacob is associated with Jesus because we say Jesus is God and God wrote the Bible instead of men. To the Christian the sixty-six books of the Bible are just a miracle. The stories that go in the stars as the real Jesus imitated the sun on his route with the planets. The constellations are for the polytheist: Babylon, Maya, Phoenician, Aztec, Persian, Greek, and Roman. We are against our penis and most people think Jesus forbade pre-marital sex.

The idea of marrying an idol, in the out of context sense, convinces us fornication is pre-marital sex. It is impossible the Bible says it let alone Jesus. St. Paul does not force his celibacy on you, but the church does. Virgin until married like Isis Mary, Virgo, Anat ......the stories of the Bible are not original they are all copied.

CHAPTER 12

THE BUSINESS OF BAAL

God becomes more a criminal each day since we must blame our ignorance on him. Try this one on for size: The Holy Spirit is the Great Spirit. The wisdom of the Popul Vuh will come back to us and we will add one "s" to heaven, and we have heavens and return to the stars. All the sacred literature connects to the days of the week and the stars. We have one book and the second commandment that controls us. All the ancients were pagan worshiping idols, so we have our duty to stay clear of them.

This is too much power for the Bible. Nobody will read between the lines and get us out of here. The criminal, punitive God is forced on us each holiday. What is the difference between Happy Easter and Happy Ishtar? One is pagan just like the three wise men at Christmas following the brightest star in the sky. Our conditioning is with words that sound bad, so we assume they are bad. I would like to live with Ishtar as the bright morning star!

Fertility and sex are the big, "sins", but we lose the knowledge of the gods. The interaction they have is tremendous and even love expressed by Ishtar after the flood is good to know about. The gods don't hate us, but we do not even have a correct history with the God we have. Jehovah is for the Jews, and they understand the Old Testament better than the Christian. Why does not the Christian read the Talmud to see what the Old Testament is all about?

The missing books, beside the four, about Jesus are all over.

Nobody wants to hear about Jesus as a man. They like his miracles like walking on water. This proves nothing 2,000 years later. Who saw it and wrote about it is sketchy. Vishnu has a name: "He who is carried on the waters of the unconscious." Mary and Martha with Jesus is a conscious and unconscious combination. Mary is Krishna (at ease) Martha is Arjuna (at work) and Jesus is God.

Polytheism fills in the blanks, but Baal shows how much the Bible is false. It cannot be the word of God with a serpent and a Phoenician devil. Too many symbols and stories add up to make Gnostic/Polytheism the American religion. Read the Popul Vuh and believe in the Great Spirit. How could these things be wrong? All these cultures have so much in common and only the Bible somehow attaches the words of Jesus to Moses. Elijah is forgotten about as John the Baptist.

These Bible characters are not as powerful as the Roman Catholic Saints. You have the Bible God claiming the flood, the volcano on Santorini, the Plagues of the Nile, and Sodom and Gomorrah. Every freak of nature is Jehovah the angry volcano God from Santorini. The explosion is what caused the flood the Bible speaks of and the plagues on the Nile. All humanity would embrace the volcano if it were Jewish. Christians claim their original followers are Satanist and what do they say about the Jews. The Jews wrote everything. They do not claim Jesus to be their Messiah. Doesn't this tell you something? The Jews and Muslims are also adversarial in the monotheistic trio. They all believe in Noah, Ziusudra, and most Americans have not read Gilgamesh 2600 B.C., the world's first poetry.

The Enumu Elish is about Gilgamesh losing his friend Enkidu. He looks for the meaning of life and finds Ziusudra/Unatapsin who tells him the flood story. Moses gathered everything he could and wiped out the idols of Egypt with his ten commandments (613 in the Torah). Now everything is an idol or devil to us.

Have you read the story of Hercules? Do you think the son of Zeus is also a Satanist? Greek or Roman orgy, no big deal? If we believe pre-marital sex to be a sin, why is it not mentioned in the 613 commandments? Not even the word fornication is in there. Most Americans don't know the Ten Commandments let alone the 613, that interact with each other. This is like taking ten laws out our legal system and trying to live by them. Think of all the problems this creates.

The Christian church has closed the door on many of us that don't intend to be celibate until we are married. This is so extreme and conveniently makes everyone guilty. Even lust is bad. Think of the gods having an orgy. How beautiful it would be to see that. Our Christian heaven does not have sex. What about my heaven on earth in Europe? This is not even possible for rich men in America.

Always guilty of lust, without the power to do anything about it. This is the obsession of the Catholic Church. They have always been against sex. The changes made to our body parts and the Bible is the trick to understanding the Osirian religion. Without the forty-two gods in the body, we are less than divine. We are made sinners by Eve. This story happens in the nude and the temptation looks sexual.

Adam does not do much so he cannot become an idol. We recognize Jesus by his cross. When we say we are justified by the law Christ has fallen from grace and we see his death as vain. The teachings of the New Testament are still not understood. We are transformed by Jesus but who has seen a good before and after example. People quit drinking or gambling and are born again.

The word Born Again has two meanings in Greek. One is to be born again and the other is to be born from above. Jesus said, "Born from above.' Nicodemus said, "Born again" meaning he would enter his mother again. If the Holy Spirit is talking to us, why don't we know there are 613 commandments in the Torah? Why do born again Christians not know the Greek of their own name? All the Bible is altered, and it requires books about the Bible to understand the Bible.

When I responded to the first altar call in 1984, I thought everybody was going to raise their hand. I did not want to go to hell, but I did not want to go to the altar. This was all new to me. They gave me a free Bible and asked me to kneel and pray. The next Sunday my friends that invited me to the concert took me to their church.

People speaking in tongues and going off in this church scared me. One woman I wanted to throw out. Next thing the prophecies, tongues, and interpretations start. One man, claiming to be God, kicks the pew in front of him. He starts rattling off the King James Bible. People are dancing and moaning. One of the most embarrassing things is the Jericho march. Everybody young and old starts going in a circle around the pews. There arms are going crazy, and they march to bring a spiritual Jericho down. They will grab you and pull you into the march.

The people at this church make me laugh to this day. I remember all the fun characters and plays we did. Everybody in the plays were gay and many confessed that they were there looking for young love. Everybody ignored the warning signs until the Pastor got busted for molesting children. These are the same people who said God would bring me a wife and a Ferrari, and all the money in the world if I would just give up karate and school to serve him. This totally fucked up my life and I am on the road to recovery.

I stayed virgin until I was twenty-one and the whole time, I had hot girlfriends. I gave up sex for Jesus and I am not married to a beautiful model or driving the Ferrari like they told me about. They would shake my head and tell me to speak in tongues. This is so weird somebody from another planet is speaking through me. The molestations add up and the only people in the church not having sex were me and my brother. We had the karate discipline. We said no to women but later in life when the spell wears off, it is all control for money and business as usual.

CHAPTER 13

BI-POLAR BUDAPEST

Being bi-polar I hear voices and I do not know if God is taking to me or not. All I gave up for Jesus: Music, karate, school, friends ....and eventually our blessed mother is a sinner going to hell if we don't bring her to church. The church did horrible things, and everybody was molesting somebody. Since they cannot get hookers, you are the free hooker. You are telling me a long-legged blonde with beautiful tits could not get those pedophiles to abandon the use of children. They could tell their fantasy to a young prostitute. We are not the free hookers, running around buying each other food for sex. It is embarrassing to be American knowing they allow these churches to set up shop wherever.

We know nothing is wrong with going to a sex worker in Amsterdam. They have an office of prostitution I went to in 1996. They say prostitution prevents rape and they have only had disease with street walkers, never with the women in the windows. The price in 1996 was $25 and in 2000 the price went up to $50. I was in Amsterdam and Antwerp in 2016 and it was still $50. The price of pussy did not go up much since the first time I smoked pot in Amsterdam. The price of so many things has gone up since the early nineties. Love is the same and there is no reason to rape or molest.

The ugliest man in the world pays the same price we do. Everybody has a chance at sex before they die. Since the government says you can do it for free, they pull the plug of money. To communicate we need prices, and everybody gets paid. Jesus hung out with hookers for a reason. He seems to enjoy their company and maybe relish their stories.

That is what I would like to hear: The prostitutes talking about the Johns. What did they do that was good or bad? In Barcelona I went to a gentlemen's club in 2001. The dancers are all photo models and charge $120 for a half hour; $240 for an hour; and $20,000 for three days. Women from all over the world come to this classy place in a quiet neighborhood of Barcelona. I saw a woman from Budapest there. She is the most beautiful woman I have ever seen.

When she dances it is $400 and hour and when she is not dancing it is $240 an hour. When she came up to me, I saw she had been dancing. I did not have $400 but on a different night she said to me: "Come on Silly, it is only $120 for a half hour when I am not dancing." I went up the elevator and she said: "You can touch me now." I grabbed her ass, and it is the most beautiful ass I have ever seen. She is perfectly proportioned. I could show you any body part if you know there is symmetry.

We went into the room, and I cleaned myself, and she said; "Don't touch yourself!" I told God if he let me lick her pussy and ass, I would do whatever he wanted me to. "I will be a Jehovah Witness or a Mormon if you want me to". I opened my eyes in missionary and went to heaven. I could only see the peripheral of heaven and I saw men laying on couches watching us. She was so perfect. I knew her face took me to heaven, and she seemed heavenly. Her body turned into light, and she had an orgasm in my mouth in the sixty-nine. I did every position and finished in the elephant. When the knock-on door came my half hour was done. She took me to heaven and gave me a kiss on the cheek.

What does it take to have this experience in America? My anger on certain drunk nights made me trigger the bi-polar. I want a woman. And why can't I have her? A law of some old men that never get laid want to ruin my fun. "Get it for free." They speak. You won't go to heaven, but you won't go to jail like an ordinary hooker. An American woman is a food whore because she is smart enough to stay out of jail.

It is important to remember that you don't have a free will as an American. If you are French, Italian, or Mexican you lose your freedom to sell yourself when you come here. We believe pre-marital sex is bad, but it is worse if you pay for it. The idea of the rapist and the pedophile trying to get it for free is perplexing. They will have such a hard time getting a woman and the Webster's Dictionary says: "Onanism is masturbation." The error of the Bible is also in the dictionary.

With all these errors we are eventually emasculated. The phallus, Osiris, in the Book of the Dead is where the soul (Ka) connects to the Sun God (Ra). If Jesus were a solar deity, we could attribute the planets to him. Now we are stuck with St. Paul for Jupiter, and he was a celibate. We need to unclog this solar curse on us. Ra, Jah, Yahweh, Yahu, and Jehovah lead to the sun. We do not worship the sun or read about it. The whole monotheistic thing comes from Egypt and Osiris is the first resurrection. His son Horus is like Jesus and Isis to Mary. The heaven or the heavens are important. Mary takes you to heaven but in the heavens is Virgo.

CHAPTER 14

VIRGINS FOR VENUS

M y life gets direction from these gods. The ancient deities are similar. They all connect with Isis or whatever woman is left standing after angry Jehovah gets a hold of them. Evil was personified in the woman and Rome is the Harlot sitting on many waters. Whenever I travel Italy, I go to their bookstores and buy other books from street vendors. At the bookstore in Milan, I bought several books of great importance. I open all the Bible commentaries to Revelations to see if anyone says Babylon is Rome. I also read Noah's sin with Ham to see if he sodomized Noah, cut of his dick, or both. If he just looked at nude drunk Noah that is not much of a sin to get angry about.

We would be in a sexual paradise in America if we would legalize prostitution and read the Gnostic Gospels. Look at what we have been through with Jehovah. Ham sodomizes his father and cuts off his dick so he can't have any more children. Jehovah kills Er, for doing evil in the eyes of the Lord, and then kills Onan for masturbating. If we are afraid to have sex with each other it is because of these lies we attribute to God.

The church could say that they are against pre-marital sex for certain reasons but don't bring God into it. I stayed virgin for five years and humped women's butt cracks and got blow jobs. Finally at twenty-one I did it and then I moved to San Francisco where I was with a different woman every night.

Missing out on all this sex has caused me to make up for lost time.

All over Europe, fifty-four cities, I research brothels and churches. I would go to pray and then the fun would begin. Every American should have this experience and the sex worker is the only woman that can civilize us. In the meantime, we feed on each other, and this is the worst. The women get rapped and babies get fucked in church but no need for a prostitute. This is sick and since we are not supposed to jack off, we better all get married young.

Marry the wife of your youth while Jacob marries four and Solomon 700. These men had sex with more than one woman, and they got married young. Virgins unite and do prostitutes that look like photo models. We need to make up for lost time. The age of the Virgin Mary when she first had sex for probably fourteen. Joseph may have been forty and she was his property. The point is we could wait until fourteen, or later, to have sex and then that is it.

Otherwise, an unmarried person is expected to remain a virgin until they die. Is that what we do now? We already have sex, and few people are virgin when they are married. This freedom from the lies of the Roman Catholic Church makes us right with God. We do not want to give up sex and we don't have to. The idea that Gnostic Jesus has the Love Feast probably means he does not mind if you make love to your girlfriend or a prostitute. The orgy is extreme to imagine.

The men cannot handle it and eventually all this horniness manifests itself. Anger, frustration, and the lowering of standards happens. I have had bi-polar outburst after leaving bars. I try and fight whoever will fight me. All because I can't get a sex worker to help me out. A whole life in a country of ignorance that believe Jesus was against pre-marital sex. I see their faces and they all seem brainwashed. They are cowards when it comes to fighting the Bi-Polar Bear.

Why go through life with fantasies that can be carried out. Many lonely people and those that have gone five years or more without getting laid. Go to the brothel and do eight in a row. Feel sex and strength come to you with a daughter of Ishtar. A young hooker gives her youth and energy to the older men, and they drink from the fountain of youth.

Get a six pack for the men and a beautiful ass for the woman. Thrusting, turning and in my case doing Ju Jitsu. It all blends perfect, and if we experience God forgiving us, we can move on to things that matter. Why do people lie and believe lies in America? We are very ignorant of the Bible and get stung by Jacob Heel Catcher instead of American Poet Jacob Mango. The sweet heel catcher or deceiver will deliver the story. The heroes of the Bible, who we are told are waiting for us in the New Jerusalem, are liars, thieves, and con artists. We celebrate them like the saints. Men who are celibate on earth and in heaven.

CHAPTER 15

PARK GUELL

The Saints of Vic, I read about in Barcelona, two Italian saints who fly through windows and seduce women. They always succeed and the women cannot resist their magic. It was funny learning about the saints with my friend, from Italy. We were the magic of Vic in Barcelona. Every night up and down **La Ramblas** women wait for us on both sides of the biggest street in Europe.

I get in fights with pick pockets and do the lovely women on La Ramblas. The magic was my friend and I on a mission. The dollar was strong, and I paid for everything since he let me live with him for five months. He does not finish well with women because he is so aggressive. He is sturdy and handsome, so he does get some women. He is a bar tender at an Internet cafe off La Ramblas.

I would leave him at night to go on my journey through Barcelona. I discovered an Alchemist Garden City designed by Antonio Gaudi; called Park Guell. It takes eight hours to walk through and the whole city is a replica of Delphi. There are eighty-eight hallow pillars that collect rain (Sarva) and store it in the parks huge belly. The pillars are for the 88 constellations 86, 87, 88 is Ophucious with two pieces of Serpents Caput. The stairway is equal to where at Delphi, Apollo swam into the cave, in the form of a dolphin and killed the Serpent Python and replaced him as the protector of the waters. He sat on a throne and spoke oracles about the world navel.

At the Cosmic Temple to the Sun and Moon at Park Guell is a

stairway with four platforms. The first is the Horned Serpent, the second is the Salamander; where Apollo as a dolphin would appear, third is the Tripod with the World Navel inside, and finally at the top is the Mouth of the Great Seer, it is bench. The lips are quivering for fear of Christ's return.

I walk around this Alchemist City with a book about it. I learned so much about Alchemy, Masonry, and Roman Catholic I put it in a trio that I use to figure things out. They have the Masonic Calvary, crosses with pyramids on top, the Closed Chapel, the Mushroom Pavilion, and the Hermana Masona (Lavandera) in the Red Sea. You walk right through it.

Europe has more resources than we do for pilgrimage. I went from city to city learning from the essence of the churches. The gargoyles on the sides of the gothic cathedrals speak to me. Lisbon, Milan, Paris, Barcelona, and Budapest were my favorites. My eyes roam from symbol to symbol and great peace comes over me. I mourned my mother's death in the Duomo of Milan. The Saints sad faces gave me great comfort and connection with God.

They are speaking to me all the time. Milan and Bologna are like the sun and moon. Bologna has the Pagan Temple to Osiris (Ra) and the Duomo is the moon in Milan. Italy is energized by its churches. All we see is a cross with no circle around it. Missing information is everywhere, and the symbols are hard to find. The connection with the past restores our history.

My learning and understanding came from matching Bible verses to art. Then I would have a vital experience with God and solidify something into my experience. I have touched the hem of his garment and was healed by the Tilma of Guadalupe (Rev 12). In Italy I am surrounded by Bible art, and it is obvious the artists are doing a critic of the Word. In Venice I saw a nine-foot statue of Noah next to a five-foot statue of Ham. I hold my breathe near St. Mark's Cathedral and contemplate the five-foot-tall Ham (that looks like Pan) with Hot Africa. The one that looked upon his father's drunken nudity. Slavery is the punishment for the children Ham, and we believe the Torah to be the word of God.

CHAPTER 16

IT STARTS WITH SYMBOLS

The excellent teachers I had in Italy were the ones that took me to bookstores in **Bologna**. I bought books by **Rene Guenon,** and it changed my life. He taught me the sacred science of symbols. One religion connects to another. Jacob's ladder is compared to ladders drawn in the caves of the Native American. Going from here to there is the symbolism. If we could turn the Bible into symbols, we would have the enemy countries of Christianity come forth especially Greece, Rome, Egypt, and Babylon.

There was always a Jesus and a Father, like El and Baal. God and Master were the Phoenician equivalent of Jehovah Jesus or Abraham and Isaac. Most of the world calls this history and they abuse women in the name of Moses. A white people look to Moses since he is a racist and his God is racist. They steal from the Egyptian and the son of Osiris and Isis becomes Jesus (Horus).

The pyramids don't matter to the lying Christian who contradict all forms of truth, every pyramid, god, legend, hero, original poetry, and books. The **Popul Vuh** is the Maya Bible but since we have the sun and moon why not use the Popul Vuh to connect us to the Maya and their sciences. You want to hear about the miracles of the saints or see what true story telling can do. **The Sun and Moon go to hell and beat the devils! We would celebrate this along with Ra the Sun God killing the serpent daily.**

3,000 years ago, this bullshit starts with a talking serpent with no wings. I'm sure Gnosis would help but we are behind the Baktun of the Star Planting (Maya). If Satan, the serpent in the Garden of Eden, was Gnostic Satan she would be a woman. **Sophia** the Greek word for wisdom is the name the Gnostics use for the Christian Satan. We could have a Satan serpent or a wise female Sophia, pure wisdom. Speak Greek to her and she will respond. That removes Satan from the Bible! And when Solomon says Sophia was with God when he created the world. All things were made with Sophia.

The Gnostic had an orgy and a human gospel. We judge them only for sex. Don't discount Nag Hamadi and the gazelle skin wrappers! The priest and the pastor go their way with Satan and terrorize the ignorant Americans with hell. God loves you but he will put you in hell. Satan lies to us, and we believe it. Michael the Arch Angel is depicted defeating him in art but not in real life.

You can't have sex is what we have, but **the reality is the orgy**. The love of the Gnostic Jesus was so great people made love to the Sun God. Remember Jesus has been changed by Constantine and others; **a myth made history**. The Bible is not accurate history, and everybody has a flood story and a hero. The racist one is the only one we believe in. Jesus got popular when they painted him white. He is an idol, so Jehovah punishes us daily and the words of Moses ring is in our ears.

We lie about the **Torah** and call the **Talmud** the devil. Every book, legend, god, or hero goes to the devil, and everything is a sin. If the church is not punished for lying and stealing, why should I fear Jehovah will kill me for masturbating? You can't even enjoy masturbating. God is watching you and he has nothing better to do than focus on a single person enjoying them self.

In Carlsbad where I live there are many beautiful women to look at. I go to the gym and see sweaty butts going up and down on the machines. Some hot women are bobbing up and down on the stomach machine and it looks like they could be doing a blow job. Then they have the leg stretching machine and the women in their leotards, G-strings, thongs, tight shorts, and revealing tops.

After the gym I go to the beach. Wash off in the waves. One time at the beach of the Army Navy Academy I saw a woman. She was a tall Chinese woman with big tits and a big delicious, beautiful butt. She bent over to get her towel and when I saw her ass; I thought I could pay her $1,000,000 for sex, if I had a million dollars. The feeling was overwhelming, and I could see myself pouring the million over her. I was out of control. She got up and walked into her expensive beach house. I thought her husband must be a stud, what would it be like to make love to her every night?

The reason I tell you the beach story and the gym story is I am in America where prostitution is illegal. How is it possible to not jack off after seeing all that ass? Women teasing you and hoping you will buy them food so they can have sex with you and risk together the flames of eternal hell.

Maybe a lap dance will help…come on America…. legalize prostitution. Call them sex workers and let us be free of jealous Jehovah and move over to Jupiter and Zeus and Baal. These are the correct order. In Daniels tree of life (Nebuchadnezzar) Babylon, Persia, Greece, and Rome are the tree seen in the King of Babylon's dream which the prophet interpreted. A lot like Joseph and Pharaoh.

We go every day horny instead of going to Amsterdam for $50 a piece. Bring $500 and do ten in a row and see how you feel. Millionaire America doesn't allow that, so the rich get trophy brides. I had the most beautiful one I have ever seen for $120, and I went to heaven. Rare countries I have never heard of and friends from all over the world making love for money. My penis has helped pay for hookers houses in Brazil; and they can buy houses with their pussies if they move to Italy.

Mean Roman Catholic Jehovah, are you going to put us in hell for making love? Or how about this one: **No fuckers enter the kingdom of God**. The whole Jesus story attaches you to Moses, but you don't believe in the Qabalah -the oral tradition of Moses.

We have an edited Bible we do not understand. We use the Christian story of Moses but ignore his oral teachings which were clean. The ugly Bible is our only ladder to God. Jacob is the heel catcher that produced the tribes of Israel. God fighter and heel catcher are the terms we use. Our master is not good to us. He takes our money and tells us not to have sex before marriage. And then only for making babies. **Welcome to the curse of the Egyptian procreation only theory.**

Babies only and no masturbation; can't waste the sperm, be fruitful and multiply, these are the ideas we have. The ancients copied each other and trusted in superstition. When I talk to American people, they quote the Bible, but they do not understand the Torah and the Prophets. The little story we know is altered and Jesus is the Sun. We copied the actions of the sun on Earth. Change one letter in son and you get sun. Let's go back to normal and quit calling the Pagans, Polytheist, and Gnostics Satan.

It is all about sex. That is the only moral we have. If a man is caught getting a $25 blow job, we call the police to put him in jail. In the old days smoking a joint was bad. What this adjustment will do is incredible. We are ignorant of polytheism and any book that is not the Bible is bad. All these options that we are ignorant of.

Jesus is what is stopping us from further illumination. We believe in him a certain way. God was never mad at sex until the Roman Catholic Church took over. **Absalom** took David's harem to the top of tent and fucked them. Solomon had a harem and others have multiple wives. They are not virgins. They have sex and it is not an everyman and women created equal. Women were tortured even if suspected of adultery. **They tried to scare everybody, but because of these lies we believe God is against sex.**

Jesus got a whore for a wife while St. Peter, our fist Pope, was crucified upside down as a political criminal. They were stealing the ministry of Mary Magdalene the wife. She would have taken control after Jesus died and our first Pope would have been a woman. It is not true she was a hooker. They changed her from wife to hooker to fuck up sex more and have us drinking it in for 2,000 years!

Moses is too young of a story and his 900-year-old Noah's is not even true. In the Torah is the warning of Abraham, Isaac, and Jacob.

These Patriarchs stole and did evil, but we only punish for sex. Trying to control the women backfired on us. Women can't give us all they want to because we punish them. They are not the goddess who is the original Inanna. Then she takes money and becomes Babylonian Ishtar. Money was given for sex on an altar and women lost their virginity for a purse of money and a handsome Babylonian man wearing the horns of a stag has special sex with you. **He blesses the forty-two gods in her body!**

We are missing out on all wisdom that has anything to do with sex. The gods threaten the monotheist but since the gods love us why do we hate them? We study only the Bible and that sick flood story. We believe Moses is good and Hercules is bad. All these happy healthy gods are sleeping. Look at the second commandment and shit or get off the pot.

We could build towers, temples, and bookstores. The fear of an idol is nothing! According to St. Paul we can go to the temple if it does not stumble anyone. I think we are afraid of the books, so I read them for you. Your penis is a grasshopper.... what more do you want from me. None of these idol books are bad and we really should read and study the Book of the Dead. We live and die, not knowing the gods are in the constellations watching us and loving us, while we are stuck with a Catholic Jehovah who kills people for masturbating. Nice guy... father figure, why are there so many problems in the world? We have Jesus (guilt) as the only resource. All books are Satan to us Americans.

CHAPTER 17

THE WORLD TO COME

When I lived in Italy, I saw people ski on the alps of Switzerland. I went to Lausanne where I was going to get a tattoo. As far as God goes-let's talk to the Talmud. I read in America about God saying: "Have you seen my Alps?", On judgment day he asks this question to us in the Talmud. When I saw the Alps on the park bench, I felt like I was at church. I even bought a Hugo Boss sweater to enjoy the show in. I sat for three hours thinking about what they call in the Talmud: "The World to Come.'

The Red Roman Pig takes the boot of Italy and turns it into a whirling axe that cuts through the bullshit. The pig is a scholar, and nobody can take him in a wrestling match. He goes to Milan, Venice, Bologna, Florence, Rome, Naples, and Lecce to see the seven heads of Satan. The Bible says Guadalupe saved the child. What about Michael the Arch Angel? He is supposed to kill Satan.

With "The World to Come" in heaven we have fire underneath with some of our friends and families in it. God is so nice and loving in polytheism, yet monotheism has a God that does not sentence masturbators to death; he kills them himself. Not put to death by the law. Why did the Roman Catholic Jehovah not kill Adolf Hitler for masturbating? The Bible says, "No weapon formed against you shall prosper." What happened to the miracle of Jehovah, the evil Sun, and Seth to me, not a god you want to wake up to.

Our American Jesus only cares about sex. We are not supposed to do it and we do it anyway. We call it fornication and that puts us in the lake of fire that St. John wrote about in Revelations. I am writing Revelations right now with the constellations on the apron of Guadalupe. I can see her with the wings of an eagle at her feet. Who is the child in her arms. The Mexican Jesus, Juan Diego? We would be free if we studied the Bible. In America other people pack your eternal parachute. Americans will believe anything. I am so glad I lived in Europe and met poets, intellectuals, and artists. In America I have been to many poetry readings and the rhymes are difficult to translate. Guadalupe is so vital that we understand it is her in the Revelations 12. 1531 AD is the page number. Now you figure it out. Ten books left in Revelations and 2012 A.D is the end of the New Testament.

If you want to break free of the Bible, follow me on this Greek Pilgrimage to Santorini, Greece where he blows up like a volcano. 1500 B.C.; Santorini caused the flood the Bible speaks of and the plagues of the Nile. Since Jehovah takes credit for world destruction it is interesting the first two books of the Bible are blown away by a Pilgrimage to Santorini (The Atlantis Plato wrote of). The other death is Patmos, the island St. John is buried at. Around his tomb are women crying and it says: "84% of Revelations is false. John gave it to a Greek interpreter on his death bed. A lot was lost in the translation."

This shows us the Bible is way off from what it used to be. In one swipe I took out the father and son in one trip to Greece. I found new faith in my own books. I continued to learn about God from the pilgrimages to fifty-four cities in eleven countries. Europe was mine and I lived in Barcelona for five months where I found the gothic art I was searching for. Eusebi Guell and Antonio Gaudi seem to follow me wherever I go. I have tattooed a character of Guell on my right tricep. He has a seven-pronged crown and carries a basket of mushrooms in a Tuxedo. He is a Mason and he funded Antonio Gaudi's work and left his name on Park Guell, an Alchemist Garden City, in Barcelona, Spain.

They toast to the Grandmaster Architect and my experiences in Greece and Spain forms a lot of my second spiritual travel novel: The

Lords of The Poison. Most of my tattoos are holy relics from the Dark Mary to her son designed by Antonio Gaudi.

Delphi Greece sunk in 1500 B.C like Santorini - The Atlantis Plato wrote about, but Park Guell has a story of a Salamander that I tell. Apollo swam into Delphi in the form of a Dolphin and killed the Serpent Python and replaced him as the protectors of the waters (unconsciousness). He sat on a throne and spoke of the World Navel.

Gaudi is the salamander because Park Guell is modeled after Delphi. On the Cosmic Stairway to the Sun and Moon there are four platforms leading up to the Mouth of the Seer. The first platform is a Bronze Horned Serpent that represent Eusebi Guell who financed the park. The second platform is the entrance to the underworld guarded by a colorful Salamander; this is Gaudi or the dolphin Apollo. The third platform has the Tripod with the Philosophers Stone in it. The fourth level in a bench that looks like trembling lips in fear of Christ's return. You can sit in it, and it is called the Mouth of the Great Seer.

Therefore, I promote my cult to the black Jesus and the Alchemy that used to be Gnostic. The Seer and the World Navel are all Masonic, Alchemist, and Roman Catholic all mixed. How does a man like Gaudi see the Bible and in particular Jesus Christ?

At Park Guell the eighty-eight pillars hold up the Serpentine Bench and there are eighty-eight constellations. Serpent Caput is the Serpentine Bench and that means the God Ophiuchus must be there. Gnosticism became Alchemy and the mind of Gaudi is one who like Dante understood. Gaudi's work is all over Barcelona. His masterpiece to me is Park Guell and the Sagrada Familia.

CHAPTER 18

CHANGES

The prophets are interesting to me, and my favorite is Ezekiel. He sees God's chariot when Cyrus the Persian was saving Israel from Nebuchadnezzar. I believe Isaiah called Cyrus "Anointed" and man does the work and Jehovah takes the credit. Jehovah held the hand of Cyrus when he saved the Jews from Babylon. How unappreciative that somebody would save the Jews from Babylon and get so little credit or mention in the Bible.

It is funny that the Kings get so little mention. Maybe in the opening they get some type of credit. But there is always a king punishing Israel. They call a pagan god a timeline. The young god is the one we want. Baal and El trade places because of popularity. Maybe it is like that with Jehovah and Jesus. Read the Old and New Testament and find Isaac on the cross. The Torah has Joseph (prototype of Jesus) to end the story. In book one we have forgiveness of the brothers and judgement day.

We do not need to read the altered Exodus! Moses (Sargon of Accad) is another copy. We don't even understand who Elijah is but eventually we will create a solar system in America. Say hello to the original Sun God! The fallen angels will have temples and bookstores. We will see how complicated the Christian religion is. Many angels and saints to keep track of. We are stuck on Jesus because he is white and Jewish. All the Gentile Saviors goes to waste, and aren't we afraid we are missing something?

We are going to live and die under Christianity alone which proposes heaven and hell. There is no comparison from Aztec, Maya, and Inca gods. Many flood stories and the interaction between gods like El and Anat is sacred to me. Baal in the Bible is a devil but if you put him in his pantheon he is like Jesus. Baal is older than Jehovah and the story of Jezebel shows what happens to the Phoenician in the Bible.

We go through this life with one book when there are many. Jesus doesn't live in the gospels only. We should be our own Vatican and study the gods. The laws, if we like them, we keep them. The main law is to love God with your heart, mind, and soul; and love your neighbor as yourself. This does not only complete the law but also the prophets. **613 commandments in the Torah and how many more in the Bible. All summed up with love.**

Eros is the oldest god, and it makes sense that we tend to ignore cupids bow. All the stars have all the stories. Without the four Greek words for love we do not know what kind of love we are talking about. In English "love" is like strong "like." I love my mother and I love pizza, or I would love one of those. The moral love is the one we are missing. To be fond of feeding the sheep or I love feeding them.

"God is love," according to St. John. Does love kill masturbators and did Jesus full fill the Torah? If we replaced "Love" for "God" much of the Bible will not make sense unless God is a racist. We favor the Jews not the Giants, yet they were created by The Sons of The Elohim or the Sons of the Gods. This is probably a cover up for the pagan gods the church does not want us to study. Even if they are like Christ, we won't study them. Our grandparents were completely brainwashed. We curse our own kind and want what we don't have.

We could lead by example and study. The idol is nothing without a book and his legend. If you read Baal first you can tell the Bible copies him, but he is pure. He does not kill you for masturbating and his wife Anat is sexy. She tells God what to do and he loves her. A temple to have sex in and make it rain. Baal goes with his seven wives, and it starts to rain. In the Pantheon is Mot the Moon. Bel Marduk is

Babylon and Phoenician Baal. We miss out on chances to honor the gods of Elijah.

Jehovah enters the window to announce the birth of a new God in Babylon. He is like the stork to them, and all the goddesses are more powerful than Jehovah. Jehovah takes credit for the Volcano on Santorini's damage, and we pick up his story from there. The best thing about the goddesses is they connect ancient cultures. **There are many flood stories and Santorini is the Atlantis that Plato wrote about.**

The original Christians had an orgy, and you believe pre-marital sex, masturbation, and looking at a woman's ass to be adultery. He made it harder to get in than ever, but he forgives you. When he saves you, you change, and then you keep the law. If the forty-two Egyptian gods waiting for us in the tunnel to meet Osiris are hearing a negative confession what are our priests in America hearing? They say, "I have not..." the Bible says, "Thou shalt not..." **Moses changed the Book of The Dead to make the Ten Commandments.**

If the Negative Confession is true, then Christians are fucked, they are going to say sorry forty-two times and meet the original resurrection; Osiris. The Exodus in the battle between Moses and Pharaoh, Daniel meets Nebuchadnezzar, and Baal meets Elijah. On every other side we are mentally blocked. We think all non-Jewish cultures and their gods are bad. "Babylon" we associate with wine and whores more than astrology. These big empires wrote first and what they wrote was not bad. These were great men and kings that ruled the world. Israel shows up and writes his story, giving Jehovah credit.

The gods tag along with Jehovah and are disguised as fallen angels. If we worshiped fallen angels, we could get the books of Enoch back. We shortened the Bible, and it is still too big for us. Maybe just the gospels would be good for length. The **Nican Mopohua is 218 lines,** and it is the dialogue between the Talking Eagle, Juan Diego and the prototype for the Virgin Mary of Guadalupe, Tonanztin. It connects to the original culture and **Revelations 12** of the Bible. If the Nican Mopohua was inserted into the book of Revelations we would hear the voice of the woman Israel, with the wings of an eagle at her feet.

The Torah is too hard for an American unless they are into law. The 613 commandments in the Torah interact with each other. They even tell you when you can kill. It is worthless to have only ten commandments that do not interact with each other. The first one "No God before me", it obviously the one everyone wants. This should be seen as the national God of Israel not Jesus. He is angry and punishing people for things we understand to be sex. We could not choose a god; we were given Jesus and the author of the word. He seems to be a Son of the Elohim and then he seems to be the Elohim replacing his father like Baal and El.

When I was a kid, I played Dungeons and Dragons and I loved the Deities and Demigods since they had images of the goddesses. I noticed they did not include the Phoenician gods, where is Baal god of Thunder and his daughter Pidray and Midray the dusk and the dawn. Where is his sexy wife Anat or Mot the Moon, not to mention El, God...A man with a spear would have appeared for El or God and Baal a Son of God that prays for you. Lotan the Phoenician dragon would be the origins of Biblical Leviathan. Kothar is the creator of the gods (Father Abraham's father Terah had an idol shop). Then Baal bows like Buddha, curls up, and Yom the serpent swallows him. Baal goes in with his axe and goes through the city of Ooze. Anat grinds the serpent into flower and fertilizes the fields (She is the most powerful goddess I have studied). Baal makes love to his seven wives, and it rains.

This is a lot like Osiris and Isis in Egypt, but we have the Ra Faucet turned on. The sun is killing us and cursing us according to the Bible. Jesus was a personification of the sun and his disciples the planets. The sun dies on the cross (Southern Cross) for three days and is then resurrected. Ra is older than Jesus, but Jah is a bridge to Jehovah. Moses was so arrogant he killed a fellow Egyptian and put the curse of Eve on us. Americans can't see the gods or goddesses in the Bible. They don't know what a Phoenician is, but they know Moses killed people at the Red Sea. He had his own people kill each other and he could not enter the promised land. Judah's land of milk and honey or money.

We live with a Bible as our God, and none can escape. We could have gotten off at Guadalupe 500 years ago. Many see the twenty-two chapters of Revelation as divine. It is so short I could write it. It is based on the book of Daniel and old St. John on his death bed interpreting revelations to a Greek interpreter. The Bible is weak compared to Polytheism which can borrow gods that know the secret of Venus. Isis lay on Osiris to bring him back from the dead. If Mary Magdalene lay on Jesus in the cave, she would be our goddess.

The two Mary's, Virgin, and Magdalene; are similar and we hooked the Ra Faucet to Seth. Virgo is the original bread loaf and lions and heroes march through her star path. The word "Virgin" attached to Mary and Virgo is the Queen of Heaven. We know she had a miraculous birth like the pagan saviors and the stars all follow the three wise men to the place of the rising sun. Mary his wife is turned into a whore and Babylon (Rome) is the Great Harlot. **A woman who has sex for money is a monster to us.**

To get paid for sex is a good and honest living. There is a need; fill it, no pun intended, and make someone you want rich. You would not be giving them money if you were not attracted to them. They are giving you their body for a small sum of money, so they like you to. Hookers get turned on, have orgasms, and even fall in love. We have a certain amount of pre-marital encounters before marriage. But not very many…I can do more in a month than an American will do in their lifetime.

What do you expect when pre-marital sex is a 2,000-year-old sin? They want to control us with their Roman Myth changed to history, yet we do not include Gnosis or the historical Jesus. The Old Testament has so many sacrifices; why Jesus on the cross? All over Italy I have studied their churches and never did I see a smiling Jesus. They want to make you feel guilt for Eve's sin. A bunch of evil slave owners and women haters put Jezebel (Chastity) in the dung. She has done nothing wrong, and Jehu doesn't face her man to woman. The Bible says two or three of her Eunuchs threw her to her death. Why two or three? We are unsure of a number, but the evil pattern of Abraham, Isaac, and Jacob seems to leave us a dirty angel to wrestle with.

Americans don't use the word Jezebel but in Israel Jehu is a bad driver and Jezebel the whore. In traffic they say: "You drive like Jehu." Jezebel makes us look for Elijah. He could not do it, so he passes the baton to Elisha, who gives it to emasculated Jehu. The Bible does not mention the El in Elijah is God even though the plural attached to Lord is the monster nobody can kill. The Christians won't let Satan die. Michael the Arch Angel protects Europe, and some countries call us the great Satan.

CHAPTER 19

MOUTHS OF THE DRAGONS

I walk up to the Pagan Temple of Osiris in Bologna with the Book of the Dead in one hand and a Bible in the other. Ezekiel calls him Tamuzzi, Baal, Osiris, and Apollo-**The Branch!** "I saw them putting the branch to their nose." I figured from the Bible that Osiris had something to do with the penis. I held Osiris and said to the sign that says: **"This Used to Be the Pagan Temple of Osiris- Now It Is the Property of The Roman Catholic Church."** "My heart is Osiris and my chest the Mighty One of Terror."

I saw my **spiritual double** in Osiris, and he comes complete with Isis. **The Boat of a Million Years is run by Thoth.** In the Bible, we call him Barnabas (Acts) but that is funny. The Book of the Dead teaches Thoth is the universal intelligence. A very important God that turns into Hermes and Mercury. Even Eros, oldest of the Elohim, is a devil to the Christian. The original followers of Jesus were turned into Satanist by the church (Irenaeus) and if you are any kind of pagan or polytheist the church will make a devil of you.

In America we do not resist the church even if they molest our children. The people that teach you fornication is pre-marital sex molest kids and you listen to them. You expect me to believe in Eve's curse. She is not my mother and I like Lilith, Adam's first wife, better. The hatred for women in the Bible comes from God. We wonder why we don't get laid much in America. Treat our own mothers to the dung.

We worship thieves and liars that tell us sex is bad. We forgive them all their lies and teach Noah to our children. They live and die ignorant of the truth. **Gnosis means knowledge.** If we studied Jesus as knowledge a more reasonable attitude might develop. Everybody that is horny is blocked from God. We take word for word the hatred and call it sacred.

In our world of Christian Satan's, we find a river where the gods meet, and mountains on which laws are given. Get into the Bible with me and say Lecce is the heel of the boot of Italy. A heel catchers delight just south of Rome where the seven headed dragon is supposed to be. A giant lifts Italy and moves the heel to Sisley where he abducts St. Cecilia, patron saint of music. The seven headed dragon opens his mouth and utters lies. Anat already killed him before the rainy season. The seven cities include Bologna where the Pagan Temple to Osiris is. In that city two men-built towers. One was taller and got shortened to be the short one and Osiris (penis) is the property of the Roman Catholic Church. This should get your attention if nothing else. The Dragon of the Nile; Osiris the first Pharaoh, is also the phallus in the Book of the Dead.

Florence opens a mouth for the dragon at the house of Dante. A man who is called the greatest theologian. The statue of King David is also in that city. Venice has St. Marks and the nine-foot-tall Noah next to his son Ham, five feet. Each city opens a new secret. This teaching expands the Bible from Rome (Babylon) to Guadalupe (Mexico). Naples has the secrets of Jezebel and Neptune. All of Italy is the axe head of Elisha. It only needs your Branch or Osiris (Baal).

This is the encouragement to you Bible students; hold on to your phallus. It will be taken like Noah's or circumcised. I saw a photo of a statue of El that supposedly is at U.C. Berkely. I went there and could not find it. In the photo I saw a black man holding his phallus, almost protecting it. This is what I do at the Pagan Temple to Osiris in Bologna. The city of two towers had one shortened and today we do not find Moses cursed the Egyptians. Nobody feels bad karma or thinks maybe the Egyptians are correct.

All three monotheistic religions have their roots in ancient Egypt, but Sumerian is older than Egypt. They have more than one god and the goddess Inanna/Ishtar. The white man's religion comes with a curse on all women. We direct these lies and stories to God, so we act a certain way. People with no history play church and pull people like me and my brother in. We learned a certain way and races in the Bible are good guys and bad guys.

Pagan or polytheistic that is the question? If the Pagan Temple to Osiris was called the Polytheistic Temple to Osiris, we would see the Lord of the Underworld has friends. Everything connects in ancient history and even the Sumerians had a monotheistic king before the Bible was written. The Bible asks us to sacrifice real history to follow Moses. We are all forced to be Jews and hate our enemies and fear their gods. In the Bible, Jehovah takes the credit for what kings do. Everything is a cover up and they want us to understand the Roman Myth of Jesus.

Jesus and the Holy Spirit enter our sinful bodies according to doctrine, but they are already there according to the Gnostic. We are being sold our salvations and there is only the road of Jesus for us. All other's gods are idols according to the Christian faith. They say Christ died in vain to follow Moses. They can't decide which is true. Are we under the law? Ironically the Christian claims to not be under the law and the Gnostics respected the law of Moses.

It changed depending on who you talk to. The idea that some go to heaven, and some go to hell is hard to believe. God hates us so much he puts us into eternal hell to suffer for all of eternity. This is pure psychology from the church who has taught us this hateful God. Zeus and the others are thought false, and their flood stories are not as well-known as the Bible. The Bible is very narrow and doesn't explain what is going on.

We have a very immature mind in America when it comes to Christianity. We do not take it seriously, but we seem to believe it. Not studying the gods of the other cultures is just laziness. We do not want to study or even read a book, so we are weird sexually. What Ham does to Noah Satan does to you. We believe in a bunch of criminals and in the end the secret is the woman.

If you can love somebody more than Eve, we can make an Exodus from the Torah. The experiment with God, writing about him, and combining history makes the journey to the prophets successful. The prophets in Babylon are seen by Nebuchadnezzar, and he says they are crazy in the eyes. This would spread to all of us who don't compare the Bible history with history. I am ignorant of many things because of my time in the church. God was watching me, so I prayed and read the Bible all the time.

This journey the church put me on led me to the gothic cathedrals of Italy. I learned the Bible from stain glass windows and patterns on the floor. The remnant of the pagan is seen in the black Capricorns and other symbolism. We can't put the 12 disciples to the 12 months of the year. They are so boring and non-sexual. In America we say, "This is a family place." Meaning nothing sexy, but the problem is America is not sexy like Europe. We go crazy to see a topless woman on the beach. I hate this about America. There are no legal hookers to party with and we are expected to get it free or by buying food. This is so embarrassing that two adults cannot come together without all this Christian baggage.

I have lived all over and every city I have made love in is special to me. It is a memory or something sweet that stays with me. I am a notch on her belt, and I like it. I don't need her to love me I just need her to fuck me. Others are different, they want to know the person. This slows us down a bit. Get to know me and then use me. The hooker is honest. It is like a mini marriage.

The memories I have of the hookers I would not trade for anything. I am glad I did not get married. The sexy women I saw on television are now mine for money. I can get the exact one I want. Otherwise, we would never meet. This gives a job to everyone on the planet and even the ugly can get laid.

Who you end up with at the bar in America is always fun. At the brothel we do eight in a row. Try that in America. But here she is the one who is going to be the free prostitute or the food whore. This is so immature and since we insist on taking the name of God in vain, he punishes us. He never said you cannot have premarital sex, but we say he did. This commandment punishes even the grandchildren. We insist on telling lies about Jesus and are ignorant of the real guy.

The whole Christian world believes the Bible says you cannot have premarital sex. The Bible has ruined the woman and turned her into a piece of property. Inanna would free us and save us in hell. In Sumerian culture everybody goes to one place when they die. It is very dusty there. Inanna helps them in hell, and she is the bright morning star like Jesus. So, we may be on to something. From Venus come these fertility gods and pharaohs! When the Bible says Jesus is the bright morning star it also says St. Paul is Jupiter and Barnabas is Mercury. They don't sound like the names of gods. That is how weak we are. We read these things and don't learn, and nobody tells the truth anymore.

The bodies of Roman and Greek Gods are incredible. I see the contrast all over Italy of Monotheism and Polytheism. The art is right next to each other. This sexual break through removes the curse of the Bible. The Bible was changed by men and altered for piety. Once again there are the tablets of Baal and Anat. If they were our gods, we would think Baal resurrected every time it rains.

The bodies of the saints are not sexy, and I have never seen the Saints of Vic depicted artistically. But I can imagine them. Other than that, they are all celibate like saint Paul. Without hookers what is their sexual release. What makes you young and keeps you happy is sex. A young hooker can save an old man's life. Make him feel attractive and keep him in shape. Since we already risk the flames of fornication, we can't say we take the Bible too seriously. The very guy that explained it is better to marry than to burn; and we all know an idol is nothing. He shares his celibacy and gives reasons why he likes being not married. Now he is Jupiter, but we do not look at any of the planets or days to the week.

The age we get married at is much older now. The "Virgin" is more powerful than her son. That is the main message the Queen of Heaven has; to not have sex. Meanwhile, the Phoenician Queen Jezebel was thrown into the dung. We see how powerful a Phoenician woman is when she chases Elijah with a knife. The prophet begs God for mercy. He is being chased by a hooker. Ironically Phoenician is the only culture in which a woman is not seen as a whore when she takes money for sex.

Anat is the most sexual and marriage is a thing of control. The Bible does not show the pantheon when Baal vs Elijah happens. If Anat were praying to El where is Jehovah? El and Jah makes and interesting name. She has the cooties Elijah thinks. He does not know better. How to deal with the Phoenician Queen? Elisha gets the branch and the axe-head, and he still can't kill the Queen. Jehu the mad chariot driver comes to kill the 400 ministers of Baal. Then he orders the execution of his Queen while she uses her tongue and emasculating knife to cut them down to size.

You murderer of your master! Burn alive in your own tower. Omri sees the enemy coming yet all of heaven can't take her down. The axe heads for three weak evil men that do miracles and tell lies about miracles. They do one good thing amongst an Old Testament story, and we forgive them of stealing, lies, coning, fake friendships, Ham but fucking Noah, and nobody gets punished for ruining my life with Christianity. Yet Onan and probably Er are executed for doing evil in the eyes of the Lord. 3,000 years later people feel guilty they are wasting sperm or having a fantasy.

The problem is in America you say and think the Bible says it. But it is the Roman Catholic church that changed it. I am an original Bible. I study the Popul Vuh (Maya), the Enuma

Elish (Babylon), Kebra Negast (Ethiopia), and the Legends of the Suns (Aztec)! The book of Revelations, 22 books, are looking mighty skinny without the Nican Mopohua inserted in Revelations chapter 12. We would hear the words of the Queen of Heaven to Juan Diego. The dragon would make sense and this story plants us firmly in the new world.

Since I have read all these books including Talmud, Zohar, and

Qabalah. I study Rene Guenon's books on symbolism. They all connect through symbols and the man becomes a god via Venus and then comes Mercury - Wednesday - and Thoth. You only must understand one idol to get out of it. We are not under that law! Love and Jesus should be enough. However, in America, we do not have enough background in the Old Testament. God did not write the Bible and it is a hybrid. Not pure, as Baal and his Phoenician family who have their story in the alphabet.

Building the pantheon and publishing the books will bring a spiritual renaissance. We will love each other and stop judging. The words in the gospel will bring us joy and enter our language of love and understanding. Many things have happened the Bible ignores, and many things have happened to Israel we don't account for. Did Jehovah punish them for not following Moses? When a king burns down the walls the Bible says God did it. But God is a man like me and you. We are the Divine Word made flesh, logos!

CHAPTER 20

A TATTOO OF BAAL

All my tattoos have myths and my own stories to bring to life to my second book The Lords of the Poison. I stand on Santorini, the Atlantis that Plato wrote of, holding a donkey in a head lock. He is Balaam my talking donkey. I have black magic in a head lock, and I am going to expose the flood story and the plagues of the Nile. Get rid of Moses once and for all. Follow Jesus in my tattoo collection: Barcelona, Valencia, Hippy Atlantis (Ibiza), Alicante, Bologna, Iroquois, Quito, Tepeyac, Montserrat, Jacob Mango Costa Rica, and a black Chinese dragon around my ankle all done by the pioneers of tattooing.

Each tattoo has meaning, and I am very proud of my designs and photos. I wear my second book on each arm; dark relics of Jesus. On the back cover is a photo of me wearing my Nike hat and holding the sign that says: "Homers Tomb." Each Greek Island teaches you something and I visited Homers tomb with my friend from LA.

I give credit to Gilgamesh for the first and best poetry ever written. I can totally identify with Gilgamesh and Enkidu. Enkidu dies and Gilgamesh looks for him. They have a great friendship and I think Biblical Esau is a copy of red hairy Enkidu. Enkidu turned into a man when the prostitute Ishtar took his red hairy hand and rubbed it across her breast. Remember Ishtar cried when the gods flooded the world. Then she parts her hair, and the waters reside. When the gods cried for us, it says they look like bloated fish. Do you feel that love for the flood story of Ham and Noah which is only in the Torah not any other flood story worldwide. We get stuck with him, Ham. Noah says, "Cursed be Canaan lowest of slaves…" What if he said Ham is brave not a slave. All Africa enters the Ark of Heaven -a spaceship can fit 144,000 but all we want is your brain…now think of Jesus and hell. You are left behind and the Ark is a Spaceship, but the captain does not get sodomized by his black son. What a disgusting story Genesis 9; and it is not even true.

There is no orgy at the local church where they dispense knowledge of Jesus. This goes around the world. We believe he is God and our creator, but the Gnostic Gospels were not put in because they make him look like a man. The gospels of the Gnostics are not all enjoyable to me and in some cases, it looks like an imitation of the Jesus I knew from the Bible. The ideas are what I believe in and since it became Alchemy it is more scientific than modern Christianity.

They refer you to the Bible and you are stuck for a lifetime. Baal is the only way out for me. His sons hump like buffalo, and each has the face of their father. This makes Baal a warm and forgiving god. He is older than Moses and much of the Old Testament was taken from cave walls.

Jehovah is too young, and he is not worshiped as an idol, so we do not know what he looks like. In the Roman Catholic Churches in Italy, I see God depicted as an old man. This is far from Zeus or a more believable image. Paganism sounds better all the time. Let the lovers love and put the children to bed early. If they masturbate do not tell them the story of Onan. Let this be our little lie of the hateful god that disguises himself as the Boogie Man.

If you are an American, it is too late for you, the orgy is over now submitted to mean Jehovah the masturbator killer. He comes through windows to announce a birth in Babylon. He exists through his three men Abraham, Isaac, and Jacob. I should say Father, Laughter, and Heel Catcher. With these three Patriarchs it sounds like they are liars. They never existed according to a Roman Catholic Priest, that I interview at Dante's church in Florence. Also, he added in that Adam and Eve never existed. He says we believe in Jesus Christ, true man and true God.

All this traveling in Italy gave me a lot of homework to do. I never heard of the Pagan Temple to Osiris until I saw it in Bologna. It is one of the seven churches. And a church older than the Bible they say. We are racist to the color of illumination. We see Seth and Horus as night and day but what about Satan and Jesus. Do you really want to give the night to Satan. But Michael the Arch Angel may have already killed Satan. He destroyed the serpent. Now we don't believe in idols, angels, virgins, gods, or legends. Satan could be defeated by Jesus, but Jesus is on the cross.

Jesus never smiles in Italy but in Lisbon, Portugal I avoided a museum dedicated to the bloody Jesus. They are the grossest depictions in the world, and I refused to see it. In Bologna I saw the Jesus with five dogs. Racism ends here I thought…the word dog is puppy in Greek. What is the relationship between Jesus and the Canaanite girl? What if she told him," Anat says hello?" They occupy the same planet Venus so they should know each other. This was the hand of the church deciding how racist Jesus was going to be to his pigs.

The word Ham means Hot and refers to Africa. The Bible is very sneaky with Africa, but they avoid Egypt at all costs. This is a theme from Moses to Solomon. We should see this relationship as bad since we could care less about any of Israel's enemies. And then we don't investigate Judaism.

I say Gnostic Jesus and Phoenician El is a perfect combination. We can even read the Popul Vuh and the Divine Comedy and imagine the hero twins doing their magic. If we look up into the skies, they will seem magical with stories. A constellation is culture hero and Quetzalcoatl is the Feathered Serpent, Isaiah saw. The wheels of Ezekiel's vision are also open to aliens and evangelist who came to be the living creatures under the throne of Cyrus the Persian.

All these Old Testament Kings and prophets are different when read together. The Bible discounts the king and gives Jehovah the credit. The countries like Babylon are a threat to us. They have **Gilgamesh** and the true flood story. Noah is not to be read to children and I can't believe it has not been flagged after all these years. Children being molested by the church that claims; no fornicator will inherit the Kingdom of God. The hookers on the street…what about jail where they can't do the rapist and the pedophile. All four put together, the John and hooker, pedophile, and rapist.

Rape is free and the hooker cost money. Hookers normally go with rich businessmen that don't have time to date. One can always find something beautiful in Tijuana. The music plays in my ears on the way home and I can smell the rose soap they use. A heaven on earth; where I point to her, and she is mine. The rapist and pedophile could get a passport and do the super model hookers in Spain like I did or go to Asia where I have never been.

In America it is just plain boring limping around with Jacob. The angel kicked him in the balls and the Bible records God punishing his people. The authors seem guilty, and it is written a certain way. Judah sounds guilty and so does David who is from his tribe. The voice of Jacob the deceiver; is our hero with his ladder. The extra Biblical books store a lot of information we should know about. All the books that were taken out have messed up and shortened history.

Jesus did a parody of the Sun God. We just call the Sun the Sun. If we started calling it Ra what would happen? Eventually we would find the forty-two gods in our body in the Book of the Dead. Look at Ra setting in the clouds. His son Osiris and his daughter Isis are in the Boat of a Million Years. Xbalanche, the sun in the Popul Vuh, could be put into the sky. The sun and moon remind us of the hero twins.

All these gods connect to the Christian forbidden fruit. But sex is the secret that pulls the gods and the planets right out of the Bible. The margins of the Bible tell your body parts. The Song of Songs I heard was compared to a Native American song, of the same length, and the part where Solomon kisses Sheba the sky kisses the Earth in the Native American song. The fertility songs of the ancient are not even dirty. They are compared to farming and the passion of Anat raises a temple for Baal.

My tattoo of Baal means a lot to me. His Father, El, has a member longer than the seas. Anat is my perfect match sexually. She stomps out the grapes and makes love as she makes war. If Jesus was Baal Jesus, we would be saying Lord Jesus or Master Jesus. Let's give him some friends that come in twelves. Only the boring disciples and no stories of twelve prostitutes. They could represent the pantheon and we could make love to the Gods. What cool tattoos we could get.

Now there is enough information on Baal to make a mini-Bible. Let's study the Phoenicians! All this trash in the Bible goes upwards and we still say the word of God for the words of men. There is nothing miraculous about the Bible. It is a collection of stories and Jesus the myth became Jesus' history that we believe in here. No Gilgamesh or Homer they are all sinners or Satan's to the Americans. Nobody worships Baal or builds anything for him. Baalbek in Lebanon is for space craft.

The idea of Baal and Anat or Jesus and Mary Magdalene are a great difference. Osiris and Isis are like Baal and Anat, but I like the Phoenician mythology better than Egyptian. All the treasures of the world are ours once we understand Bible history and honor the kings and queens that created the real stories the Bible copies. While Israel is getting thrashed by God, they still call the foreign kings, God. If Nebuchadnezzar burns down the walls of Israel, the Bible says God will do it or did do it.

The problem is we are so ignorant of these gods we can't even piece together our fake Christian history. In conversation we do not talk about these countries or know where Babylon and the Bible come together. Jehovah punishes us again for building a tower according to the lie, but they do not call the Tower of Babel the Tower of Babylon. All history and symbols including Ezekiel's comic street theatre, are lost to us. We know the Ten Commandments and that is about it. Find the real El that was Phoenician and see if Phonetic thinking and alphabet will not cure the confusion.

We must remember our Christian masters tell us about every god on Earth and every expression of God is fake or Satan.... except for their Jesus. The one that makes you feel guilty for sinning and then kills innocent people for masturbating. Ra the Sun God masturbates with both hands to make the Nile flood. Think of what Moses does to the Nile with all the blood, frogs, and death. It is an attack on the penis of God and the Pyramid. The Nile is the Dragon of Osiris and the piece of shit Bible forgot to tell you that. So, believe the false Bible and die. Liars go to hell and for an American that is big. Our whole religion is based on stealing and lies.

The sky looks different to me, and I see the belt of Orion who was stung by a Scorpio. Osiris and Seth are a parallel; so, with Baal or Bel we are back to the stars and a God like Zeus who encourages the worship of other gods. Think of how selfish Americans are compared to Italians...that is my experience. I get home to California and everybody I know has spent all their money on something stupid and all we can do is go out. Big deal ...I like to stay out all night in Barcelona, Madrid, Lisbon, Paris, Milan, and others. The friends I have that are forever and faraway.

In America I feel I am being used all the time. Nobody is sexy or wants to look for women. Drink expensive beer and go broke. Another night of drinking only.... thank Baal I have a passport. This lifestyle gets me down and every night in Europe has love if I want it. Being told what to do is excruciating when I see a woman I want. In a perfect world I could proposition her and back off if she says, "No." Or go to a hooker. In America there is nothing to do but jack off your entire life.

The kids of today know nothing of the 90's when women strutted the Sunset Strip all sexy. Now the kids who missed out on sex in the bathroom have never been kissed. The government has stunted our growth by approving Christianity. Phoenicians could approach each other with money so it is ironic Queen Jezebel is called a whore when her culture had no concept of it being bad. They saw the beautiful concept and ruined it for the world. Our hatred of women fuels this fire.

Now women have pussies that can't buy them houses. They can use them after they pay the church for the marriage certificate. Then you can fornicate but don't lust after a woman. All the attractive people walked by us, and we wanted to love them. But there is no communication without money. Either the man or woman should get paid, and this would stimulate the world economy.

It is funny some women go on so many dates before they know who is the one. If a woman approached, you immediately what would be wrong with that. It makes the man feel attractive for a change. The lie of Christianity is that there is a reward for virginity. I noticed in Italy the Virgin Mary does not smile, like her son. They celebrate death and try to poison our minds with guilt.

My first lessons came from the church and then I caught up with them by studying the Bible. They have a few things they want you to believe. They use the thin books that don't tell the whole story. All these years of history are hard to understand but I feel something is not right. We use Jesus to tell the story of history. We make up stuff to fill in the blanks. People walk around without the circle of illumination around their heads.

We should have the Bible and the serpent under our feet, not above our head. We don't really understand it. We don't use the characters of the Old Testament in conversation. We don't know what the stories really mean. In passing we don't say anything to each other religious. It is only Maya, the tangible, the Indian says. Not part of the unimportant world but the spiritual.

All religions connect and say the same things, but Jesus is attached to Jehovah, so we stunt our own growth. Jehovah saves on the cross and the sun died on the Southern Cross for three days first.

What came first is of no importance to modern Christianity. To understand the Bible their way we must close our eyes to even our own history. Phoenician Baal prays for his friend on Earth. He prays to El the Compassionate for him to have children: "All of his friends have children why should he not have." Baal says to El. Interceding on our behalf like Jesus at the right hand of the Father.

This also warms my heart that Baal thinks of me and my friends. What if all your friends got a new car? Baal interceded like a champion for his friend. Anat approaches the bench, and the gods talk to each other. I feel Baal has compassion like his father for me. He saw what I don't have and interceded for me. Phoenician Baal is like ancient Jesus and the twenty-two letters of the Phoenician alphabet correspond to the twenty-two paths of the Tree of Life.

We get everything back with Phoenician Baal that the Bible misplaced or hid from us. Osiris and Isis, the penis and the neck, are like Baal and Anat. That is why the woman is the secret to immortality; Isis lays on Osiris to bring him back to life. Think of Baal as Osiris and your member. Is Baal a connection of the sun to the soul? The Ka (soul) sits on the right hand of Ra (Sun).

Baal is a cleaner god that comes back every time it rains. If we missed Melchizedek, we could see what he had going for him with the complete couple Baal and Anat. Melchizedek means the King is Righteous and he comes from Salem (Peace). He worshiped El Elyon, God Most High. Solomon (Peace) is called Melchizedek in the Psalms. Jesus is Melchizedek in the Gnostic. In the book of Hebrews, Jesus in like Priest Melchizedek.

The idea of Melchizedek that is important is: "He had neither beginning nor ending of days." And he was a Canaanite Priest of **El Elyon**: "God Most High." There is a good chance he was a pagan and a polytheist. We do some weird things because of Christianity. We don't talk about the gods, calendars, and history of the Native Americans. The Bible is too big for its own shoes. Claiming Jehovah will protect Israel. No weapon formed against you shall prosper! This criminal and punitive God is part of a pantheon of saints and angels. Then in hell is Satan and the fallen angels and demons.

CHAPTER 21

UNDER THE CURSE

J esus as a man or God on the cross is very weak. We see how many of the thousands of crucifixions done by Cesare on the Apian Way. Comparison with Alexander the Great who crucified people in Tyre, after seeing Baal Melkart welcome him in to destroy the Tyrians who dumped hot sand on the Macedonians. Baal is fair and says with a gesture to the Son of Zeus: "Take them!"

These other gods are all shifty for the Lord Jesus Christ and he is the only Lord. Don't we think that this might have been convenient since they are trying to control us? One way of thinking and one code to go by. Somehow all world myths are false, and the gods are bad. So many gods in the world with one good story after another fill the need for Father. Now we worship a book, the Bible, it tells the end of the world or worlds.

When I was at the **Pagan Temple of Osiris,** I realized the church has control of our members. What was taught in this temple? And why does the black Virgin walk the **666 archways** once a year? To remember Isis, the neck, and Osiris at a temple that is now the property of the Roman Catholic Church. Nearby is a church where I found a message from the Virgin Mary. **"If you call Abraham a friend, a little angel will sit on your shoulder."** The Virgin Mary-Abraham means Father so figure it out with your own father.

My father died when I was nine. This emptiness or void caused me to first take solace in karate and then the church. God is the new

Father; but does Jesus go to his Father in the Bosom of Abraham? Who is our father? Why not El or Dagan? The Abraham who sacrifices his son is our father. We see a sacrifice from the Father of Monotheism to kill Isaac. Jehovah wants to test his faith. The same story of God and Jesus is told but the forgiveness never comes, and we are under the altered law we call God's law.

Keeping only ten of the 613 commandments is what we have. Don't murder and don't commit adultery we think we kept. To tell a lie seems very forgivable and once we see Jesus as a Solar Myth turned into history, we see the difference is great. We have an idol to bow down to, but we don't understand it's book. We are supposed to not have sex, not lie, and not covet but the rest is forgotten. Two-bit scammers open a church, and nobody questions their intentions. To make money and use psychology on the people.

This book shows what part of our inherited tradition is a lie. It all makes sense once we pull the sexual thread out. We had Osiris and Isis in us but later the Jesus that was in us is taken out. We get the Holy Spirit and Jesus once we are saved. The Gnostic and Hindu teaching show us that God was already in us. This whole fake history of Adam and Eve keeps us attached to the story. They sinned and now we need a savior.

In my own life I think of sex all the time. I see women that would be perfect for me, but I have nothing to say. I can't normally proposition them but in the gentlemen club I can. The same flesh I see that drives me crazy and makes me so frustrated is available for money. All the sex we miss in America is because we believe Jesus was against sex. The hatred of his father against the masturbator Onan and Jesus sliding it in with to look and lust. The whole sex thing is bad, and we blame the Bible for this information.

Many years ago, we could have taken the fork in the road to be Gnostic. We would have no concept of sin and less attachment to the church. We would have been focused on knowledge of all kinds and we would be wiser. The Gnostic respect the Jewish law and Christ fulfilled the law. The real Jesus was first a man. Then Constantine turned Jesus into his own personal war God. The average American is not about to say, "They made a mistake." But now we have the four Gospels that are really two. Two pillars on the throne of Jesus and all other books are false according to the Christian. Anything that does not make him God is bad. The idea of one God only is strange, but we say Christ died in vain and keep the commandments.

Everyone likes Moses. Islam says Christ is a prophet, but Allah spoke to Moses. The Jews rely on Moses and so does the Christian. Not everybody needs Mohamed or Jesus! All three monotheists agree on Moses. This is where I ask the Christian to read the oral tradition of Moses called: Qabalah. The Talmud and the Zohar are also good for the people of the book to study. How does an American Christian know the Bible is true if he has not read the Quran? We should hear from all books and not have the forbidden fruit and the book burners lighting their matches. So many things are forbidden that point to the other cultures we don't hear about in the Bible. The Song of Songs crosses over from black to white and Ethiopia to Israel. A sacred book read at Lebanese weddings. It puts together Father Sky and Mother Earth.

Knowing about Solomon and Sheba helps me understand why Egypt is called the black lands for magic. Sheba is like a goddess and the dialogue they have is divine. In the New Testament we have Jesus and Mary Magdalene, but they do not dialogue much about love. "Oh, that he would kiss me with the kisses of his mouth." Their love is sweeter than wine and she is one of his women that stands out to me. They say Solomon wrote Ecclesiastes on a bad day. I think he missed Sheba. We miss that love since we edit for piety. Penis becomes a foot, and the vulva becomes a navel.

We have all kinds of desires that could be stirred. In our church many had sex anyway. If we did an orgy, it would have been more convenient. I desire many people that I do not want to know for some reason. A woman could be exactly what you need but she walks by. We have nothing to say to each other. "Do you want to fuck?" Can be said at any gentleman club but one must be ready to pay. In real life we do not get to choose our partners like we want to.

The woman is a rib instead of a goddess, so we don't get laid. No praise to the woman, just blame and slavery. This goes to our mothers and our sisters. We believe all of this is Eve's fault. Look at Jezebel in the dung! This is where they are taking us sinners who won't believe that we are the Sons of the Elohim. We force Jesus and his holidays down people's throats. Gnostic is not even a word people are familiar with. Look at the punishment we have brought on ourselves sexually.

We can't just look and choose. All this work to get laid takes a lot of time. One can fuck more hookers in a week than most American's do their entire life. One after another or many at once the women flock to the money. Try to buy her with food and dating and see how long it takes you to get laid by your monogamous partner. It ruins everything the waiting. We are willing to teach that one goes to hell for fornication but if you pay for it you go to jail. The one man got a slut, so he doesn't go to heaven the other got a whore he goes to jail and hell.

Probably American women are not going to want to put out with all these eternal flames bullshit. God loves us too much to put us in the fire forever. The women may have walked into a church and heard the lie of fornication. Horny young people are afraid to masturbate. Older people and cripples can't call sex workers to love them. All of us would be so happy if we learn this book and understand the Bible.

The church has done all the evil but with Baal we can escape them. An older God with an older Father takes us back to the beginning. We do not apply a timeline to God and the Bible is short 800 years according to the Mayan calendar. We bring this angry God to scare people, and nothing seems to happen. People continue to sin against each other and even make money doing it.

The way I am telling you to make and save money is prostitution. Every night we can get laid if we have the money. It is a lot cheaper than dating. It gives everyone a job and extra income. This American Christianity is old and indifferent to the gods of the Native American. Pyramids, constellations, and calendars are of no effect to the cross. We have hurt ourselves by not studying any of the cultures in the Old Testament. To know what they did and how they did it is important.

Along with the interaction of gods and planets is the history that pieces like Gilgamesh have to offer.

After reading love poetry to the different goddesses, I found nothing dirty. The Bible is the dirtiest book on sex. Ask Ham about Noah's drunk body or Lot about his horny daughters. I know some men who get turned on reading the Bible. These things are not true, and no flood story has slavery attached to it. The evil Moses wrote the first book about creation and the second about Moses. He wrote his own story, and he was the angry God the people looked to. Many men go to the mountain to get a law, but we only know Moses. This shows us how powerful the word "Pagan" is. We classify them as idol worshiper. It is a trigger of something bad to our brains. Polytheism sounds better, while Jehovah is jealous, Zeus encourages the worship of other gods.

My own experience creates faith for me in this book. I see so many women I want to be with or just taste. To be linked to the same person for a lifetime is not natural. After two years the spell may wear off. Since I know I want more than one woman, my way of thinking is not too off. We have already lost our virginity to someone other than our spouse probably. And who wants a bloody virgin? Better to pay her like they did in Babylon. This would be the next step towards sexual freedom, and we don't have to say sorry to God every time we lust. It makes us guilty all the time.

We think after 2,000 years we have figured Jesus out. It is the opposite. We get further and further away from the truth. The Gnostic Love Feast compared to today's sinful trio is great. People had so much love it spilled over, and the Gnostic Jesus has a smile. He is happy to be attached to the sun and all those forbidden books. We have a weak thread to Moses and the Old Testament. We are limited by that selfish and jealous God. If Jesus could stand on his own two feet, we would not need all these fake miracles.

We need to make an exodus from Rome (Babylon) and look to the gods of the Native American. The Holy Spirit and the Great Spirit could be the same. One Greek god links us to all the Sun Worshipers.

Building temples to these gods is a good thing and gives America places of pilgrimage. The idols have legends, and those legends are in books. Why not have a whole pantheon support you and get the feminine side of Anat. This completes the man, and the Great Harlot and Mary Magdalene is of no effect. The word, "Virgin" is the title we all look to in this present age. Virgin Mary of Fatima or Guadalupe are all stories told by the angels that are in them.

The woman is or was property and the goddesses diminishes into myth. They must hide deities like El and Baal from us. I feel at home with them since they are like the Bible. They wrote their laws separately they did not put them in the holy book. They are out of date, but we still use them to judge each other and show that Christ died in vain if we are justified by the law. Or ten commandments as we know it.

The law in my body tells me sex is good for me. The lies and jokes of the Roman Catholic Church keep us guilty. They know we will never question them since we feel the guilt. It is for us Jesus died and took the whip. Now we respond with a relationship to an anti-sex God, and judge others accordingly. This power could be taken back, and sex could be used for good. Many people down on their luck can have an extra income. Men wont chase women around the bars anymore. They can go to a gentlemen's club and fuck their brains out. This prevents rape and can possibly turn a few child molesters from fucking the kids. If we had an option…but what is our option? Go online or go to bars looking for other people living under the curse? They must hide what they do or not tell anybody.

CHAPTER 22

BATTLE FOR THE BOOT OF ITALY

I think every day in America: "Will I get laid today?" In Europe or Mexico, I can just do a sex worker, but America says in its Bible: "No premarital sex and no paying for it." This is funny men who were not virgins for their wives are going to tell me I cannot give my partner money. This fucks everything up! Now we cannot communicate unless we go to a restaurant where many women are known to drop their panties. This is the only legal way to do it. How inconvenient I must date one woman and let her believe we could get married. I only want sex and I am willing to pay her, but she has no price.

If hooking became normal, we would be honest with each other and get laid all the time. Usually marriage is a bait, especially for the rich, that hooks the believing woman like a fish. "It will all be mine." She says. Then she is a long-term whore, but the man must convince her into doing other women if he wants to mess around a little bit.

With prostitution in Amsterdam, I did eight in a row. A year later I did eight more. Three years later I stopped there for two weeks. I had sex all day and all night with a different goddess. I had to get it out of my system. America is people who believe they are going to hell for fornication, and they do it anyway. They judge all others by an on old Egyptian curse called the Egyptian procreation only theory. That is why the church teaches us wrong and we are so impressed with their Jesus.

Take note of the upside down cross of St. Peter. Satanic symbol for the first Pope; how hard to figure out why Jesus said: "Get behind me Satan!" To the Other Disciple of John's gospel which has seven competitions between the Disciple Jesus loved and the Other Disciple. John the Gnostic beats our first Pope in his gospel. Did Jesus leave this to be read at his second coming?

The church changed the wife of Jesus, Mary Magdalene, into a whore. They wanted to steal the ministry from her when Jesus died. They make her into a plain whore, and she was not said to possess great beauty. This is the neutering of the church and the only rule we follow. With all this shady stuff in the beginning I can see why selling forgiveness was needed. It is not like a negative confession where one says they have not done. In Christianity we lie and steal and say sorry. This accounts for many problems in America. All religions are measured by Jesus, and they all say don't have sex.

With so many warning signs and so few people who appreciate Gnosticism we are in a rut. We are not going to have an orgy and people may still die believing in the trio of no masturbating, no pre-marital sex, and no lusting. These are the trademarks of a Christian, and the rest of us are just along for the ride. The church is not going to liberate the women; we must by making an exodus from Rome.

We have all the basics from the Roman Catholic Church. The beliefs are there but Protestants differ in idolatry. They keep the second commandment the best they could; but the white image of Jesus is the one we all know. We would recognize him more by his appearance than by his words. The end of the gospels is portrayed in art. Always sad with a tone of death to it, and no saint or angel looks sexual. They are sad and look lonely without the Jesus that was inside of them when they were born.

We go without idols, saying Christ died in vain, and artwork to prove like the Muslim we are under the law. The idol cancels out every god and culture hero. It makes us a people of the book. The idol now has a book, and it is the original revelation. The Bible is clearly written by men and all its miracles are suspicious. The most racist book ever written, and it curses Africa. What kind of karma is that? A

Red Sea full of dead Egyptians, that we don't study, and the cradle of civilization under water in a flood caused by the Volcano on Santorini. All this anger could have been expressed sexually by Anat. She is not evil or judgmental.

I am surprised when the Bible says, Jehovah destroyed the world because of violence. I would think it would be because of sex. This is the main guilt that they use on us to keep us down. We need their savior who says all other faiths are Satanic. Then he comes to live inside of you and saves you. All Sons of Elohim do this, and therefore every country had its mythology. We ignore everything with the word "Myth" in it, including the Roman Myth of Jesus. I love Europe because the people are so curious. They want to hear about myths and their history. I have shared many intellectual conversations in the big cities of Europe. We share art and poetry and much of my writing inspiration comes from these cities I have lived in.

If we had statues with stories attached to them, we would come to love the gods. We are so narrow and uptight with our fake Jesus religion that includes only works about Jesus in the gospels. Gnostic and every other thought are false to the Christian. They take chunks of history and say they are bad because they worshiped idols. This makes us look so naive when we travel. I remember in Montserrat in Spain I saw the million-year-old sawn out mountains. I thought the world was 3,000 years old according to the Bible. This left a bad taste in my mouth for the church. I was not balanced, and I am missing parts of my life I gave to Jesus. Including my virginity which has no reward since I am not a piece of property.

We grow so old with our thinking and find evil heroes in our New Jerusalem and a Serpent from the Garden of Eden in Gahenna. All religions and calendars line up with numbers. Orion's belt is the three stars known as the three wise men. It is so obviously a sacred place, but the Christian's deny the gods in constellations, and we all suffer for it. You can't even see the gods in the night sky or imagine the god's doing battle to make the sun rise. We have all the books on these other cultures, but we are so Christian we do not take them seriously.

We go along with this because we are too lazy to read. What if there was a Gnostic Church that read the Gnostic Gospels? Temples to the pagan gods of other lands and the literature known as the Bible will expand and multiply and grow. We put the missing sixty-four books away and they appear in Enoch and other books. All these books are necessary to understand the Bible; not one way whatever they say.

The Nican Mopohua is 218 lines of dialogue between the Virgin Mary of Guadalupe and Juan Diego. It would be a good addition to Revelations 12. The voice of the Virgin I can hear calling me Mikey. I have been led through numerous Catholic Pilgrimages by her sweet and understanding voice. She represents the love of a mother to me and is my connection with the Catholic Church. I listen to Mary and the pilgrimages have taught me esoteric secrets. We can't have just one savior when the evidence of Christianity being false is so evident.

This way of thinking opens me up to new experiences and freedom. I believed so many lies of my church. They promised me God would give me a beautiful wife, career, and family. We were all to be rich. They told me to quit karate. They told me my straight A grade average made me prideful. Give it all to the Lord Jesus Christ they told me. He will make you rich in this lifetime and the world to come.

Stay virgin until you are married, no matter what that age is. No more movies, secular music, or dance. Dancing leads to sex they say. When I got saved, I had an adult black belt in **Isshin Ryu Karate** and good grades. All of this went to nothing since they told me I had a problem with pride. I started reading St. John in the Bible and became a type of Bible expert. I have read stacks of books about the Bible. In church it is just business as usual. They don't intend to set you free from the curse of no pre-marital sex.

They will use it on you until the day you die. You will always be lusty, but we misinterpret the gospels and don't listen to St. Paul. If we were Gnostic, we would have forked off a long time ago. Gnostics don't even have a concept of sin. How refreshing we would not be dealing with a 2,000-year-old sexual curse all the time. We believe since Jesus there is no pre-marital sex. Since Gnostic's had orgies, we see how far we have fallen and how mean Jesus is to put us in hell for not believing in him. Also, we must believe in the upside down cross of St. Peter. All crucifixions go in vain except for the cross God is on. The devil must have enjoyed this.

I paid my tithe and offering. They never told me to invest or look for a job. I was to serve the Lord Jesus Christ only and he will hear my prayers. I told Jesus I wanted a model for a wife and a business career. The church sent me on a mission to Rome. I see how small Revelations is and how we can't understand it to this day. Joke is on us the Red Roman Pig ate Revelations at the tomb of St. John, Patmos, Greece. He found seven cities in Italy and conquered them with laughter.

He calls the Duomo in Milan; **Melchizedek Manor** since the pig did battle with the giant that created it. Outside is Drago Verde - a green dragon water fountain - where the pig drinks the Holy Water. The pig is buff, and one time saved a woman from the Golem of Prague in front of the torture museum.

One day the pig decided to wrestle the giant for the boot of Italy. The pig carries the she-wolf into the woods and wrestles with a goat. These are the three pagan animals of Rome. The pig is like Ra the Sun god or Samson. The pig brings his trio into Melchizedek Manor and invites the gods of the Moon to acknowledge Apollo. The pig says, "What about Enoch and Elijah?" Nobody could hear a thing from Jesus or those aligned with him, saints and angels. We allow demons and devils the right to do anything they want. They break the rules and hurt us all.

They teach us we can't have sex with our girlfriend or boyfriend. And we pay them to spread the good word of Jesus. Are you an expert on Jesus or the Bible? I think you know the answer. We only believe in the post Irenaeus Jesus. When the Gnostic were called Satan by the church they changed to Alchemy and got more powerful. Does Jesus realize this? That he was more powerful than he is or ever will be.

The followers went to a Love Feast where the oldest god; Eros surely visited his polytheistic partners. How cool it is to be polytheistic.

I can see the moon and read the Popul Vuh. I have read legends that make the heavens come alive. Ophucious and Serpent Caput are the last of the eighty-eight constellations and this maybe Jesus killing the serpent. The church and its puny sixty-six books are nothing compared to Park Guell: Barcelona, Spain! Eighty-eight pillars in the park drink rainwater and store it in a crypt. They support a Serpentine Bench that has writing from the Virgin Mary of Montserrat on it: "Oh country rich in treasure, do you smile at me, her eyes, her forehead, jealousy be gone."

The jealousy is powerful in my life. I see things that I want, and I save money for them. Others get jealous of this and think I am rich. What I learned about the jealous is they want you to fall. They are not happy with the clothes on their back or the car they drive. If we were sharing it would be different and my riches would be your riches. You get to ride in the car and eat the good food. Italy has an economy, especially in the South, based on barter. They have an overflow of something they produce that goes to friends.

Up to two hours from my friend Enzo's house we still get free fish. **Lecce** seems like a heaven on earth. The people talk like Jesus and quote the Bible without realizing it. I told them the story of Jonah and a whale appeared while I was speaking. They said I was their Messiah; the Big Bible Giant from America, they called me. For seven months I taught them the Bible and I had plenty of time to study.

Any city we go to we find a giant that lives in the Cathedral he or she built. The abduction of St. Cecilia was done by the Greeks, and they had sex with her. They refer to the many abductions of St. Cecilia. As if she got laid all the time. The Matron Saint of music goes with all kinds of peoples. The seven cities offer her lodging from the Roman Dragon who is afraid I will go to **Lecce** and grab the heel like Jacob or Achilles. Greek verses a heel catcher in battle for the heel of the boot of Italy.

CHAPTER 23

THE AXE OF ITALY

I will be like Gilgamesh 2/3 divine and 1/3 human, and the bull of heaven will be Baal Hammon: in the Song of Songs. Solomon bought a vineyard at Baal Hammon. The giant divides a leg of Peleg and abducts St. Cecila. Then he uses Italy as an axe. He cuts the horns of Baal Hammon off between the temples of Apollo and Venus. The giant and the pig leave Revelations and cut their way through, counting books until the Song of Songs. The pig holds his boot of Italy and imitates the giant.

Handing Italy over after living in it seems strange. In my mind I can visualize me doing this. Covering the islands with the axe of Italy and expanding Rome to the size of my axe is necessary. I can turn the sixty-six books of the Bible from within the Bible. Lord Elohim is free from Lord (Jehovah). Let the angels go free. Turn them back into Elohim.

This whole story of Italy and the axe can be told with the pig as the hero. He carries the axe and wherever he goes he honors the heel. Imagine the Roman Catholic Jehovah is going to kill the pig for masturbating. The pig straddles the boot and jacks off the heel. Milk and honey come out two things Jehovah can't resist. The pig fastens a swastika above Naples so the boot will turn and flip over to cut off **Baal Hammon**. We need to expand from Rome. Much has happened since the seven headed dragon was left in charge. Probably Sumerian

Apsu or a water god is responsible. The pig can take his boot, grab it by the heel, and cut off the heads of the seven headed dragon.

We are all responsible to know the city of seven hills is Rome. The Great Harlot and Dragon are there. The fact that we do not know this in America is sad. The pig could bring Italy to us. There is more than just Rome and seven headed dragons, upside down cross for the first Pope Peter. We are completely blind to a tiny twenty-two-chapter book called Revelations. The problem is the Christians have no hero to kill Satan. **They let him live and prosper since he is the father of the lies.**

These things crippled my poor heart in church. God loves me and he will make me rich I thought. They talked about the riches we would have on Earth for serving the Lord Jesus Christ. Everybody thinks he is against sex, and we pass a sexless life in America. They keep sex from us by making us pay the American food whores in anything but cash. Now the women are no longer sexy, and they steal all the time. **We are forced into Jesus and Noah, and we have no choice.**

The American's don't think that this influences us. We believe everything differently and are very horny and awkward people. Teaching these sexual curses to our children turns us out all fucked up. God is a big concept or idea to wrestle with. It put a lot a pressure on me to not masturbate or have sex. This is just too much for a young person to deal with. Lose your virginity to a whore and call it a day.

Many hate women because they cannot get laid. This leads to resentment but if they have the money, they can do seven super models in a row. What I love about hookers is they do not care what you look like. The most handsome man and the ugliest man pay the same price. I have got free sex in Amsterdam and made friends with them. It was so natural for me. These woman haters and rapists can go to hookers not us. We are the free whore, and we are so stupid we celebrate going to hell. We see sex on television, and nobody is punished. But we still believe the Bible and are too lazy to study it. Ignorance tells us what to do and this is the best we have.

I am glad I did not get married in college so I could experience the Budapest Woman in Barcelona. She took me to heaven, and she is the most beautiful woman I have seen in my life. Others should see her and have an experience with her and go to heaven. She is pure blonde light and reminds me to spend my money on experience and not just things. Hookers almost never say no but it is their body, and they have free will unlike the American woman who will sell her free will for a hot dog like Uncle Esau.

Somebody will always take advantage of good-natured people. You see God on the cross, all bloody and beaten and you feel he did it for you. Why was another sacrifice needed? Before Jesus, hell did not exist…he brought it with him so you would believe in him and give the church 10% of your income. Everybody wants a Bible, but we only believe the Bible. We disrespect all ancient cultures and teach people Jesus saves from hell.

Hell cannot be true if God is love. Why do we even have children if there is 1% chance they will go to hell for eternity? Stop having children if hell is true! Don't risk them burning eternally with Satan and his demons. Do you think this might be the church trying to scare you? There is not proof, and Jesus spoke of Gahanna as a funeral fire not eternal flame. You just die and they throw your body in Gahanna for cremation. Other fires in the Old Testament became hell and they have the usual lie to scare you since Jesus can't stand on his own two feet.

We are still not willing to study the Tibetan Book of the Dead or other books that might enlighten us since it is all demonized by the church. The church just wants your money they don't care if you live or die. America is the fertilizer for Christianity because people are so ignorant of the Bible. We are under a curse I am showing you how to get out of. The evil God of the Torah has never killed a masturbator, but the church, Bible, and dictionary all spell it out: "We are all doomed." But are we smart enough to know we would all be dead for doing evil in the eyes of Lord. Everyone one of us killed by God personally for onanism.

The second fact is you don't go to hell when you have sex you go to heaven. The church turned the myth of Jesus into history and started controlling us a long time ago. We are born into this, but the church is not going to read it to you. But in America the church still teaches the trio! Do you wonder why it's hard to have sex with an American woman, who is taught she will burn in hell for sex? This has been in our stick in the ass culture and now we are on a liar's boat using Gods name in vain and staying a virgin for Satan.

The Virgin is unapproachable, she is young, and better than you attitude. The whore wants to fuck you for money. The virgin you pay forever. And this is how America teaches you go to heaven until the church marries you and then it is okay. Everything depends on sex. The Bohemoth (Hippo) in the book of Job used to have a big cock. Now he has a tail. This ruins the description of the Hippo since he was edited for piety.

All these symbols are in The Temple of Debod in Madrid (see the Lords of the Poison). The Hippo is led in procession looking for the original Bible. Americans are not familiar with Osiris, and they are emasculated by the church. They took your dick and free will and you did not put up a fight.

An Italian woman is protected by the Pope. She can be a prostitute, but she cannot have a pimp. The Pope says: "You can't tell her what to do with her body. She has free will." This is so beautiful that an Italian woman has free will and can use her body to make money. Nobody thinks it bad, and one can make a lot of money in Italy. Italy is much sexier than America. People dress up and clubs are elegant. In America I feel I am in a trap. No premarital sex ordered by God and no prostitute to relieve my sexual frustration….and no jacking off. This is what we believe the Bible says and it does not. They should teach the Bible in High School, so we have a fighting chance against the wicked child molesting churches. Nobody can protect us from Noah. He is nude and drunk before the Father of Africa.

The Bible is so out of date we need other books to interpret what it means. Generally, an American believes he is saved by Jesus. The Jesus out of the Gospels is fake to them but they don't read even their own book. It is so cruel people take advantage of us in America because we are so ignorant of even our own culture. It seems like they have never read a book or believe in the gods of the Native American. We could be polytheistic and have the gods of all cultures teach us their wisdom.

The Great Spirit made the rocks in the Grand Canyon red by eating buffalos by the handful. Why don't we have stories about the Holy Spirit? They all connect through Greek and Roman mythology. The Indians have flayed saviors and **Quetzalcoatl**, the Plumed Serpent. He was crucified with a cross in his hand. He jumped off the cross into a funeral pyre and shot out of the Grand Canyon to become Venus (Bright morning star like Jesus). His city **Teotihuacan** which I visit in my first book Nine Days to Healing a Spiritual Pilgrimage is built in 100 A.D. right after the time of Christ. Time changed for the Christian with Christ and for the Aztec with Quetzalcoatl.

All the gods and Jesus connect when we put a circle around the cross and it goes back to the zodiac to jump start the solar system. Also, the days of the week are the gods. We could celebrate every day! Keeping them demonized in the longest list in the world is the list of Christian devils. We are ignorant of our own God, but we think he says other gods are bad.

My training in the church was to pray and read the Bible. I was very interested in Solomon. The Proverbs helped me find my way in life. They helped me make decisions. If we added them to the commandments, we would be sure to keep them. As custodians of the Bible, we have failed! We don't even know why Jesus did not explain pyramids. He did not talk about the cosmos or how he created the world. We exalted the man Jesus to God Jesus; but he was both God and man. We lost the man side and that is one reason we do not read the Gnostic Gospels.

To the Christian mind the Bible is a book of racist documented miracles. The whole solar system has stopped, and the sexual gods become the non-sexual angels and saints. All are celibate like Paul in Christianity. We are virgins waiting permission from the church and they take our money for this. We accept things that nobody saw as true, even if they are bad. The racist side of the Bible makes Jehovah look like a miracle working war machine. He is always punishing people and taking the credit for what kings did to Israel.

The Christians like to think of their enemies burning in hell when they disagree. This is so cruel and abnormal to put your creations into the eternal fire. These things are made up to scare us. If there was any truth to the Bible, we lost it and have the three Hebrew children in Babylon as our religion. Bow to the statue or be thrown in the furnace. Just like Christianity bow or burn. In America we lie to people with psychology knowing the average American has a weak background in any kind of critical thinking.

Nobody can explain the church away. They keep going and dumping their evil ways on us and we can't stop them. What if the woman you want to have sex with goes to church. Your chances are getting smaller and smaller. She is being taught a woman is lower than an animal. This hatred for the women is seen in the monotheistic religions. Unfortunately, American women don't know who **Inanna** is; but they know Eve. The only evil mother we will ever know as we try and please God.

CHAPTER 24

COILED UP DEVIL

B eing exposed to miracles taught me Christianity is false. When somebody pretends to be healed, they are faking it and it is all a scam for money. People prepare for the afterlife with Jesus. They have led a good life…no murder and no adultery. Lies and stealing is the American way. We are in a stolen country and teach our children a false history. We think to make people white is to save them. Being white or American means you believe in the curse of Eve but not Inanna. You don't have sex, you try to tell the truth, and God in the Bible is against sex according to the Roman Catholic Church.

Everything in the Bible has a symbolic meaning and a link to another religion. When a prophet sees a UF0 with Cyrus the Persian Messiah on it we don't even see the familiar gods underneath the throne. Anointed to do God's work and save Israel from Babylon. Even an eye is a symbol; imagine Ezekiel's chariot with the wheels intersecting wheels. They all have eyes in them, symbolic of life and intelligence. The other countries are on the other side of the prophets, but we do not see them or see the flying saucer.

The good news is this, I have solutions in this book. Polytheism sounds better than Pagan but either Jesus and Satan are brothers or there is more than one Son of God. With the Pagan gods like Osiris, we have the life of the Nile, which is contaminated by the story of Moses. They put him in it and copied the story of Sargon of Acad. The volcano at Santorini plagued the Nile not Moses. Moses is a name used by the men that wrote the book. He does not even seem real, but he led the Hebrews into Canaan and cursed that as well.

Do you ever wonder why American's steal so much and try scams all the time? Where I live there are the guys that borrow from everybody and don't pay it back. They have scams where they tell the people at the bar their tools just got stolen from their truck and collect money from people. Just a waste of money and time with a bunch of users. The Bible has these tricky characters doing all kinds of evil, but it is kind of a book of war. What they do is forgiven but Lord Jehovah is still waiting to return and kill masturbators and forgive thieves.

God laughs at us because we are not having sex every day with a different person. Young people are forced into long term virginity, and they can't go to a sex worker. If you are horny everyday have sex every day. But wait for your wife is what we teach. Jesus believes even though he hung out with and married a hooker we should be poor virgins. He could have been sending us a message on an easy way to make money.

Why do I say God laughs is because the Christian only knows the ten commandments. Number three is to not take his name in vain. He will punish up to the third generation. Our grandparents lied to us that Jesus was against pre-marital sex, and we believed them. We tied up our children so they would not masturbate. And we believed this stuff. This book shows where the Bible errors with history and has obvious lies. It is a hateful, shameful book, and I think we would not know the difference between Satan and Jesus if they changed their names.

Satan means adversary, so Jesus in the wilderness with the devil for forty days fasting produced an inner battle. The only place we hear the voice of Satan is the Testament of Job. He talks and has a character unlike the Bible. If the serpent in the garden of Eden is Satan, then it is a small Satan. I imagine Satan as the ruler of hell but in Italy they are careful to not show God and Satan, or we will wonder why God does not defeat him. Or why America is not covered with the art of Michael the Arch Angel killing the devil. Or celebrate Ra killing the serpent daily when the sun comes up.

The clogged toilet of America is the Bible. We could use it to build temples to gods and teach history correctly. The story of Jesus produces such weak testimonies and being a church kid, I am used to nobody calling you on your lies. Since America takes the hooker away from the rapist and the pedophile, we are the free hooker. They go after us and our children. They rape them in church since the best America has to offer was a lap dance. The real sex and the kind you that won't get in trouble is hard to come by since we don't have hookers having sex in America 24/7 experience. Think of ugly men, poor men, and worse.... the hooker will do them all and you don't have to worry about it.

The way it is it seems like American men will explode from getting so horny. You can film a hooker and turn her into a porn star. So, we should all just start filming it to stay out of jail. How fun but the pre-marital sex that puts you in hell is what Jesus Christ ordered according to our idol of the Bible.

This cannot continue if we do not update our Bible. We need to know it better and learn the Gospels. Since we are not under the law but under grace I say if we want the 613 commandments of the Torah, we can study the Talmud. Since we barely know the ten commandments it would be good to get rid of the stories in the Torah. Moses was a disgusting individual and he copied from the pagans all his commandments and plagiarized stories. Even Moses himself is copied from Sargon of Acad.

CHAPTER 25

TRUTH

I could expose Bible lies all day; but the church is all around the world. If we would have forked Gnostic instead of Catholic, we would not have a concept of sin and we would be knowledgeable. The Catholic want you dependent on them and therefore they lie to you so much. I think American's are ignorant and don't see the obvious psychology behind the stories. Heaven and hell are motivators. They make you do good things. But would a living loving God put you in hell for not believing in Jesus?

In America we don't even understand the evangelist and their totems. The four Gospels are just the same as their endings with the crucifixion: a scene seen all over Italy. Only the Gnostic Jesus smiles but we hide history and anything pagan just to stop sex. In America that is our only moral. We react to others having sex, but we are not smart enough to save our asses from hell.

Americans go around minding their own business even though some people will burn in hell. We don't cry for them or try and convert them, but we wave the sixty-six book Bible at them and promise them miracles. With this sexual pressure on us we cannot communicate. Men communicate through humor, stories, and lies. We must buy the entitled woman a glass of wine or dinner…maybe a few dates and we will have pre-marital sex. Maybe we should say: "Don't sleep with your wife until you are married. But until then do whores instead of people you find drunk at a bar."

The quality of the men and women improves, and we give each other the rare gift of honesty. No lies about marriage…just a quickie for money. We can have all the sex workers we want. Every so often you see one, but she just walks by. Many doable people pass us on the street, but we can't offer them money. Money is the only communication unless you want to get married to somebody you don't know. By the time I see thirty doable women that I cannot fuck unless I go through getting a number, dinner and drinks and then it is still a maybe.

The whole dating thing is so funny. We eventually lower our standards and are happy to get loved by one person. This ancient superstition is not created by God. If you want many and can't have thirty in the brothel, then masturbate and pray the Roman Catholic Jehovah does not kill you.

When prostitution is legal an ugly man can go with a perfect ten. Doing one woman after another makes you hornier and hornier. This experience is had by many in Amsterdam but what does a Christian do in Amsterdam? They stay in the hostel and hide from the Jezebel's. This opportunity to go with so many beautiful women from around the world can't be had in America. Even the rich are screwed and figure it is not worth the risk.

To punish two consenting adults for sex is weird but it shows how much control they have over us. It could change and they make up new lies or pretend to have discovered something new. We should break free and learn our history and not look at **Pagan** as bad. They have changed the Bible so many times and we need the cave wall Bible that they copied in the first place. We cannot explain so many things and it looks suspicious these men with little training lead us. They could be teaching us the truth and help kids in school.

Instead for me it was the: "Let God do it for you." All these miracles coming my way I thought. Then the money goes to the church, and they get richer. Sixty-six books they hold in their hand to control you. Knowing you will never question Jesus or the Bible. The Bible is really his book, it could be called the Bible of Jesus. But what about the other countries? They are all fallen angels with mysteries that open a new Bible for us.

The gods fit right in, and they connect. Stars and constellations come back to tell the story and we figure out what the Bible says and spoke. To change many of the elements of Gnostic to Catholic we see the church uses psychology on us. We are in fear, yet we have hope. The whole 2,000-year-old story has blinded us to the truth.

I believe if America and the world has freedom from the three sexual lies of the Roman Catholic Church, we will be different. Now what you want you cannot have but you disobey the church either way. If we were all sexually satisfied and could be satisfied anytime we want, we would relax. American's look very tense and stiff. They think drinking alcohol will relax them, but they don't try sex. Why even go to a bar in America to look for women. Go to a gentlemen's club or brothel where you can express yourself and feel the freedom.

In 1996 I was in Amsterdam for three days. Once I was smoking a joint and drinking a beer while talking to a cop about the hookers. All these things legal in America we imagine there would be a riot. Smoking pot and drinking beer outside while shopping for hookers. A collection from all around the world; you can't go wrong. I have had many fantasies and none of them could happen in America. I want others to share this happiness and take our freedom more seriously.

To have some old man tell our youth they can't have premarital sex is just sick. He is wasting our lives and even immigrants suffer. Funny a Mexican and Italian woman come to America. They can both have sex in their own countries for money. Once they get to America somebody else is going to tell you what to do with your dick or pussy. They lose their free will and ability to make money with their body. All to satisfy an ancient criminal and punitive God who married a hooker (Not Ashtaroth the wife of El).

CHAPTER 26

HOOKED ON HOOKERS

Jesus hung out with hookers. He should have got twelve and made a second set of disciples. We lose money and communication with Eros and physical love. The hooker makes you younger and helps one to feel good about themselves. We cannot get it easy without money and this gives us a completely different life. The sexual frustration and the unwanted virginity go away, and we can live out our sexual fantasy.

The three lies that keep us down have to do with controlling our bodies. We feel guilty all the time and are under the Egyptian Procreation Only Theory. We are only supposed to have sex to make babies. This is the culture the Roman Catholic Church got its ideas from. We curse Egypt and have no problem with the God of Moses killing them. We also curse the Holy Land where Baal lived. All of this is in the book, and we don't have to believe it. It is just the way everybody thinks. We are born into a hypocritical society that celebrates sexuality but under a curse. Do we really take it that seriously when somebody on television has sex? There are certain limitations, but it is clear they are in bed together.

These examples of how living under the curse has stopped us from knowing more than the book of Jesus. He did everything, created us and the world...Quetzalcoatl created us from corn. These gods are common, and Jesus is not as unique as you would think. We trade in our history for the Ten Commandments. "No God before me," is the first. Everybody wants this one for control, but it defines the jealous character of Jehovah. Next is "Idols" #2 and this kills all art. No expression of the divine but we know the idol of Jesus and his Bible.

It is all about him and the third commandment is:" Do not take my name in vain." We do this on a regular basis to keep Christianity running. In America we don't tell our children we are against sex; we tell them God is....and continually take his name in vain to prove it. Almost the whole Bible is full of sex, and we don't know it. We have been trained on how to interpret the scriptures, but we need the Gnostic Fork to go left and take care of the devil and the dark side once and for all.

Babylon is a seven headed dragon controlling us and there is no hero to save us...but the Red Roman Pig can do it with the Pagan Temple of Osiris on his head and an Italy oar in each hand. He sits in Melchizedek Manor in the moon church called the Duomo. He eats books and understands them. He has the power of the *Popul Vuh,* and he can read calendars. He has a spaceship in a tree. The Sun and Moon verse Draco and Hydra! Where is Rome, the City of Seven Hills? The constellations are above her, but she calls my mother a Virgin Mary. I am a child **Juan Diego in Revelations 12.**

The pig wears Egypt like a crown and stands on the tall tower. The pig sits on any throne in the Bible. He sees the lamb on the throne at the right hand of God. They say he is Jesus, but it is you and me at the right hand of God since Jesus is God. "I and my Father are one." Follow me to Bologna and the **Church of St. Maria di Servi** where I would receive the magical message from the Virgin Mary: "If you call Abraham a friend, a little angel will sit on your shoulder." The Virgin Mary...

Abraham means, "Father" and it is said he is a friend of God. When Jesus says, "I go to my Father." Does he mean, "Go to my Abraham?" **God Most High; El Elyon,** is the other choice. Jesus could have been talking against tradition and we did not understand. We assume his father is Abraham and there is Isaac the human sacrifice. Everything happens in the book of Genesis that we need to know.

Isaac was a sacrifice and Joseph was thrown in a pit by his eleven brothers. He rose to sit with Pharaoh and judged his brothers. The elements of the New Testament are already in the first book.

How much we need to study and not rely only on the men gifted in the sixty-six books. They do not know mythology, the Apocrypha, or the Quran. They make up stories and read a passage of scripture. We think they have covered everything, and they are ignorant as well. Without exposure to these other books, I don't see how these men can be experts in the Bible. If we gave them a test, what would they really know?

Not learning the Bible in High School is a big mistake. Later we can be tricked by what it says and does not say. Reading the Bible makes us smart. Many stories are good, but they need to connect to the outside and to reality. There is a big world out there for us to explore. We need to regain curiosity and lose the laziness. "Somebody else will do it for me." Should be an American expression.

I hear few Christians produce an original testimony. They used to do something and then they stopped it when Jesus came into their lives. Jesus has not told them that since we believe he died in vain and are under the law we consider all religions false. We don't know anything about ours, yet we judge theirs. It is hard for the lazy mind to keep track of all the Bible has to offer. Cross referencing scriptures is a good way to study.

There is a difference between understanding the whole Bible or a part of it. We are too ignorant to understand the whole thing at this point. Knowing what they want to do helps us analyze the stories. They are man sided and against all religions except for their own. This blocks us from getting a more realistic view of where we came from. The Satanic child's story of Noah shows how much we are willing to forgive the Bible hero. He is based on **Ziusudra**, the **Sumerian**, so it is not that he is made up. They changed his name and his story. Only in monotheism do we regard the curse of Ham as being God's words. God cursed the Holy Land and moved his people into it. We determined who the good guys are beforehand, no matter how evil they are.

Just having faith covers it, but faith in what...in who? Hebrews eleven is the hall of fame for faith. Before Jesus they had faith in Moses and later Elijah. It is tricky when I say believe and obey the law. When they say we are not under the law this is not true. We don't even have the word fornication in the Torah or the Ten Commandments. Yet we speak for God and say, **"No pre-marital sex."** This is not what we want, it is what God wants, and the Bible has been created into a lie.

Remember the Gnostic Fork; we would have been less dependent on the church. We are so dependent on them to interpret the Bible for us we can't do it ourselves anymore. Pray and read the Bible. Why are we so ignorant of the truth if we do those two things? Books are left to interpret, and we can't even interpret the book of Revelations. These skinny pages predict our future and tell our past. The heaven or **New Jerusalem** we believe in and the hell we have been told waits for liars and fornicators.

An eternal fire with Satan and the demons motivates me to believe in Jesus and be saved. If hell is not true or we don't burn in Babylon like the three Hebrew children. They saw Marduk (Baal) and Ishtar (Inanna)! But they did not burn nor was the smell of smoke on them. A Son of God appeared in the fire. When they say Jesus is the only begotten son, they could also refer to Dionysus. Who is in the fire? And what statue did the King want them to bow to? There are many gods in Ezekiel and Daniel, while Isaiah carries an extra Messiah (Cyrus the Persian). The Torah was done, and the Old Testament was done, and we added to it.

We don't agree with the original authors, and we should believe in a new Bible that we can understand. The curse continues if we call the edited Bible, God's word or words. Man wrote it and printed it. There are many gods and many books about them, and we are held together and fucked by this Roman Seven Headed Dragon.

Take your freedom from this book and remember there is an error in the Bible. We are free through the portal of Onan because his story can't be true. While the Catholic Church believes in Christian miracles, they have a pattern for telling lies like Jacob. Once somebody dies of masturbation, we will believe the Bible. Until then it is like a fine cognac or cigar to tell the story of Onan and Er to somebody who is afraid of sex and God.

They messed up our lives and we believe the Bible says to tithe your money to the church. Anybody with an audience can take an offering. We block the true gods in order to serve somebody who was inside of us when we were born. We close our eyes to the planets and the days of the week. The church has weakened us over the last 2,000 years. They know true history and we don't. This is not information from the Vatican library. It is mostly available online and should be researched more seriously. How sure are we all these Gods are fake and who are we to say another God is fake. Look at ours all dolled up with blood and thorns. We impose this Jesus on the world. He is the creator of all the thing's pagans' worship, but they are our forbidden fruit.

One God speaks in the Bible according to the Christian. We don't say, "Moses said" or "St. Paul wrote." Usually, we don't know the author but ascribing the Old Testament to Jesus defeats everything he was fighting for. This "God said." Is very cheap and we don't have a lot of gratitude for the truth. They apply his name to everything, assuming the Bible says it. They also use confusing language. One "s" in heaven (heavens) makes us polytheistic. We learn the constellations and the planets. Apollo is on the moon not Jesus; we still believe in mythology, but we are taught it is not true.

We should see and read about the gods relating to each other. If we collected the saints, angels, and demons into a mural, how somber, just like the art I saw in Italy. The artist puts in his opinion to the Bible verse. The non-sexual collection of judges that tell our women they are cattle and go with the other monotheists in a search to stop their own sexual urges. The answer is Mary Magdalene. If she was beautiful or did what the goddess Isis does along the Nile, nursing men or "Nursed all of the fish of the Nile." If Mary Magdalene did this, she would have the power to raise Jesus from the dead in the cave.

Since neither Mary is sexual, we get the word "Virgin" but not the

Latin "Virgo." We have only one moral and that is sex. You don't have to lie to us about sex or take God's name in vain and curse even our grandchildren. We live a boring life in America with our sex workers out of work. Do you really think most Americans are virgins when they get married? We should be with hookers not somebody's future wife. We lie to woman to get sex and they train us to lie.

Nothing is smarter than making up with lost time by honoring the free will. Other countries have it why can't we?" I have been with the most beautiful woman in the world. She will go with you to. If you are in a wheelchair, she will fuck you. On with the list of ugly, drunk ...whatever, she will take your money for sex. To deprive us of this and threaten to put us in jail for using our own bodies is sick. Waste of a life not knowing the women of the world or having dreams come true. No fantasy is forbidden!

In America some people get laid a hundred times in their life. In 1996 in Amsterdam that would have cost me $2,500 and I could do this in ten days. More in a month than your life...and there is no ugly in Amsterdam. Just bring your money and a smile. If you are not virgin for life or for spouse, why take women out to dinner when you can fuck as many as you want. Don't run out of money, you can't do this in America. People are free outside of our own country. Adults can pay for sex, but American's think the Bible says it is a sin. They teach fornicators will burn in hell and lie that fornication means pre-marital sex.

What a waste of money on beer, searching bars for loose women. Every night we come up with the same thing and there is no solution. We pass so much time with a beer in our hand we grow bellies. We get depressed and smoke more. We talk about early death. When I was in Prague, 2001, they told me: "**When a country gets Americanized the women stop having sex and the men start smoking cigarettes because the want to die.**" That is a perfect description of me. In America when I see a hot ass, I light a cigarette. A week before in Budapest I went on a Low Brow tour for my thirty-third birthday. He showed me where the men and women came together in a Piazza between two sets of apartments. The woman makes you dinner and you have sex for ten dollars.

This Piazza would be a heaven for Americans to go to since they associate sex and food. Food is payment for sex to keep us out of jail. Once Budapest was Americanized the prostitution stopped but the mafia uses the women to rob tourist. Walking down the main fashion street I see the bodybuilder mafia and a beautiful woman grabs my hand. She says, "Will you buy me a drink?" If I say yes, the drink will cost, $300 and the bodybuilder guy walks tourist to a nearby ATM to pull out the $300. She likes the good stuff.

To be Americanized is to stop having sex but look at the Hungarian woman in Budapest. She changed from a hooker with dinner into a thief. The food whores in America don't tell you if you are going to get laid before dinner. You must impress them and let them do all the talking. This is boring compared to sex but a little dinner on the table keeps us out of jail. The thing is you are not taking eight women out to dinner in a row and fucking them. Who has time for all this dinner.

A food whore fucks and feels guilty about the restaurant food still in her stomach. She has nothing to show for it. She stays out of jail since we reward the bad investor. Hookers in Italy are buying houses back home. They pay them off with prostitution. In 1996 I talked to a prostitute working in Italy that made $3000 a day doing blow jobs. A bunch of them are paying for houses back home. A women's life in America is impoverished by these laws. How come in the countries where it is legal, they have no problems?

CHAPTER 27

THE GREAT HARLOT

I was in Amsterdam in 2001 on Valentine's Day. The women dress like whores and the Dutch women look like goddesses dressed up. These beautiful days strike memories. We fear the impossible. The whole world is still revolving and nothing bad happened taking money for food. I wish we were mature enough to embrace this kind of love. I am never going to meet her online.

It is weird that our only moral revolves around sex. We judge everybody as if they were married. The control the church has over us is overwhelming. We look at this book and simplify the esoteric secrets of the Old and New Testaments. Even the gospels are four pillars for Christ's throne. They are Babylonian deities in the book of Ezekiel - all attached! If we knew the symbols, we would have eventually read the polytheistic stories. These stories are in such harmony when I follow Isis on my writing adventure. I went to her Temple in Pompeii and felt a vibration I did not feel at the other temples. I saw her husband's pagan temple in Bologna and the black Mary is Isis.

America is the aftermath of an emasculation. Murderers and thieves are tricking us into worshiping them. The characters of the Old Testament at war or doing bad things to their Queen. The hatred toward women is old but it comes back to haunt us. We don't get the love they want to give us. We could read them poetry to **Inanna** instead of the Virgin and her sons. The woman would be blessed by Babylon and has **Ishtar** on her side! Forty-two gods and goddesses in the body anointed by the John with the horns of a stag. A small purse of money goes for the virginity and every woman became a whore in Babylon.

Rome is called the Great Harlot in the Bible and since I have lived years in Italy, I saw it all. Prostitutes all over the streets and parks of Milan. Up and down each side of the street are the transexuals and the women. Choose your side and take a walk on the wild side. When I bounced at different clubs our car would wait in line to leave with all the cars asking the line of women the same thing: "How much for one how much for two of us and even three." They tell the price, and the car moves onto the next woman. It takes forever to get out of there, but I get to meet all the street walkers.

How they dress makes the night life come alive. Hair and body parts everywhere and the price in 1997 was thirty-five dollars for a half hour. All kinds of people come out to hook and the discos are full of horny men. To not have this in America is cruel and it leads men to be aggressive liars dangling money in front of slave woman and her kids. I promise money if you will have sex with me for free. Then the man is stuck with one woman forever. I can't believe prostitution is illegal. It is a harmless thing I have seen all over Europe. Who would be so stupid to volunteer their women to the rapist. He is horny but he can't get laid online unless he calls an escort. We seem to allow this, but it is not a celebration like it is in Amsterdam, where they protect their women.

In America you are the free whore. He goes to jail for paying and for raping. So, you are telling us to get it for free. When we are desperate the penis does the thinking. "Get her, I don't care what it takes!" Men lie to women and eventually this leads to divorce. All the tricks with dinner and drinks lets me spend even a hundred dollars to get laid. And then break her heart repeatedly until I find the right one.

Some lie is told early in the relationship and women who know how to work a man's ego will do well in life. The hypocrisy I am removing from America is we don't have the television telling us one thing and the Bible another. If we are dammed for sex, then don't show people on television getting away with it. Do we believe our favorite actors and actresses are going to hell?

If one character on a sitcom knew the Bible, I would love to have him teach the Gospels with wisdom. He could solve problems with the teachings of Jesus. In America we do not believe in study or checking facts. We are the most trusting people on the face of the Earth, and we are ignorant of spirituality and religion. The Bible is all we have, to blow away every religion on Earth and at this point America is under a punishment. "You got to be married," God said? This is something that happened with our children. We never tell them it is a lie to get them to behave.

This study updates this out of date and hurtful philosophy so we do not associate God as the punisher of love. To pay for physical love is such a big deal for us but we risk pre-marital sex for food. We could go to hell for doing what the people on television do. This is hard to believe but since what another believes determines your life get ready to masturbate your whole life away. A woman is so hard to get but in the 90s it was different. People had sex in clubs, and I remember the Sunset Strip. Women's asses hung out of their jeans, and everybody was sexy.

Now I return to the same places and the young people are not hooking up anymore. Nobody dresses up and you meet less people than when it was sexy. This man who decides that I do not have a free will when it comes to my own body, who is he? I want to see his face so we can all know who ruined paradise on Earth. Having what you want and loving what you see is adults loving each other.

In America, they put it all on the children. "A child might see it." Then the child is always there since we don't have good gentlemen clubs in America. Other countries do what is normal and the happiness that they have is what I want. We will live and die in America. What will happen today that I don't have control of? I would like to pay for sex everyday but that means taking Mr. Passport out and flying around the world. Why is America so advanced and yet so stupid on sex?

You don't tell a child he is going to die in the fire of hell for having sex or masturbating. We need more educated threats or the truth. Suffering God to be the devil all the time makes us stupid. We are using psychology that comes from the scriptures. It seems to say something but what are our New Testament commandments? What can I and can't I do? Traveling helped me to evaluate this stuff when I saw sex workers in other countries. They seem happy and rich, and this is what some people are meant to do. Others rely upon it for survival.

In America an adult woman has sex for an hour with a guy she brought home from the bar. When it is over if he gives her money $200, is that a bad gesture or act of appreciation? When they freed Onan the thief, they killed Onan the masturbator. Now the church says masturbation is a sin, but they steal like Onan. Now we have a bunch of thieves not afraid to steal but they are afraid to whack off. This is so petty, and I wish we desired a pure view of God or had it in us to resist the lies. They had to tell us something but that doesn't mean it is true. To free the mind is hard work when you must unlearn the church.

The freedom I have by understanding Onan is grand. I remember it was a lie that he was killed for whacking off. How many other lies are in there? The Bible does not say what we think it says. We are free if we had a Bible and no cross to bear. The church turned us into fornicators. We worship wood and stone just like a pagan. Many saints and gods cross over and at one time the world was under the blessing of the gods. It produced beautiful poetry with Gilgamesh and then the story of the "hero thieves" of the Bible.

The exposure to this brainwashing shows we do not learn much on our own. The church provides the racists stories and tell you Jesus wrote them. Look how stale the saints look, and they can't fight the devil or make love to a woman. This is all of us and I cry for us. The paradise I had in Europe after my mom died is every man's dream. I lived in Barcelona for five months and every day I had a different girlfriend.

I was a bouncer in 1993 in San Francisco. The bar is known for its exquisite women. I had sex with a different woman every night for two years. Then I worked at a club, and it was the same for the year before I moved to Italy. Then I left San Francisco and wondered why I was not having sex all the time. Being a bouncer is a great way to meet women. I had two old chefs from Italy cooking at my apartment in North Beach every night at 2am knowing I would bring home a different woman every time for dinner and desert. They would leave at 5am and I would never see them again.

Then I saw Amsterdam and loved Italy for their great women. This traveling was inspired by sex and God. I wanted to know if I could do whores. And I knew Jesus hung out with them for some reason. I imagine him happy with them after hanging out with twelve fishermen. I would love to hear their stories and know what they liked about the other John's. We have a double punishment that we cannot do whores or women we are not married to. Once this is through everybody's head we can move along and heal from a tremendous lie. God loves you enough to let you have sex, but **fornication is not a ten commandment.**

We wait for a longer time to have sex than the Virgin Mary. She may have conceived at fourteen years old. The virgin that appeared to Juan Diego was fourteen years old. They may have had sex at an earlier age. We cannot wait to be married if nobody wants to marry us. The Budapest woman will do you and sit on your face. You could have a real fantasy instead of just masturbation.

Since we are doing it anyway, but not as much as we want to, it makes sense to legalize prostitution and make a spiritual exodus from Rome. The seven headed Babylon dragon is still there, and we forget Revelations 12 when the Offspring of the Virgin Mary was saved from the water that came out of the dragon's mouth. We have freedom but the ignorant teach us Jesus was not pleased with sex. Then the shame and darkness of having more than one lover; once again we are doing it anyway so let's unlearn the shame and put my book into practice.

The hypocrisy of introducing the lessons of sex the Bible and the Roman Catholic Church has to offer is gross. We walk around having sex like it is no big deal, but we think fornication is pre-marital sex. This lets us have sex and please God by loving each other physically. I did not have to know the Budapest woman for a long time. She is already impressed with me since I have money. On a slow weekend get a call girl and let's stop using the women at the bars. This is our only option in America since nobody is getting laid without money. People get desperate and settle.

Two adults knowing what they want is common. I want to have sex with many women that I see each day, but nothing happens. We are going to live and die with few notches on our belt. It is not natural to do only one woman, and everybody has a past. The good news is Americans don't get very jealous of their partners past. They are all the exes that are partially forgotten. People start fresh and don't expect you to be a virgin; but God does, they think. So, we are all bad and shamed.

Knowing each other this way makes way more sense. **Not every relationship has to continue to be a good one.** We know more than one soul mate and we are missing out since we believe and respond to premarital sex being a sin. If we did not have 2,000 years of anti sex and anti-woman culture, we would be happy in and out of marriage. Would you rather your husband cheats on you with a hooker or a regular woman? It is better if he cheats with the hooker because she is all business. The regular woman needs wining and dining, a promise to leave the wife, a box of chocolates, love cards, and roses. He is spending money either way, but he doesn't share his life with the prostitute.

No pre-marital sex but we do it anyway. We disrespect our false God by telling lies in God's name. Nobody seems smart enough to catch them. This has been passed down from before our grandparents. The curse of taking God's name in vain continues with us whether we like it or not. **This book is the only way to freedom; there it not another book like it.**

Our perceptions of God come from our fathers. And Father Abraham in the Bible is holding a knife to his son foreshadowing the sacrifice of Jesus. What would please my parents? What if angry Father Abraham is going to sacrifice you for masturbating like the kids in the 60's with the various lies and masturbation detectors sold to prevent children from masturbating.

We believe a lie, and this is a shame. We block out all religions for Jesus. We learn nothing of calendars, gods, zodiac, or pagan legends that seem like Jesus. The lie of sex is the worst. We start with a love feast or orgy and now we can't even touch ourselves. Now with this book we can believe the truth.

My sexual frustration on a given day is like a clawing demon inside of me. I realize I cannot get a hooker and the government says to get it free. Now free is never free with women and once you are a friend there are a lot of favors to do. All this work, the looking, and worst is the scary proposition. Women are afraid of men and like to do online dating. When I see a woman, I want her and that is all I know. My penis does not understand why we must go to dinner and start a relationship. If there was no law, I could take her the second I see her, and there are many women on a given day that I am attracted to for sex only.

CHAPTER 28

PAGAN TRUTH

In Amsterdam often we don't speak the same language. This is not a problem. Everybody understands their part. Money for sex and without jealousy. No monotheistic God to sign you up with the church. The only way he likes it is the married sex. Single men are not supposed to masturbate but the married man is free to do whatever. The church marries you, so they control you. With a prostitute it is like being married for a half hour. It is the only honest relationship and if it were legal in America, I would not have saved my virginity for my wife.

The wife I dreamed of looked like the Budapest woman. She was perfect like an angel in every way. Her long legs were like pillars holding up a perfect heart shaped bubble butt. It is almost painful to look at her she is so beautiful. Now I live in America where we teach pre-marital sex is a sin in the Bible. We are ruined by this and cannot know the real God or the Gnostic Jesus. All this Bible trash was dumped on us, and they won't set us free.

I would send my Bible back to Rome and say, "Feed it to the seven headed dragon." I don't believe in your Satan. **My hero moves the heel of Italy in the Bible.** The boot goes from book to book counting numbers and turning pages. There is a war in heaven, and we don't read the stars into the book of Revelations. It is so short I cannot believe we consider it miraculous, and we ignored Guadalupe in the Bible 500 years ago; in the Baktun of the Hidden Seed.

The book of Revelations keeps repeating itself. It does not have a precise ending. We delay the return of Christ and put it at the end of the world. What a scam that puny book of Revelations holds us all together. We don't even interpret it. The story is so unbelievable...and so obvious. The scary end of the world is just some war. The lake of fire for Satan and his angels is weird for me to think there are American people who will go to hell. We see them on the street, and we don't even take it seriously. Nobody cries for them or tries to get them saved yet we are supposed to have the love of Jesus in us. Since Jesus is God and God is Jehovah, we inherit all the evil of the Torah and don't even try and understand it.

The right hand of the Father is also strange that our Ka or Soul would be next to Ra, or the Sun. Jesus is a parody of sun worship. And the lamb on the throne is you and I but we are not connected to Jesus anymore. He has been absorbed by the Father and you sit on the throne next to him. **This is symbolic of the Ka in Ra.**

There are chakras, gods in the body, and stars that connected us to Osiris and Ra. **Osiris was the first resurrection and Isis brought him back to life.** We went a step further than to say the woman is a help maid. More of a slave or a piece of property; in some countries can't drive a car or vote. Men and women are equal spiritually, but the Bible proposes all this divinely ordained slavery. The woman serves the man, and the Hamite is a slave; we curse Canaan with our faith in Noah.

Noah is not even a real story! It is a copy of **Ziusudra** (Sumerian) before the flood; and **Unatapsin** (Babylon) after the flood. Noah shows the arrogance of Moses and even it looks like Ham fucked Noah like Seth fucked Horus. These Bible stories have ancient counterparts, but we pretend the Bible to be a magical book. It tells the future and records miracles involving war. We watch Israel's history, and they don't seem to have this magic with Hitler. **Hitler said, "I will destroy the God of the ten commandments."**

We act like all the Bible promises are still good, but this requires us to lie about history. The line in the Bible that shows how it was edited for piety is sex. The one thing they changed consistently was sex. We have an edited Bible but what God said was sexual. Just because man lies about God does not mean God is not true. **The punishment of the third commandment is the one we should be working on.** God does not want you to have pre-marital sex and then pass it on is what we believe that is not true about God.

This makes life stale, and every day in America seems the same. Boring beer parties and no women and it is very expensive. Other countries are not as tight on this stuff and people have more elaborate parties without worrying about the children. Everything in America seems to be for the family. "A child will see it." Is the controlling mechanism. Anything adults do will be seen by children and children are everywhere. This makes it so boring that a bar is the only place you must be twenty-one. Then what happens there? We are supposed to hook up for that pre-marital sex that will put you in hell. Or be safe and get married. We are not a sexy people that is not our thing. We don't even question why we are here.

They have spread Jesus so thin making him the answer for everything. They explain away science and history with God's miracles. Even the devil gets involved when he planted the traits of Christ in the pagan deities that were before him. Anybody can figure out that they have been telling us lies. The time I spent studying the errors of the Bible is a lifetime. Most people are not interested in the sacred book.

How much the culture of Christianity has affected us? Years of people believing sex was bad and now on American television we see people doing it with no punishment. Nobody is expected to be a virgin by a normal American man. We must get over the past and this does not seem to be a problem. We don't normally get jealous of our lover's past. The table leg was once covered since it was considered sexy. With this book we have a way out and can return to true history and learn Gilgamesh.

Who decides what we read, and are people reading as much as they used to? The Bible won't help us until we understand it. The Christian does not know the Old Testament very well and they avoid the sexual stories. I heard the story of Noah told at the **Vatican Museum** last year. I waited for the part with the curse and why Noah cursed Ham. The tour guide said' **"Ham was teasing Noah about being nude."** And that is it…no explanation of slavery or racism. Our God is a racist and we hear Philistine, Canaanite, or even Greek we react like we were taught they were bad people. And we decide this without studying a thing about what Canaan used to be before the curse.

That is what we should be going for. Study El, Baal, and Anat and the whole Bible must change. Elijah defeats the ministers of Baal by calling fire from heaven. If we were not brainwashed to not like certain races, we would see Baal sending lightening to Earth. When this little competition on Earth was done, Jehovah replaces Baal, if the Bible mentioned the pantheon of Mt. Zaphon, we would have to rewrite the book. **We know too much now to go by the old Bible.**

This ugly story that does not change or get better ends with the bloody massacre of God. A book that makes people money has a bad ending to the animal sacrifice story. They made money off this and we adopted this strange religion by putting the New Testament on the Old one. We are waiting for Jesus to appear since Adam. I understand there is no historical record of Jesus, and some say he is Horus the Egyptian. We are holding a book that has done us no good when we read it brainwashed. We see things a certain way and make excuses for God.

When we see the crimes God's people have done, they seem very sneaky. Having the word "Heel Catcher" or "Deceiver" for Jacob is not enough. We still say what he did was okay and then we reward him for wrestling with an angel and seeing a ladder to heaven. These stories that confess horrible things about Jacob are powerful. He gets away with all this stuff and we forgive him, but we judge the **Aztec God Quetzalcoatl** as a bad guy. All the god's and culture heroes would teach us history and give us their wisdom.

The Bible is not enough to say we have answered all the questions about God. Mayan calendars and their God, **Hunab Ku** (One giver of movement and measure), give us framework for history and heroes that kill their devils. Just like in mythology. Who is the devil of Jesus that temped him? When does Michael the Archangel kill him? They make Satan bigger than he is and the unsaved are going to meet him for eternity according to the Christian.

In Sumerian everybody goes to one place when they die. It is dusty there and the granddaughter of the two Gods that created the world will visit there, **Inanna**. Venus brings us relief in the afterlife but originally there was one place we all go to. There was no heaven or hell. Who deserves to burn in hell? What kind of sins would they do to merit burning for eternity? It is harsh. As it is written fornicators burn in a lake of fire. We call ourselves fornicators when we have pre-marital sex. Our destiny is sealed, and we did not measure up. We teach this separation from God to our children and curse their sex forever.

They say God will never be pleased with pre-marital sex, lusting, or masturbation. This puts a curse on us until we are married but if a married man lusts after another woman, he has already slept with her. This makes all of us guilty and the angry Jehovah is never pleased. He wants your money, body, virginity, and soul. He wants to be the only God you go to, so he does not get jealous and start punishing. With all this it is a miracle Americans ever get laid at all.

Why do this to the young people who will never know the sex of the 80s and 90s? They could have a model prostitute and a memory like the ones I have of beautiful woman crawling all over me. Different languages, different tasting pussies and asses, and I become a notch on her belt, and she is on mine. But what did you expect love and marriage and sex to go hand in hand? Why does a woman fall in love after they have sex? How many lies has the man told her especially about marriage and money? The woman is careful, but she falls into the same old trap. Dinner and drinks may lead to sex. It takes on a form of payment.

The drinks we buy women and the lies we tell them are awful. Women waste their time with men who only want sex. They want to borrow you for as long as possible. Then women settle for a mediocre man, and he tells the lies of marriage to her. The prostitute is the only honest one with her John. The pure physical relationship is so complementary that for a small amount of dough I am having love with the goddess.

This can only happen in fantasy and since the Judeo-Christian tradition is opposed to sexual expression, it is not going to happen like the **Gnostic Orgy**. Love inspired by Jesus and the real teachings on the Old Testament by a people that were smart. The twelve ignorant fishermen of Jesus occupy the twelve months and the twelve tribes of Israel. They are not sexy and did not ask him hard questions. If a philosopher was there, we might have learned something. Now Jesus is a monster that puts you in hell for not believing in him. He puts fornicators in hell. Then his father kills Onan for masturbating.

CHAPTER 29

THE CURSE FROM THE CHURCH

We have the scriptures so twisted and nothing new has come out of it. How often do you hear the Bible applied to a problem on television? We really do not know it and history waits for us to open our minds and read books. Our lives pass under this sexual curse, and we do not know any different. Travelers notice that all the boogie men in America are false. In Amsterdam we drink beer, smoke pot, and love hookers in a safe environment. Because of all the lies they tell us in America we expect the same bullshit all over the globe.

A foreigner might say Americans do not know how to enjoy life. They only go so far, and the individuals are very similar. This **procreation only theory** is a block to us, and it is an old way of thinking. We need to update our faith into something that is concrete and solid. By adding books like the Enuma Elish and the Book of the Dead to our faith we are more balanced. The church created a scary God that kills and curses people. Jesus is saving us from this harmless God. Jesus created hell not Jehovah! We are put in it by him depending on our status. This is so obviously religious psychology; they scare us with hell to bite the hook of Christ. Once you believe he is the Bible incarnate we suffer all the ill hatred of his Father.

This religion does come to us externally. We smile and act sweet to people in church. In Italy gargoyles protect the gothic cathedrals. One can learn more outside the great gothic structures than inside. A Mason's Bible that includes the pagan deities. Alchemy and other sciences come from Gnosticism, but we don't even give it a try. Not even to compare or study the differences between Gnosticism and what we believe today.

These things are very valuable to us, and we have more information now than before. I see a universal Jesus who does not conform to Moses. Remember Moses is agreed upon by all three monotheistic religions. The prophet and Jesus are not revered but Moses is. All the evil that Moses wrote has erupted to the hate of women. The very people that gave us birth get the blame while the lazy male has his slave. Women should study Inanna and the goddess in general. Eve is to blame for all this craziness, and it is men who wrote and organized the Bible. I would think since Moses is the important one, we would all convert to Judaism. Study the Torah and the Talmud; we could see what some of that stuff really means.

Polytheism gives us back the gods of the Native American. They even have a flayed savior and Quetzalcoatl. The Romans and Greeks would lend us their wisdom and the early religions have so much in common they are more likely to be true. The shame of history is that we are ignorant of the gods in the Bible. The legends connect us to the stars, and everything is holy. Now we have false forbidden fruit and deny the Gnostic Jesus of the Love Feast. This love and, Eros, is the oldest God.

When I see a woman's hot ass in the grocery store, I want to devour it. Eros is alive and well! It was the same since the beginning, we saw women and desired them. Even the angels left heaven and had sex with women who produced the Giants (Nephilim). We are so strict in America on condemning sex while exploiting it. In Europe they protect their women with whores but in America we are the prey of the ugly rapist. He can't go to a hooker or even beat off, so he rapes an innocent victim.

Besides rape there are other things to be concerned with. The rage of sexual frustration makes men fight at bars. They drink to kill the pain, but the truth is we believe God does not want us to have sex before marriage. This means he cannot bless our sex if we think the Bible says it is bad which it does not. No sex is a lie of the Roman Catholic Church who changed the Roman myth of Jesus into history to control us.

Do you want to go your life without expressing yourself sexually? Then turn around to an old ass lie that goes back thousands of years. Our parents and grandparents put these curses on us when they lied about God to us. The Bible has all the answers, but we learn the Bible from the preacher, and he only wants to be rich.

The story of Jesus is so small and must be told four times. There is not much to even suggest he existed, but we follow him anyway. **Irenaeus**, the church father, calls the Gnostics Satanists and we miss out on the Gnostic teachings just to tell the lie that God is against sex and pre-marital sex is fornication. I feel sorry for us Americans that we are not hooking up anymore.

In the 80s and 90s I wore my hair long and had lots of women. In San Francisco I was a bouncer for three years and got laid every night. Older people used to tell me about the 60s and 70s about how much sex they had. Around the year 2000 life grew dark before the dawn. Fashion changed and people stopped having sex. I was a bartender in different cities watching it happen. The only hope for us is prostitution. The horny men of the French Quarter in New Orleans watching the tits and ass on **Bourbon Street**; would make money off love. It is a crime a woman must do it for free to stay out of jail. The American pussy gets presents and food but no money. When God asks her, "Why have you had premarital sex?" She thinks the Bible says it is a sin but does it anyway.

Explain the Bible to the space aliens. Tell them we judge each other by what is not in the Bible and take God's name in vain to enslave people and tell them lies. It is all based on faith they say. This is very easy to see we are not sincere in our faith. We don't really believe in hell, and we don't have a Gnostic Bible to see what the real Jesus was like. Once again America has no curiosity and most American's do not know what a Gnostic is.

The years of good sex for me are not over but we remain under this curse in America. Choose between sex and God. One is a sin and the other a lie. We read the Bible and even remember the racism against Egypt and an Egyptian is meaningless to the Christian. They know the Bible is a black book painted white and that was when it got popular. The false things we say God said in the Bible are too many to count. We are clogged up, but I am a spiritual plumber. Imagine the seven headed dragon in the book of Revelations walks through the Bible. He gets to the part where it was Jehu's men turned the house of Baal into a urinal. There is an axe head attached to a branch.

The Phoenician Queen is thrown out a window and hit the dung. This was a cowardly ending for the match with Elijah who called fire down from heaven and runs from Jezebel. All these races are expendable people to Jehovah. They are his inventor, and they are more powerful than the God of dirty tricks and criminals. We forgive all their crimes no matter how bad they are, and we figure we are okay if we don't commit murder or adultery. Telling lies is second nature to the Christian who has never seen eternal hell.

CHAPTER 30

THE BATTLE BETWEEN THE TRUTH AND THE LIE

These stories, in the Bible, motivate us. They are made for the simple. People don't check their facts and there are no good Bible timelines to match it up to the Babylonians and Sumerians. They are older and have better literature. Baal is everywhere yet the Christians have the upside-down cross of the first Pope and an upside-down Bible where God is the devil. The studies of Phoenician El are interesting that nothing comes before him. The Bible claims to tell the whole story. El is an idol and this is what happens to the gods. The Americans should learn what a fallen angel is. They are the sons of the gods that left heaven. They lusted with their eyes and the giants poked out Samson's to make it even. If we say Zeus is a fallen angel just remember all these lies are to hide sex. Angels and saints don't make love, but the gods do.

If we used correct terminology, we remember the Gnostics are called Satanist because of an orgy. The fallen angels lusted with their eyes. Sex is the only moral we have in America. We don't have sex, but we lie and steal all the time ...not to mention taking God's name in vain. Our children grow up with this nude drunk Noah and it is a racist children's story. Noah is nude and drunk just like the pastors of my church were with the children they molested. They told me not to go to the prom, since dancing leads to sex.

The crimes the innocent must suffer because men cannot do hookers is incredible. The government wants us to harness all that frustration into getting a wife or husband. We are under the curse of Egypt but there is a way out. If we continue to tell people pre-marital sex is fornication, and fornicators burn in a lake of fire, we are stunting their growth. They are going to have untold issues.

We don't let Jesus stand on his own. Hell is necessary to scare people into believing and giving their money. Have you recently heard something new from the Bible, besides this book? They quote a basic story and teach Jesus again. They never want us to open a Bible commentary or concordance. The message is so simple, and it ends in Jesus saving you from your problems and forgiving your sins no matter how great they are.

Eventually we find many subjects in the Bible that teach obedience. A person like the Wizard of Oz is behind it. Men making scary sounds with their Bible lies. Look at Daniel and the three Hebrew children. They did not bow to the statue in Babylon and when the King threw them in the fire they did not burn. Is this not the message of the Catholic Church? Bow to Jesus and Mary or burn in hell. In the book of Daniel, not even the smell of smoke was on the three children foreshadowing our God who would not put us in hell forever.

Other examples are Joseph forgiving his eleven brothers on mini-judgment day. The stories of Jesus are already in the Old Testament, and we rarely show crucifixions in art even though there were many. It would be an interesting mural for Julius Cesare and Alexander the Great. Christianity has touched everything. We don't know these guys because they are not Jesus. Like Moses the miracles are in the Bible but not in the war. In real life the Bible turns out to be false. Emperor Constantine made Jesus God and everything before him is false to us. Extra Biblical books have the true secrets and connections to other countries.

El and Baal as a new Father and Son couple gives us something that has not been tampered with. Stories of a God saving us from draught and infertility. Several gods are like Baal and his tablets show

how false the Bible is. We don't get the whole story of the Bible we just feel guilty about Jesus. Once we understand the Bible it is under our feet instead of above our heads. While we believe the world is flat at one time we pass on these lies from the church. Monsters will get you if you leave. Since the Bible is written as a history book and not myths, we get stuck with the mean son of bitch for God.

It is not true the Bible or Jesus really said the things we think, but since we think so we get judged. If a space alien asked us if our Holy Book permits pre-marital sex, we would say no unless we had read this book. We think it is a sin and we celebrate it anyway, and we don't even realize the words pre-marital sex are not in the Bible, but fornication is. **Not in the ten commandments or the Torah!** But we ruin our sex lives and the spiritual orgy that would happen if we were all knowledgeable about Jesus.

Instead, we watch the violent short story of miracles and the cross. The church makes a lot of money off him, but they teach Jesus cancels the gods. Even America is proud to have Apollo on the moon, but we don't know who Apollo is. He is a sinner since he is not Christian but if he looked like Jesus, would we know the difference? The same story told four times and art all over the world. Welcome the teacher from heaven and follow his laws. Love freed us from the law and Jesus said, "Don't judge or you will be judged." The law is more alive than ever, and the three monotheistic religions believe the Torah is the words of God.

"Put no god before me...." And then we all line up to play judge. 2,000 years later we think we have mastered the teachings of Jesus. Love your brother and fulfill the law. Stop telling the lie about sex being bad to make us guilty and see what happens in the world. As I say sex is the only "sin" we react to. If somebody is telling lies or stealing, we take that for granted. Any spicy sex story gets front page news.

This heaven on Earth could start with studying the Quran, Gnostic, and Pagan. Make the preacher responsible for this knowledge. The Bible is too short. Much has been removed but now it is interesting as history. We don't even use the wisdom of Solomon which would fix the world and teach us how to think. Otherwise, they must lie about history to make the Bible true. Nobody wants to hear about the Sumerians and Babylonians because it will mess up the story of Noah and slavery. The slavery is based on another sexual sin, and we see looking at our father drunk and nude to be punished with Africa (Ham) being the slave?

These things in the Bible are simply not true and we are bullied into saying Christ is Lord or we go to hell. The worst part about the way, truth, and light is he thinks he is the only way, and this turns to gods that were turned into fallen angels into devils. Everybody who had sex is removed so a child won't see it, but Noah has the angry voice of a nude drunk man awoken to see what Ham had done to him. **Probably Ham sodomized him and cut off his dick.** That would make anyone mad but just for looking is the angry voice of God we know.

He does not let us have sex with each other even though that would make the world beautiful. We believe this and teach it to our children. They don't pray or read the Bible, but they go to church and watch it on television. Christianity is powerful in America, but Americans are ignorant of the Bible. They can't help you or heal you if you are down. They know the story of Adam and Eve, the commandments, and the cross and that is about it.

We eat the fruit with Adam and realize we are nude in the middle of the Garden of Eden. Shame starts as God hands us our clothing. Still, we don't have the strict trio we have today. It is worse for us even though we don't obey it. Belief needs to be qualified as belief in what? To believe in Jesus is to believe the Bible. What if somebody is Gnostic? We show great ignorance waiting for Jesus to return. This book of Revelations is so small and will repeat itself when there is a war in heaven. We could link the stars of the **Tilma of Guadalupe** to the constellations and put a marker in the Bible to know Revelations 12 happened December 9, 1531, A.D. in the **Baktun of the Hidden Seed.**

We would finish the Bible in 2012 A.D. and the second coming of Christ could be Quetzalcoatl. Or the parody of sun worship could mean the sun came out the next day. But 2,000 years later we are not even curious about the truth. Religion will continue to shape our lives and bring us under mind control.

Pyramids and calendars are not used but the Bible is, and we are not sure what happened where. The same symbolic animals could represent many countries. The idea of judgement day is scary since we have not learned the gospels. He said, "As you have done to the least of these you have done unto me." This takes the person we hate the most as a measure of how much we love Jesus. He said that the law and prophets is fulfilled by loving God and your neighbor. Yet we insist on being ignorant of the lies the church must tell us to stay in business.

The complicated teachings of Moses are long and drawn out. He takes credit for history and finds a God that will follow him. Since we teach Jesus is God, and in particular the God of the Old Testament, he is the leader. The number one and most powerful God is only known on the cross. His teaching according to us is that all others are fake. **320,000,000 Hindu Gods** are now like Gnostic, Jew, Muslim, and every faith on the planet are all the devil or the serpent in the Garden of Eden.

This is a crime to introduce us to this jealous deity. All other gods disappear for the Protestant. No saints, which resemble asexual gods, and Mary Queen of Heaven and Angels is also fake to England's invention the Protestant religion. The followers of Jesus can turn anybody into a Satanist. The Gnostic and Jew both agree with the law, but the Christian is not under the law but grace. He says sorry after he sins against you. God lets him lie and steal not to mention they molest children while teaching us we must be married and get our one shot at a sex partner for life.

Too much control they have and have had. To scare us with hell from the sixty-six books and collect an offering. Jesus and Krishna are in us when we are born. They awaken that which is within us. We all have the Divine Breathe and the Heartbeat of the Universe. Jesus and the Holy Spirit don't enter you at baptism. They are in you; and being sold to you by the Christian who makes a lot of money of off scaring us with hell. Feeling guilty about Jesus when Adam and Eve did not even exist is sad. We have so many resources to understand the Bible. We could build things to educate everybody.

In the old days when a God or an idol did not predict the future or failed them in some way, they get a new one. This is what we should do with the Bible. Study the Popul Vuh and we study all the gods associated with the Sun and Moon. Every polytheist could enjoy the adventures of the Sun and Moon in hell **Xibalba**. Names of Greek and Roman Gods could appear and follow them on the adventure. With the **Popul Vuh** we get a book that attaches us to the unadulterated stories of the **Hero Twins**. We have them above our heads, but we do not revere or study them.

The whole world is against us converting more to Christianity and the Gnostic fork will bring us back to where we are supposed to be. Just reading the Bible is not enough. We must study books about the Bible to interpret it. It is like we have a computer disk but not a computer to put it in. They don't teach us the Bible in High School, so the church gets first stab. "Do you want Jesus in your life…. or do you want to go to hell?" This is how they put it to me when I was fifteen. I did not want to go to hell, so I raised my hand. Years later after living in Italy for a year and a half, I did not believe anymore. I saw the art and the esoteric symbols, and I became a Unitarian. I believe all religions are good and if we take the sexual curse off ourselves the Bible will make sense and we won't be victims to the rich religion of Christianity.

Italy offers the best of both worlds. Outside of the church in Florence is the man god, Hercules beating the shit out of Nexus the Centaur. Nexus stole the wife of Hercules at the river of **Evevenus**. Hercules chases him down to the river saying, "Nexus your plans are not as swift as your feet." He beats him with a club. What if Jesus punished the church for telling lies and stealing? He can't even beat the devil. Michael the Arch Angel must do it.

The devil must be happy with Christianity since he has God on the cross forever. He never smiles and never looks happy. Only the

Gnostic show the smiling Jesus. All through Italy is the crucifix. Bloody scenes and suffering all to forgive our sins. Sin is a concept of the Old Testament. But we were not going to hell we go to Sheol. Jesus saved us from nothing…. the hell he scares us with did not exist until he did. It is just the story of the three Hebrew children in Babylon.

With his hands held back by nails he cannot even masturbate. Why do we relate to this image as the image of the only true God? It does not make sense and it is still the story of Abraham and Isaac. We see from the beginning this story of a Father sacrificing his son. The angry God put his son on the cross so we would not go to hell. Some believe and some don't, but in America we are an embarrassment. We are cheap and lie to each other continually and in my own life I compare my friends in Italy to my friends in Carlsbad and there is a big difference. We value a friend more than his money and the using is so common people don't reach out as much in America.

Every American seems to want something, but they don't really help at all. This puts them in the user category. If I need them, I can call them, but they won't feel my pain. In **Lecce** we were a community and family. This brought them financial prosperity that poor communities in America should know about. Not much happened on 2012 A.D.; it certainly was not the end of the world. We should know the stars and constellations in the book of Revelations and start interpreting the Bible symbolically.

Freedom from the fake laws and stories of Roman Catholic Church will refresh and clean us. We have an evil father figure who is going to punish us for idolatry. The God of the Old Testament did not keep his promises of protection for the Jews. To have the other life that I had in Europe helps me compare and understand my boredom in America. We have children always watching us and there is no good adult entertainment. Sex is the last of our worries and connecting sex to a different sound "making love" is better. Sex sounds dirty to the American and that is because we are inexperienced. Anybody who has made love knows what it is all about. But you want me to believe making love to my girlfriend, who is not my wife, is a sin?

CHAPTER 31

THE SHAME REMAINS THE SAME

People want sex so badly, but they do not express it. If they could have her and him, it would be a dream. Never in these red-light districts I saw in Europe was there a fight. People behave and not everybody has sex with a prostitute. America demonizes drugs and sex but that does not stop the rest of the world from making love and paying for it.

The fantasy is for us to explore with no sexual shame. Remember I am a spiritual Catholic and I believe in the Roman Catholic Church. I only change the trio of masturbation, pre-marital sex, and lust. That is too cruel of a God to put in charge of your children. They learn that the kid has sex with the father in the stories of Noah and Lot. They are so gross the stories and Moses is such an evil man but now we have an escape. Sex is the key to the esoteric secrets of the Bible. Expand past the basic stories of Revelation. All of Catholicism is based on this and the art shows the esoteric secrets.

We can go to church, but the old Bible does not have the Gnosis. We owe it to Jesus to hear his human story. Polytheism brings back the adult love and missing history. I have read the ancient love poems and they are not dirty. The Bible is the dirtiest book of all, and the characters are all evil.

We can do better as a country to not take God's name in vain for money. Then lie to us about the Native American gods and their legends. We get this white Christianity from a legacy of horrible men.

Since the Bible does not say sex is a sin, we can figure Solomon had 700 wives. Did Solomon have pre-marital sex? He had more than one woman and therefore we don't read Solomon in church. People will figure out they are being lied to.

Sex is everything in the Bible that was hidden or distorted. We are twisted to and if we had a relationship with Ra the Sun God we might understand. **Gods (forty-two) are in your body!** We connect to Ra when we understand the **Boat of a Million Years.** What if we have to say a negative confession to the gods in the underworld? With Jesus you are forgiven no matter what you do, and it is a free for all.

People surrender too much to the church and have such a low expectation. If we had vision of what it would be like to escape these old superstitions, we would be different. Traveling Europe and living in Italy gave me a comparison and something to hope for. We are so shut down people not only don't have sex they don't make friends. People are happy after they get laid, and they are a pleasure to be with. How about a sexually frustrated person? Somebody telling you what you can and cannot do with your body hurts. They have stopped our love and called any physical love sinful.

Otherwise, we pass each other, and nothing happens. No memories of some enchanting night, and no new experience. We are not virgins when we marry normally so we are afraid of doing too many people. We want to have a small number but there is no need for that. We have misunderstood the Bible and the book that promises freedom from the law enslaves us to it. Every word of even the New Testament is law to us. We did not get the saved by grace and walk in the Spirit.

I am afraid to lose what all ancient religions have in common. We judge the idols and don't read their books. We rely on Moses but don't listen to the Jews. Everybody is a devil including the gods. This is too much power and we should be reading more than the Bible. We all assume we know what it says and much of it is hidden knowledge. We are so easily satisfied with any so called "Bible expert" that it shows how weak and ignorant we are. They make up anything and then praise Jesus and all these cults appear.

Monotheism is as strong as its weakest link. The Jew, Muslim, and Christian all have sick and twisted views on sex, and they are in control. Be free with God and remember if the Bible doesn't say it, we are getting more hogwash from the Roman Catholic Church. We assume the Bible says many things it doesn't say. The church doesn't try and teach us much and they must compensate to make Jesus look like God.

Therefore, the Gnostic gospels are less accepted, because Jesus looks like a man. Forcing us to worship this crucified individual that claims to have created the universe. We make God up based on the Old Testament, but we follow only one little law that says the others are bad. If we had the love including physical love the world would change. We get more upset about sex than other sins. People are brainwashed to think sex is bad. Try and proposition a person in America you are attracted to. We miss out on so many opportunities because we don't have the communication.

We have done this to ourselves but now is the end. We acknowledge the ten commandments don't include fornication. Fornication is more of a spiritual adultery to God and never is it used in context to mean premarital sex. They have taken it too far with masturbation being bad and they try to prove things the Bible doesn't say. It is hard to find the right person dating. In a gentlemen club we can choose based on looks. How many people, including the rich, can say they have had this experience in America?

I know we don't approve of bad treatment of woman, but the Bible is the devil's book. The word God comes up in the Mayan prayer for the morning and it says he loves us. Everybody has God but we are the only people that believe Jesus only is God. We attach the cross to the second commandment and go around calling everything an idol. Jesus is an idol, but the New Testament says we all know an idol is nothing. This blocks us from the idols of God but not from their books.

Are we so brainwashed that we don't even have curiosity? The stories of Greek mythology and Zeus have helped me greatly. I live in a world that thinks the Bible says the trio. I am the only one who knows what fornication means. This is lonely and any woman I meet in America has been poisoned by the church. Zeus helps me relate to other gods and the planet Jupiter. We have gods as the days of the week and the planets in the solar system.

Each planet tells a story, and some have many moons. The plural Elohim (Gods) in creation sounds like there were gods in the garden, including the serpent. This puts us towards the aliens and astronauts that we are going to meet. Let's not call the planets, days of the week, and sacred calendars Satan. This is the power of the church. They call the original followers of Jesus Satanists. The other monotheists are hateful often to each other and they all have one God. The first monotheist was Sumerian before the Bible. This 800-year period, the Baktun of the Star Planting and Baktun of the Pyramid, are **the missing Baktuns of the Bible.** The Bible starts with Moses and the Baktun of the Western Mountain. We are missing stars and pyramids.

All this lost information could help us and fix our problems. I don't think people physically loving each other are committing sin. We get less mad about war than sex. In the countries where it is legal, I am usually the only guy in the brothel unless it is outdoors like Antwerp and Amsterdam. Not everybody is going to become a slut or a whore. But when you make love to your boyfriend, I don't think God is mad. Tell the rapist to masturbate; Jesus won't kill him, but his followers will. War after war and they think controlling the trio is not good?

Prostitution makes money appear out of nowhere and saves men so much money, one woman becomes twelve women. Women can buy a house with their vagina and the American woman has nothing to show for it but food and gifts. A salary is different, and you meet more people. The prostitutes in Italy told me how much they love going with the handsome Italian men. Think of all the gross sins only a hooker can handle go to "free woman." And dinner whore…. porn is okay but prostitution is not? We go to jail if we pay to make love. We have nobody to protect us from getting horny. Sex offender wherever you go.... we don't know what you did. Did you rape a woman to a bloody pulp, sodomize a child, or pay $10 for a blow job? They don't care it is all the same to them. If I get a blow job for free it is okay even though we believe that is fornication. I go to the jail of the rapist and pedophile?

Adding money to sex doesn't change anything. The women get rich and maybe the slut does more than the whore. We are smart to exchange food for sex in America so we don't go to jail, but it could be so much more fun. Some of these cities are twenty-four hours and if you can't sleep have sex. In Amsterdam and Antwerp, they have sex workers from all kinds of different countries. Going around the world is going around the world in these cities. Without going to those countries, I sample what a sex worker from there is like. Sexy accents, great bodies, and pure passion steams the pink windows of the red-light district.

Brussels, Belgium I went to in 2001 for five days and stayed drunk in their red-light district. It was so cheap I would have sex between each beer while carrying on a conversation with a guy at the bar. Every time the sexy bartender bent over to get a beer, I got horny and would leave to have sex and then come back. I did this all day and kept a conversation going with the same guy all day. Supermodels were $60 an hour and they have all kinds and countries. This is the most beautiful experience of my life living this dream and I want America to have physical love to.

Legalize it and everybody gets a job. We get married too late in life to wait for sex and have only one person. The women I have been with have left a mark on me and enhanced my self-esteem. I also became a very good lover and I like to show it off. This is what we all want. But focus on the problem here with the $10 blow job. The guy putting you in jail for not doing it free is telling you what to do with your money and your body. The world's oldest profession is not good enough. The judge is not supposed to have pre-marital sex or as he might call it fornication. He figures he is going to hell for sex but not to jail unless he pays. What right does a fucking fornicator have over me. He has sex and is going to hell, but he looks at me and says, "You pay money…. that is not an acceptable form of payment."

The nerve people must judge us. I tell them an Italian woman has her free will protected by the Pope so she can be a prostitute, but she can't have a pimp. They can't tell her what to do with her body. If she or a Mexican woman come to America, they lose their free will and become like an American woman fornicating for food. Think of how it is in countries like Spain and cities like Barcelona they have street walkers and brothels all over the city. One night a man paid me $3000 in 2001 to take him to all the brothels of Barcelona.

None of these cities have any problems and the women seem so happy. Having sex while other people have sex makes the walls move. These twenty-four cities produce money and give the rapist and pedophile a place to go. The prostitute handles all kinds of men and seeing all of this taught me that sex is not a big deal. These women do it all day and our God hates us so bad he clamps down the masturbation detector. Why do we live in the past and keep the curse of Eve attached to us?

We have outgrown the Bible and we know more now than ever. After World War 2 we should get a new Old Testament. Hitler is forgiven if he asks Jesus, just like the thief on the cross. This is not a good message and where are all those racist miracles from the criminal God. He kills Egyptians, Philistines, and Canaanites with these wondrous war miracles that allow them to take land and kill innocent people who do not believe in their God.

In the war there was no Red Sea or the story of Samson killing the giants. It is as if God went on vacation or switched sides. If we were polytheist, we would all have Zeus to help make sense. The Bible is not good, and it is too hard for us to understand. Which Lord are they talking about and in what language? Baal is Lord and is Phoenician and his name works like a title. The Old Testament uses Lord for the Elohim. If Baal, Bel Marduk, or Jupiter comes in we align planets, aliens, and stars.

We see none of these evil miracles in history, but legend has them.

Not having a Talmud to interpret the Torah is like wining people to Jesus without reading the Gnostic Gospels. We don't know the difference and Jesus is only God since Emperor Constantine crowed him king. Before this there was no one book that tells everything. Ancient beliefs had so much in common. Now we have lost the wisdom, just like Sophia and Solomon.

Where we go from here is up to us. This book is the one chance to be free from the sexual trio that is used to control you and fuck up your sex life. Guilt, shame, and the idea of going to hell trouble us. Women are not as free as they would be. It is the pressure of the Bible and Christianity that make us guilty for sex. The Bible does not say pre-marital sex is a sin but the whole world thinks it does. By taking this exodus from Rome we keep Jesus, saints, and angels but we understand the gods they were copied from. This teaches us the culture of the countries we are ignorant of.

CHAPTER 32

UNITE WITH THE GODDESS

W e don't talk about certain cultures and history seems to get shorter. If these lies are in place, we are never going to grow. Stealing and telling lies has become a way of life for the Christian in America. You don't know even the New Testament, but you go around spreading the white man's lies. No sex is the final message we get anytime Jesus appears. A man who hung out with prostitutes and told the ones without sin to throw the first stone is now evil Moses coming down the mountain. We don't learn only from the laws of the Torah but by the stories.

The stories are about destroying certain kinds of people, but we feel it is good for some reason. Nobody feels sorry for the ones God is destroying. When the Jews are punished it is for not keeping the Torah. The prophets witness Nebuchadnezzar collecting his taxes from Israel. They go into exile and the gods are everywhere and they worship Bel or Baal. The Bible leaves out important details and Jehovah takes credit for what the Pagan Kings did in real life. He switches sides to punish Israel when Israel is losing. We put all this bad karma on our children and add them to the children of Father Abraham.

The man with the knife raised to his son is the father of the three monotheistic religions. A Catholic Priest in Florence, Italy told me, "Adam and Eve never existed. Abraham, Isaac, and Jacob never existed." He says Christ was true man and true God. I interviewed him outside of Dante's church and he sold me some books. Every question

I asked him had a similar response about Christ being true man and true God. Who goes to hell? "Those that say Christ is not true man and true God." Every sin and every religion got this response. This priest was the Parocco of Dante's church.

The decision to take Jesus as myth or history is up to us. The history looks weak, and his story is told in the stars. The serpent is already dead (Serpents Caput) in the hands of the healer (Ophiuchus). When is Jesus' going to kill the devil? How did a little talking serpent get to rule the underworld? Every god looks like a Christian Satan, but the devil goes back to the time of El and Baal. All the secrets we lose and the holy things we cannot interpret. So, few people can apply this basic wisdom. Remember Solomon and his 700 wives are blocked out for sex.

With Solomon I learned his story and Proverbs when I was a young Christian. Whatever your problem was I had a proverb to help. Ecclesiastes is another book I love. And I refer to my dick and balls as the grasshopper and caper berry bush. We miss the esoteric language in the Song of Songs and the book of Job. It is a different kind of wisdom, and it would be good for us to know this. The church does not have a grasshopper, but Phoenician El has a member longer than the seas. Osiris is the penis in the Book of Dead. The Bible emasculates us but if we trust the Phoenician pantheon, we will get a new view of the Bible.

Phoenician Baal is Bel Marduk in Babylon and Marduk is the 12th planet. Look at how Baal or Bel connects the stars and the apocryphal stories of Bel and the Dragon. We lose this Phoenician Jesus that prays for us on Mt. Zaphon instead of Mt. Sinai. The Bible is a dirty book, and it teaches God is not your Father until you are born again. Until then suffer for Eve's sin and blame the woman for everything.

Baal holds a spear of lightening and makes it rain. He battles his dead brother Mot (the Moon) God of infertility. **The Popul Vuh** called the 400 drinking boys killed in the orgy **Motz** after they die and become the **Pleiades.** Without constellations we cannot connect the countries and find religions that we call Satanism if they are adversarial to the Roman Catholic Church. We know what our parents taught us, and they were taught by their parents. When will we stop taking God's name in vain by assigning his name to our lies? We are ignorant but if we were smart, we would not tell children God is against sex. Teach them birth control and to take money instead of food. If you want to get married get married. Was your American wife a virgin when you defiled her?

Bloody virgin you are better than me since you have never had sex. American virgins expect a reward in heaven for avoiding fornication. If fornication was one of the ten commandments, I could see teaching the way we do. 613 commandments in the Torah and not one of them is fornication. We could be Jews and have pre-marital sex and lusting is not the same as adultery in Judaism. That would seem to be a cruel commandment from Jesus; now he is law. The whole book is law.

Each story reaches out for another god and dies. The church has idols, but they use idolatry as an excuse to condemn other religions. How could they all be false? And is that what Jesus was teaching when he said he was the "Way"; this could be **Tau** or the last letter of the Phoenician alphabet. When I lived in Milan in 1997, I went to a bookstore behind the Duomo. There are many books on Jesus and other religions. The covers were half Jesus and half another god. They compared the teachings. I wish I would have bought all of them.

Now we have the Way which burns all other Ways in hell. Even Baal who prays like Jesus for his friends on Earth is part of this bad guy thing. We understand the enemies of Israel are called God in the Bible. We don't even hear the voice of the prophets. Moses and St. Paul are the same voice, and all the books are God. This study shows the Er and error, but we assume the Bible is perfect even though it has been changed. It takes a lifetime to study the Bible but if you want to understand Jesus you will need more than the Bible.

The story does not even seem true, but here we are believing it and teaching to our children all over the world. The sex is evil... lies come out and get full attention. America throws stones at its's leaders if they cheat. If they lie and steal this is sort of the forgivable sins that

American's do to each other in greed. Everybody wants something materialistic from each other, but nobody is giving. No other country would trade a friend for a small amount of money. In my life I watch people I know juggle friends over small amounts of money. A friend could be a friend for life. They could help you when you are down.

The fact we don't have sex and stop other people from having sex is like a mission. When people come here from other countries and want to use the system nobody tells them sex is sin. So according to our own beliefs the person is going to hell, and we encourage them to have sex as much as they want. Even to the point they don't need to work. Why don't we tell them the lie that fornication is pre-marital sex like we do with our children?

Men can't get laid, and women can't have orgasms. We wonder why with this boiling hell that is said to be eternal. We are so fucked up we can't even talk about sex or proposition somebody. Many men I know have gone years without getting laid. After a divorce I offered my friend a hooker if he drives us to Mexico. He could not do it. This would have erased the memory of his ex-wife completely. He could have gotten out of heart break and loneliness with the power of the hooker or Ishtar. She makes men feel good and fulfills men's ultimate desires. Never can a rich man in America do many in a row unless he pays them. The main thing is communication comes with money. No can change to yes by adding more cash.

I am so happy I paid extra in Hamburg, Germany to a German hooker. She quoted me double for what I wanted, and I told her ok if you do it for an hour. It was the greatest experience and this night in Hamburg lasted 24 hours for me. I partied so much and went from apartment to apartment fucking women. A night out in Europe can't really compare to America. What do single men do after they leave the bars in America? It is a sin, but we do it anyway and show it on television. It is as if we believe two different things so why poison our children with the lie of fornication and cast them into the dark ages.

We don't even read what we have let alone all that we should be reading. We are so ignorant around the world of what the Bible really says and means. If people say they love Jesus, why do they confine themselves to the gospels. Four books about him when St. John said the books about Jesus would fill the world. Instead, not only do we not recognize St. John's message we don't even know the gospels. We think the Bible is the one good book and we understand it to say other Bibles are bad. This is the only book; all else is Satan.

They use the word Satan for anybody that disagrees with them. By now the forbidden fruit is so much that we have called the devil. While not applying one teaching of Jesus on television, nobody is a Christian actor in Hollywood. What if a Bible student had a show and used the Gospels to solve all our problems. When I heal or I teach the Bible I am like an expert that can see the whole story in the Phoenician alphabet. What if I was a character on a show that knew the Bible and heals people. This is who I am. A camel through the eye of a needle, all things are possible with love, and God is love…are examples.

These things would unite us to the God that is love instead of Moses. We will finally be free from the law that doesn't even have the word fornication in it, but we teach that it does. More ignorance and more lies ruin a people. Our God will kill us for jacking off and we teach it its bad. Be free from all of this when you let Jesus stand on his own two feet and the old God of Moses. He surrendered to Hitler and punished his people. Now we don't want anything to do with the Old Testament until we learn Ra kills the serpent daily.

We have a talking serpent (Gnostic Sophia) that was turned into Satan. We cannot defeat her and don't even try. In Egypt Horus kills Seth to start the day and Seth kills Horus to start the night. Ra kills the Serpent daily and we don't know the afterlife in the Book of the Dead. These missing books hurt us, and we are going to die someday. We call all religions false except for Christianity. What if we don't enter the Boat of a Million Years with Osiris or confess to the gods of the underworld?

It could all be true, and we are so brave to take a stance as a monotheist. A Christian usually knows nothing about the Talmud and the Quran. They say they are false, but they don't know why.

America promotes racism by favoring certain peoples and staggering this wicked totem pole. Give more money to the rich than the poor for school and everything is racist. Equal treatment of people is difficult in America. America is so racist it is hard for me to get assistance of any kind. This is called a cloak of many colors that provokes racism and jealousy. This will cause hatred and violence. Once a person is poor, they want a non-racist president to help American people like they help immigrants.

Like I said people don't listen to reason or apply the most basic logic. Once I lived in Italy, I knew many things of my country were not true. The things an American will believe a European won't. In Italy it is more settled. Americans are not wise like Italians. Nobody including my own mother could save me from Jesus. He was going to give me a beautiful wife and a fancy car and all this material stuff. Jesus wanted me to quit karate, even though I was teenage black belt, because it made me prideful. My straight A grade point average went down after quitting karate. And this is how Jesus ruined my life. Men tried to molest me when I was fifteen and I was stranded in the land of the ignorant users who do not care about anything but themselves.

Capitalize on everybody and break the commandments of Jesus with no fear. We don't know or care what the pagan holidays are we just want to look rich and white. The slaves, the bad treatment of women, and other crap is what our father is all about, America should convert to Judaism or read the Talmud. Christians don't know their history and they have way too much power. By teaching you the Bible says pre-marital sex is a sin they have already ruined your life. Imagine the life of the polytheist in Rome or Greece.

Sex with the goddess and Ishtar will be a reunion with the Babylonian gods. They were waiting for us to come around, but we are stuck on this Jesus guy. The only begotten son of God is a title of pagan Dionysius. Bright morning star (Venus) is used by Jesus and Pharaoh. Bel aligns the constellations and Venus is my favorite planet. All the women associated with the sister planet take on different forms and legends as they help to shape history. To be ignorant of this spirituality on the other side of Christianity is to miss everything. We would all have something in common.

The sex in America is always under a curse because people do not know that every relationship doesn't have to continue to be a good one. We know a lot of people in our lives, and I can remember women from twenty years ago that I had sex with. The hookers in Spain were so out of my league I have dreams about them and remember a feeling I never felt in America. To be free is so good and who is this old man telling me what to do with my money and my penis? I'll bet he believes pre-marital sex is a sin.

It is so good to spend time in Amsterdam and hear all the different languages spoken. My apartment was in the red-light district. I walk and walk looking at the women and smoking pot. In America we go to a restaurant or a bar, and nothing happens. A night in Amsterdam is full of mystery and party. The most beautiful women in 1996 were $25. In 2000 the price went up to $50 and when I was there in 2016 it was still $50. **The price of everything went up but pussy hasn't doubled in price for 21 years.**

The fact that we do not experience this kind of sexual adventure in America is sad. People who travel to Brazil and other South American countries have brought me great stories. I want to go to all these places, and it makes it hard to get married knowing all these young women want to sleep with you. The adventure from one country to another is like eating different food. As an American aren't you a little curious about what it is like? We sit here in this country eating and drinking but no love is in the air. God won't even let you masturbate let alone have sex with a woman that is not your property.

CHAPTER 33

THE CHURCH AND HELL

This is a waste of a life and sex is the fountain of youth. My friends at the gentlemen club look younger after spending time with several sex workers. We must be so horny in America from all the sexy women we see; but you can have them. Pay them and tell them the truth and if we don't judge, men and women will be equal. When the woman becomes the goddess men will get what they want. Eve and the **Wicked Woman in the Box** is not a good story. Moses intends to blame the woman for sin and then treat them like shit until Jesus got here and called the Canaanite girl a puppy…the church changed the Bible to say dog. The Muslims also say the women is lower than a dog and for these reasons I am happy to be free of monotheism and being a pagan or polytheist is not bad. The Gnostic Jesus is the real one and his disciples had a love feast or orgy, and all the goddess stuff is clean. Do we imagine Sumerians did not exist? The Bible is a new book of lies that the whole world believes.

Those that don't believe where are you? Everybody in America is a Jack Christian. They have sex and drink, but they go to church. The lies we are exposed to are heavy since they deal with God. All we can know and imagine is related to our earthly father. Giants are memories of adults in childhood. We all relate to the serpent in the Garden of Eden as a tempting penis. They are probably describing sex and this story of two people that never existed we treat as history. The man gets his rib slave, and this is the mother wife. Men seeking their mothers and not getting laid. Of all the evil American people do they punish themselves for sex and teach it is okay on television.

The story ends that without this book we will be a slave like Ham. Nobody seems to be able to keep track of the Bible and Bible history. If we read the cave walls, we would find the Bible. Stories of El and Baal later copied in the Old Testament. To not consider the gods of the pagans as evil is a start. Each story has a hero defeating a devil or dragon. The Dragon in Revelations is in Rome, but nobody dare disturb it. 2,000 years since the volcano went off and **Quetzalcoatl** founded **Teotihuacan**. All kinds of things have happened, but we don't think the book of Revelations is done. It is a short story that I could write myself. Why don't Christians talk about the dragon that sounds like he comes from Greek Mythology? Christianity has no hero, so Satan lives forever. Jesus can't kill him, and Michael the Arch Angel has had numerous opportunities to defeat his opponent.

We keep the devil and hell alive to scare people. Who knows what happens after we die? Most people accept death as natural. We trust the church who says all religions are wrong and we pay them. The Gnostic fork requires study to get knowledge, but the Christian never knows anything about the Old Testament. It should be taught in school, and we should all read it once. To have no options but the crooked cross of St. Peter is horrible. John tricks Peter in the book of John. There is Gnosis in the Bible!

Building temples and statues bring these deities to life but it is not idolatry to read their books. Jesus won't be jealous, that is his criminal father you are thinking of, and I find Jesus to be like Phoenician Baal. They are sons of God, and they intercede for us. When Anat comes along Baal is like the story of Osiris and Isis. If Mary Magdalene laid on Jesus and brought him back to life she is like Isis. He would join the club, but nobody wants to lose their slave, and therefore men don't get laid.

If you would only pay for it the quality improves. As hypocritical as it gets, we judge others and put prostitutes in jail. We think you must be married but we "fornicate" sometimes and say sorry to Jesus.

This book removes the wall of sexual shame and guilt the Bible has put on us as a culture. We believed in a lot a bad things, but we were always fucked up with sex. We have done horrible things to our children and the child molester can't go to a hooker either. We have no protection from the rapist and child molester. Our victims are in a pile of fuddy duddy faggots!

To put others through this life when there is a 50% chance of burning in hell is wrong. If hell is true stop having children. One of them might go there for eternity. It would make sense to stop producing all together. The fact that hell exists is necessary for Jesus to save us from something. Once again hell is an invention of the church. It is so obviously a lie. If God knew he would put us in hell, why did he create us? This is the motivator of the church.

The blind confidence we have in the church is incredible. They told us the world was flat and monsters would eat us. We know the world is round, but we think the church is honest. They are getting money all over the world for a misunderstood savior. Now we know more about history and the Bible needs a complete overhaul. The time does not make sense and the church does not want us to make sense of the Bible. We were three or four stories, and the lesson is the same every time. Our country is so big and so many people are affected by Christianity. We do not really have a choice as we follow our Christian holidays with no pagan interpretation.

We miss out on the stars above us and the Sun and Moon. The gods all over the world are waiting for us to stop following the commandments. They are changed to idols and fallen angels that fucked women and produced Giants (Nephilim). Everything is based on sex even the original sin. The Bible characters break all kinds of commandments and Moses tells his people to kill each other. These evil men own God and we are brainwashed to thinking Zeus is an idol. We have such a lazy and ignorant interpretation of the things, but the language is understood. Jesus doesn't want you to have sex and he will put you in hell for not believing in him.

This seems the church invented it and keeps the "No God before me." We think this still applies to us and we ignore the teachings of Jesus and St. Paul. There is a way out, but we cannot be the bitch of the church. Pray and read your Bible and learn on your own. Christian's never talk to me about the prayer and Bible reading miracle. They know what their pastor taught them and that is it. Ask God for guidance and read Proverbs and Psalms; you will have a testimony like I do. Things were shown to me that changed my life. It is not just the story of Moses and Jesus. The wisdom covers all subjects, but we don't use it.

If Solomon were a celibate, we would read his wisdom. Since 700 wives is the same as having pre-marital sex, we hide the sexy king. He is named after the city of Melchizedek, Salem. Another teaching that is way more advanced comes from his wisdom. The Proverbs and book of Wisdom would help us raise our children better than masturbation detectors and lies. We are so worried about sex and every other commandment we bury. We don't explain it we just ignore it. **This book saves people from the evil part of the church.** We can know our god and the gods of other countries. They all have something to offer.

CHAPTER 34

BI-POLAR BRAIN

Being born again and bi-polar is weird since I hear voices. We speak in tongues and do interpretation and prophecy. Growing up I read Solomon because I wanted to be wise. I could help people with their problems on any subject by using Proverbs. Hearing voices and the voice of God is like a mix of the Bible and my brain. I notice the prophecies sound like the Bible. We are listening to a voice in our heads, and I must ask if it is God or me. If I must decide, I pray but what if I do the wrong thing?

Hearing God and following what I thought was his plan for me.... that I become a writer. I went to Italy and pursued my goals. I learned incredible wisdom about the Bible and the Catholic Church. I came back to America, and nobody received my message. I stayed Catholic but did not go to church. I think of when I was fifteen and heard about hell at a Christian rock concert. I raised my hand and started going to the church with my friends that brought me.

People give up their secular music collection and donate their time and money to the church. The church came in my life when I already had it all together. However, this mission for God that I am on has distracted me greatly. **I would run around Rome like I was in the book of Revelations,** and I taught the Bible to the Italians, and they said I was their Messiah. In Europe people love my books and I wish I could translate my poetry better. In America I give out poetry tee shirts since nobody will buy them. Americans check the size and to see if the shirt is cotton, but never do they read the poetry on the tee shirt. In Italy they beg me to write in Italian and my friends in Mexico have my books interpreted to them.

Americans are more a television people than book people. We read captions under photographs on the internet and get some knowledge. A book can be a complete mastery of a subject. A guide or a Bible to something that in book form we have the knowledge of the **Maya** in the **Popul Vuh.** We should be taught all these books and a quit demonizing every culture that ever worshiped an idol. I cannot believe the Bible has no pyramid and Jesus did not do any miracles until he was baptized and filled with the Holy Spirit. Up to age thirty he does nothing and then we can trace his miracles and titles to many pagan gods. Yet I cannot have sex with my girlfriend and pay her. This stops the whole show, and we are all slaves of Satan taking God's name in vain.

God did this and God did that; he is mad at you…. he is going to punish you. That is how they take his name is vain. They assign God's name to a bad purpose. He punishes the grandchildren and that is what we are. Ask you parents if it say pre-marital sex is a sin in the Bible. They think it says it is a sin just like the rest of the world. Even the angels wanted to have sex with women. Samson stays with the prostitute until midnight and his name means Sunshine. Why don't they say he was not married to her? Or why did God stop killing masturbators like Onan?

After the revolution that this book will cause we will never lie again. We are all fucked! We are in the same boat and the whole world agrees on the ten commandments, but they don't revere the Book of the Dead. When a Christian is too lazy to study something he or she lies and says it is Satanic. If you disagree with the shit, they make up you are following Satan. If you listen to the wrong music, you are Satanist. This whole Christianity thing seems like our parents trying to control us. We let them and lose the Egyptian magic and the gods in our own bodies. All the planets line up against us and they are called "Idols" or "fallen angels" we don't believe in the myths of our own solar system or look to the Babylonian and Mayan calendars.

We are so ignorant of these things anybody that controls us has Jesus in some form. They disrespect the law and do not interpret it according to the Talmud. They use the Christian interpretation for the talking serpent and talking donkey and all the curses are sexual. Why do we admire Israel for stealing from their brother Esau? A red hairy guy like **Enkidu.** His story is with **Gilgamesh.** The world's oldest poetry is dragged down to red hairy Esau. A horrible story of two brothers who wrestle in the womb and did Jacob wrestle with the angel of Esau?

We admire him since he had only four wives. Just like Solomon, is the man a virgin for each wife or only the property must be a virgin? Today we believe both men and women should be virgin until they are married. It is equal and women are not considered property, but they don't get equal treatment. Funny the best god was a woman; Inanna and we do not worship her as the bright morning star. Virgin Mary is virgin and that is what makes her different from Isis, Ishtar, and Inanna. Virgin and no sex, it's all I hear. Without knowing the story of the Virgin Mary, I can hear the virgin in her name.

They don't let her teach sex nor does her son help a lot. We are better off with the Torah then Christianity today. There is more freedom, and the 613 commandments have an exact number. Since we think there are only ten, we figure, "I have not committed adultery and I have not murdered." We think we are good people keeping the ten commandments and the funny thing is pre-marital sex is not one of them. **Fornication is not in the Torah.** What law did Jesus free you from? The whole Bible is law and we do not apply the wisdom of St. Paul. He explains things more clearly than anyone in the Bible. "We are not under the law we are under grace." The teaching of grace gets swallowed by the ten commandments. It is not just murder and adultery there is the first three which are the most important. The ten commandments are copied from the negative confession in the Book of the Dead. In our Bible the first one "No God before me" is what everyone wants. They represent what every king and control freak want you to believe. We believe God has contacted us and he commands us. This is not taken seriously by the Roman Catholic Church.

No God before me is what Moses said and others want to be in control. The second commandment about idolatry puts Jesus in the frying pan but St. Paul said it is ok. This is the death of art, statues, gods, fallen angels, angels, Buddha, and tiki images. They are all Satanic as well but if you believe in more than one God you are polytheist. The graven image sounds like he was thinking of Egypt.

When Jezebel was queen of Israel and Ahab was king, she erected a statue of Baal. Elijah descends from heaven and anoints Elisha who anoints Jehu to order her execution at the hand of her own eunuchs. This story is so evil, and the hatred toward the woman, Eve who bit the apple, is now the Phoenician Queen Jezebel. She finishes in the dung and in her life, she chased the prophet Elijah with a knife. **One could say the prophets rib came back to haunt him.**

The story of Noah and Ham or Jezebel in the dung is hard to explain to a child. Since we do not trust the Jews on their own history, we make up lies. Lazy people get into it since you can sin and say sorry. If a man beat, you to death and said sorry what would that mean? King David suffered after God forgave him. So, in our lives we think we need no law, but the ten commandments and we miss out on the 613 which give a balance to the law. Our problem is we think we have studied the Torah when we read the ten commandments. Moses is a bad guy, and he drops off a lie called Jacob. We believe all people of faith are good just for believing in God.

This is how the church tricks you into surrender. Once they have you the gods of history are all false and we fall back in line with Moses and the second commandment. This is like you take a bite of an apple and swallow the whole thing. The principal of totality is in the apple and once you bite it you must believe the whole thing. All we must communicate with Jesus is a false Bible. Made up to scare people and cause them to surrender to a Pope or king. Now we cannot use the wisdom anymore since they messed it up. The people are too lazy to study, so we have no updates. We teach the Bible is true and the trio comes up. Spilling the seed on the ground to steal is bad but not spilling the seed only. So today we steal all the time, but we are embarrassed to jack off. This is a measure of the damage the lie has done to our relationship with God.

The Maya talks about God but nobody connects Jesus to that God. All the cultures have Gods and Sons of Gods but what we are missing is Mary Magdalene. If she raises Jesus, she is Isis and he is Osiris, the first resurrection. Can we afford to dismiss the Book of the Dead just to keep Bible history? Keeping us racist like Adolf Hitler who said, "I will destroy the God of the ten commandments!" Did he? Where are the miracles of the Old Testament people ask? The ground did not open to swallow the enemy. The sea did not part and then close on the innocent Egyptians. The Philistine giants (Nephilim) were gathered to be killed by Samson. Now the Jews are gathered and our God that kills the masturbators was no match for the Nazis. We believe God is so powerful in the Old Testament and he has all the characteristics of the devil.

We don't even know who or what the devil is. The serpent in the garden is Gnostic Sophia or Wisdom. So, the Gnostics call her wisdom, and the Christians call the serpent Satan. If the serpent had wings, we could say the second coming of Jesus was Quetzalcoatl. An empire of Satan and eternal hell according to Revelations awaits us. Eternal doom and pain in the flames of the *inferno*. We teach our children this along with Noah and Ham like they were bedtime stories. When I was a young Christian, I read every Bible commentary in the library to look for what happened to Noah. "To look" only is too severe to result in slavery. I figured Ham butt fucked him since he was nude and drunk. Noah woke up so angry it could not be just looking. I read the Talmud where it said that Ham castrated Noah so he could not have any more children. Also butt fucking and cutting off the dick are the stories of **Horus** and **Seth**. Remember the Bible is copied but we are so brainwashed we believe it anyway.

Christianity stole my life and made me suicidal. I never should have let the church talk me into stopping karate. My grades and goals went into the toilet so I could serve the Lord Jesus Christ. My life is sort of an experiment and since I am a teenage black belt, I never really quit karate. It helped me balance out all the church bullshit and lies. It kept me balanced and protected me in my travels.

Since I like dragons, I go to Rome to kill Satan. **I bring back the boot with me and it spins in the book of revelations cutting off the heads of the seven headed dragon.** The churches are involved, and I conquered Italy and turned it into an axe to kill the seven headed dragon. People back home are not intelligent enough to know I am a culture hero like Quetzalcoatl. I slay the dragon and wear his fancy hide. Yet nobody will recognize me for my messianic message.

After I pinned down the dragon in Rome, I went to Mexico City to see if the Woman Israel is Guadalupe in Revelations chapter twelve. I published my book Nine Days to Healing a Spiritual Pilgrimage. After my mom died, I went to Guadalupe for healing, and she healed me and told me to write the book. I recorded everything from the peyote experience at the temple of Tonantzin to the constellations in the stars of the Tilma.

This book shows how Revelations 12 is December 9, 1531, A.D.; in the Baktun of the Hidden Seed. This shows us where we are in the Bible, ten chapters to go and the Bible is done. What has happened in the last 500 years? For me 2012 A.D. ended the Bible. But how valuable the stars of the apron of Juan Diego the first saint of the Americas or the Indian Saint; he is buried in the Old Basilica at Tepeyac, and he is the child in Revelations 12.

Once one knows the Bible like this it is quite fun, and Revelations 12 happens in Mexico near us. Why not bring the Bible over and let the Great Spirit meet the Holy Spirit? Polytheist can help the Monotheist understand their own Bible. Do you really think Jesus is the key to your salvation? He fulfills the law in you, makes you love people, and then you keep the law, and it is heaven. Since we only know of ten commandments, we should expect crimes all over the world. How are we supposed to follow the 613 commandments if we only claim to know ten? There is something you are supposed to do and duties to fulfill and treatment of each other to look at.

CHAPTER 35

PURE PAGANS

O nce a Rabbi saw his enemy and his donkey stuck in a pit. At first the Rabbi ignored him until he remembered the Torah. It says, "If you see someone's donkey fall into a pit on the Sabbath help him get it out." The Rabbi started to help his enemy with the donkey, and they talked a little bit: "Pull here and push there." Finally, they get the donkey out of the pit and the man offers the Rabbi some wine. They drink and become friends and the Rabbi says: "Blessed be the Torah! I follow your laws and gain a friend."

This is such a good story for the 613 commandments and us. We don't know them, so we have no idea how much God wants from us. Everybody loves the first commandment. The second one sounds like art is bad but without art we would lose history. All these artists in Italy have some esoteric code or message in their art. People have no idea how much Italy has things like this. I kind of re learned the Bible living in Italy. The bookstores, Italian Bibles, and mostly the Pagan Temple to Osiris in Bologna; are the things that fascinate me. Nobody else on my pilgrimages understands the esoteric. They buy food and look while I read art like I read this book.

The hidden meanings and insights are adding up, but we do not get that in America. We know that Jesus is an idol, and we worship him anyway while pretending to have this powerful Old Testament God chasing us down with the ten commandments. He wants us to worship him and not read Greek mythology. A new flood story would get rid of slavery and that is what we are. Just as Ham looked at nude drunk Noah, we see a story that is not even true is attached to Jesus.

Jesus did not know much about the Old Testament, and he did not predict the Bible. The word "Word" is the opening of St. John; it is not the Bible it is the concept or idea of God. The Bible impresses people that have not read much. I have read the Divine Comedy in Italian. This is way cooler than the Bible. We call everything we don't understand or study or try to study Satanic. If Satan is the Lord of Hell and Osiris is the god of the underworld, we have reversed good and bad. Night and day and all other contrast are messed up. Satan according to the Christians has all the gods that ever lived. 320,000,000 Hindu Gods or idols are demonized by the church.

Ignorant people think everything is bad until they try it. The ugly old men in church against sex can't get laid so they fuck up our lives and say no orgy and no love. We go every day in America in this hell trying to prove to our fake Jesus that we are good boys and girls. Sex should not determine if you go to hell or not. Even the rapist is partially forgiven since rape and being a John will both put you in jail. He can't get a prostitute so what do you suggest the rapist do. He can't masturbate and spill his seed, or he might die like Onan.

What do you expect the rapist to do without a prostitute? He will explode and go crazy. They used to lie to us and say masturbation caused blindness and hair on the hands. They might have thought God would kill them for "Doing evil in the eyes of the Lord." Our preacher molested five little children and he was married. If he went to a blonde hooker with big boobs and a heart shaped ass, he might forget the little children and fuck the hooker. This would be good for all of us. Don't let the man own you like a mule be a hooker. Hot businessmen will give you a lot of money for missionary.

Why not do several women, men, transexuals, and everybody going against the Egyptian Procreation Theory; Gnostic orgy instead, what was the orgy of the followers of Jesus like? Imagine the love of those who have the real Jesus and the Gnostic Gospels along with all known literature. They were not limited to Moses like the three monotheistic religions. They had an orgy called the Love Feast and it has the word love in it. Imagine the love we would have to have to go to church and have sex. The church father **Irenaeus** would be a great idol for the church to remember who called the original followers of Jesus Satanist. Because of sex is why we are all fucked up and blame Eve for all our problems.

Irenaeus should be a statue to remember why we reject every book about Jesus but the Bible. Look at the man that stopped the orgy and identified sex with the devil. The Gnostic orgy was not the devil but Jesus, the true man. Why can't Jesus be a man God like Hercules and Gilgamesh? Since we have Allah, Jehovah, and Jesus as the three Gods of the three monotheistic religions that don't agree with each other. They all have something good to offer but it is time for America to learn Moses. His oral tradition is Qabalah. The 613 commandments are explained in the Talmud.

So many books we are missing that are blocked or edited for sex. Remember we are on the side of Irenaeus. If we had an orgy in church people might say it is diabolic. What was the Gnostic woman's orgasm like compared to the Christian? The Gnostic has no concept of sin and believes evil spirits created the world. So many gods have created the world, but we show loyalty to Jesus whether we like it or not. Christianity is forced on us in America and we never talk about the pagan holidays or connect the twelve disciples to the months of the year. Connect the gods to the days of the week. Venus's day is Friday, but we forget the bright morning star every week. Ra kills the devil seven times a week and we are waiting for Jesus to come back when the world ends.

The Gnostic woman is free to express herself with no guilt. When I teach people about sex and the Bible, they often brag to me about how sexual they are. I listen to many lies of people trying to impress me, but I am learning Americans don't have sex anymore. Since we lie and take Gods name in vain to make our guilt religion work, we don't get to have sex. Not like the Gnostic woman who has Sophia in the Garden of Eden. We are completely weakened by Eve who came out of the man Jehovah created. She is responsible for the fall since she ate an apple, and we refuse to use symbolism to kill the serpent Satan.

The church has changed so many things and taught so many people to lie. The people remain ignorant of what they are taught in their own history. It is very hard for me to have an interesting conversation. They are the most brainwashed Christians in the world. They are sure they know it all and repeat to me the Bible story. We talk about the Tower of Babel, or The Tower of Babylon and it is different for me. I love Babylon and I imagine that tower to teach all languages known to man. Educate people and teach children Latin by the age of seven. Get us world wise and not just America wise. I even notice America changes good food from other countries into shit. We have so much to learn from the Europeans. Christianity is a ferocious and evil religion made to steal money and create lies.

Jesus is based on several pagan gods that we don't believe in because of Moses. We have only his God. All other faiths are false yet Moses himself is a copy of King Sargon of Acad. The laws are from the Book of the Dead. The whole Bible is a hybrid and as big as the Bible is, and used to be, it is false. It did not prove true in World War 2, and it is not going to save anybody now. The Gnostic woman is born with Jesus in her. She is taught Namaah the Ark Burner - Noah's wife burned the Ark down three times. The Gnostics respect the law of Moses, unlike the Christian, but they are not so evil and stupid to believe a bunch of lies from the heel catcher.

None of these things match history and to study Babylon or Egypt is exciting for me. I am behind the scenes with the Bible reading about how Babylonian exile looked from the perspective of their King. The prophets are crazy; Ezekiel eats his Torah and starts preaching like Moses while Isaiah the prophet walks through Jerusalem nude for three years. He says, "You women with the outstretched neck." And it is explained in my Bible commentary that these women had an outstretched neck because they were looking to commit adultery. This makes me laugh so hard, but the reality is they were looking at the prophet Isaiah nude as a jay bird.

This is hilarious what the judgmental people think. The prophet is crazy and yelling out crazy shit. **He calls Cyrus the Persian the Messiah.** But it is always the woman's fault when they see Mr. Nude for three years in Jerusalem and see his penis. He has some psychosexual problem, and he curses the women for looking at him. He curses their jewelry and wants them to get a fatal disease.

We know the prophet Isaiah for predicting Christ. With **Cyrus** already in there, is he also not the God on the throne of Ezekiel? Baal is everywhere under his different names since so many people worshiped him. He is the original God and in the throne vision or UFO of Ezekiel, Marduk the Ox is one of the four living creatures now associated with St. Matthew. Since the vision is coming out of the North, we see a man on the throne and the four living creatures underneath the throne; that has wheels full of eyes (UFO).

This Bel Marduk is Baal and the 12th planet. Marduk and Jehovah both wear the asteroid belt like a hammered-out bracelet in the **Psalms.** Which means they both hold the sun like Ra the sun God. We should learn **Ra in the Book of the Dead** and the original resurrection Osiris. Moses beats the Nile but that is Ra's phallus. **I heard in school Ra masturbates with both hands to make the Nile flood.** Moses curses it but The Lords of the Poison (lulu.com) shows the God of Moses did not cause the plagues of the Nile the volcano on Santorini, the Atlantis Plato wrote of, blew in 1500 B.C. and caused the flood the Bible speaks of and the plagues of the Nile.

On the cover of the Lords of the Poison I am thirty-three years old holding a donkey in headlock and a black whip in my right hand. I posed on Atlantis with the talking donkey of Moses. Balaam blesses the Jews and Balaam beat his donkey three times. Since I think the serpent in the garden of Eden is Quetzalcoatl without wings; Balaam the talking donkey is in a head lock since my writings are taking on meaning. I hold a whip like Michael the Arch Angel and posed with my friendly model. I am claiming Atlantis for America and hoping we become Gnostic someday.

So many people I know have no idea what a Gnostic is. We

go through life pedaling around and the whole world believes the Bible only. The dead God speaks from the pages and his son is the Isaac of Abraham. Tied up like Ezekiel in Babylon. Do we miss the symbolism? What would happen if we studied the symbols in the Bible? We would turn Pagan in a second. There are pieces of Jesus scattered everywhere. These other gods go grey, but America keeps Jesus alive, but they do not know the Gnostic teaching that you are born with Jesus in you.

This is very different from what the Catholic Church proposes. The Holy Spirit and Jesus enter you and Jesus was helpless without the Holy Spirit. The trinity is its own little pantheon, but monotheist believe Jezebel deserves to die in the dung for buying Naboth's vineyard. We know it is all about sex, but we are to believe a queen took some property and Elijah descends from heaven to fight her. She chases him with a knife, and he wanted to die. He anoints Elisha who anoints Jehu to kill the Queen. She says to Jehu, "You Omri, you murderer of your master." Master means Baal and Jezebel is a daughter of Anat. Jehovah used his guy Elijah to do it and they could not. She erected a statue of Baal, and this is idolatry.

What if idolatry was a good idea to make as many images of as many gods as we can so we learn God around the planet and not just Israel. The gods and the saints of Italy interest me since I learn the story of the saint of the city and make friends talking about Padre Pio in Foggia (See Lords of the Poison on lulu.com). Idols everywhere and I on the cover of my own book…. on the back I am wearing a Nike hat and holding the sign at Homers tomb.

All these pilgrimages taught me that people don't know what to expect but for me they are fun. I saw the Virgin Mary of Montserrat at the monastery in the mountains. I tattooed her face on my left bicep and will never forget how the Lords of the Poison got its name. I saw the black **Morenita** in the monastery and I saw the Ganges River behind her in a vision. I thought she was a Hindu Goddess and I felt pulled to the river. I kissed the ball in her hand and forgot to kiss the one in the hand of the baby Jesus. I imagined salt was thrown over my shoulder and I heard the Morenita speak to me: "My Son will kiss you in Mexico City."

A year later I go with Julio to see the Tilma of Guadalupe at Tepeyac in Mexico City. On Christmas we went to the Cathedral of Mexico City to see the Lord of the Poison, a black crucifix in the cathedral. The legend of the Lord of the Poison I found on the ground outside the cathedral. I picked it up and read it and understood the Lord of the Poison forgives cigarette smokers. That could be a kiss but listen to the story. **The Lord of the Poison** was white, and a priest kissed the feet daily. He would not forgive or absolve a thief who murdered his victims. So, the thief put poison on the feet of the statue. The priest came and went to kiss the feet of Jesus and the statue turned black. Jesus absorbed the poison or as they say, **"The sin that impedes you from the eternal."**

The thief refused to give back the stolen goods. The priest said to him, "You can't bring back the dead, but you can return the stolen items." The thief has a plot, but Jesus saved the priest from the poison by drinking it himself. Is this the kiss I was looking for? The black baby Jesus in the lap of the **Morenita** is now The Lord of the Poison in Mexico City! This is what happens to me on all these sacred pilgrimages that I take. I would love to do more and study Fatima and others, but I have heard four times the Virgin Mary.

I encourage people to do this and with my first book Nine Days to Healing a Spiritual Pilgrimage I go to Guadalupe to be healed from the grief of watching my mother die of cancer. Julio led me to the place of the Peanut Tree (code word for peyote) and said: **"A tree that once was but no longer is."** This spot on the pilgrims guide to the seventeen spots of healing and five spots of apparition is where I was healed by Tonantzin/Guadalupe. The tree I knew was a symbol of the parent and the peyote is the Peanut Tree that was once was but no longer is.

To show how much I learned on this pilgrimage I realized Guadalupe was *Tonantzin.* Juan Diego, the Talking Eagle, goes to Tepeyac to see *Tonanztin* and takes the peyote. She will appear to you If you go alone. When Juan Diego saw *Tonantzin,* she was in the form of his dead wife Maria Lucia. She was fourteen and they recite their wedding vows. In the Aztec marriage when you say I do, she says; "Buy me a house." This became the tent shaped Basilica at **Tepeyac** where the **Tilma of Guadalupe** is.

The image of the fourteen-year-old virgin Maria Lucia is what I saw at the Peanut Tree. Maria Lucia became Guadalupe and the house at Tepeyac is what the American woman could learn from the Aztec Maria Lucia. **"Buy me a house."** Goes with the wedding vows and when you read Nine Days to Healing you experience all this peyote or Mushroom Mary that is the true story behind the legend.

It seems people do not want to connect cultures. We do not value the Indian wisdom and since we only like Moses we are stuck with the law that we do not read or understand. We pretend to and every person says yes to the question, "Have you read the Bible?" Never do I find people that understand it like I do. Since I was a kid, I knew the Bible like nobody's business. I help people in church, and I was like a teenage Solomon healing everybody with my proverbs and parables.

I could have gone into the ministry, but I wanted to drink and fuck. Now I present America this book. Something you will never find if I die and don't finish it. People will still think God killed Onan for masturbating, they will think the Bible says pre-marital sex is a sin, and finally is it really the same to lust as to fuck somebody's wife. To look and lust is what I love to do. I love to watch a woman with a hot ass walk or ride a bike. These things frustrate me in America since we have a Bible that has screwed us since we think the ten commandments say we should not have sex or make love. This is so sad our years on this planet are passed with the trio; the misunderstandings we have about the Bible that stopped the orgy and started the stealing. Onan steals the inheritance by not fulfilling his duty and that is why he was killed. He did not masturbate he pulled out. This would make it look like wasting sperm was a sin. Make a baby every time.

Why not lay an egg and fertilize it? But do I really need to sell sex? We love it and the orgy is better than putting masturbation detectors on our children. Are we smart enough to figure it out on our own? If God kills masturbators, we would all be dead. This is the freedom we have with Onan and Er, not to mention Jezebel. The Bible is not pure and cannot be true. Osiris is the first resurrection and Jesus is based on his son Horus.

CHAPTER 36

AXES

Now we see a pile of books the Bible says are bad. Malachi 3:16 is the **tithe** chapter. Anyone you give the book to owes you ten percent of their income. The one who gives the Bible is going to interpret it for you. He is like God. But on the Gnostic journey we go internal. In America people only know what the preacher says, and I don't hear the Bible quoted much on television. We have an external religion so they can sell Jesus Christ and the Holy Spirit to us. But who is the father? Abraham?

This is where we are fucked up in the father image. Remember Father Abraham is evil, and he is going to kill his son Isaac. This is the Father that Jesus knew, and he became the only son when he died. The final sacrifice is Jesus, but Quetzalcoatl taught his people to not sacrifice, and Osiris taught against cannibalism. This avatar of Jesus or Quetzalcoatl come into this world and some people acknowledge the culture heroes of the world and some say they are Satanist.

According to the Christian everybody is a Satanist. This is the hell gun they taught me about in philosophy class in college. They point the hell gun at you, and you do what they say. No American can imagine Jesus standing on his own two feet. We need to lie about him and his father. The hell gun will put you in your place and since I have read the Divine Comedy, I have a reference. I can see the flames and the stories of Dante are incredible. We miss out on this using only Christian books to interpret the Bible.

Remember without this book you are doomed to fuck and be called a fornicator. Scary word for the wife of Yahweh. Even calling Queen Jezebel a whore is funny that she was a queen. How much did she take? What does a blow job cost? The Bible is full of lies and the devil of God hates the woman. We don't know or care about this because the church has left us completely up the creak without a paddle. This book makes it clear the Gnostic faith is necessary to come out of this hell with the evil criminal God. We can't do anything, and we don't know any better.

I did my life is reverse. I went to college for a B.A. in Italian Literature and moved to Italy. I traveled first and then found my job as a photographer. This was smart since everything was cheap back then. I lived like a millionaire in the 90s and everything is best at the beginning of an artistic movement. In 2001 I lived in Barcelona for five months. I saw everything about **Antonio Gaudi.** Later people lose vision, and it gets commercial, but the fresh movement is the best.

I want to return to a life of travel and exploring new things and new people. I would not mind owning some property in Italy, I have a good idea of where to go. The wisdom I have from almost four years in Europe is incredible. In Italy I meet so many people and have so many connections but in America very few support me. When my mom died, I went to Europe's gothic cathedrals. Saints frowned with me, and I was comforted. Since I have experienced the miracle of Guadalupe and published a book about it, I want more. I wish churches would read Nine Days to Healing and invite me to their country and church to write another book.

The woman Israel of **Revelations 12** speaks to **Juan Diego** in the diminutive. **Tzin** is the diminutive in the Aztec, and it also makes one a Lord. Juanito Diegito is the Juantzin Diegotzin of what may have been the voice of Maria Lucia saying, "Johnny." Little John is also a tzin, but this is all in the **Nican Mopohua.** The dialogue of Revelations 12 woman and the Talking Eagle; I'll bet you did not know that was in the Bible. A talking woman with 218 verses in the Nican Mopohua which is perfect for an American because it is short. Americans need a Bible they can understand and not one that cancels history since the church changed it.

The **Popul Vuh** is also another Bible of the **Maya** that has enchanted me with the stories of the Hero Twins. The Sun and Moon perform all the miracles and I published a book called the **Mangolishis Popul Vuh** about the Popul Vuh's similarities to the Old Testament. There was a source before all this stuff we believe in comes about. A lot in common but the countries we are not supposed to know about all have a black marker through it. The church has called so many Satan that the truth "Satan" and "Baal" having their myths copied is no big deal to them. They copy names of pagan gods and apply them to Jesus, but they want to claim the pagan gods are bad.

It is so obvious how much they like to keep history down. They are always forgiven no matter how much they lie. We could do better and know the truth and at least have a chance to make our own decisions. Especially about our bodies and sex. They are dropping a heavy bomb on us that our grandparents believed in and passed on. Now we need something new. Fill in the blanks of the Bible and figure out where all this stuff comes from.

I need the Bible and Italy as an axe to chop up the red Satan with seven heads! The seven hills of the she-wolf, goat, and pig. The three pagan animals can use the axe and so can you. Imagine you are holding Italy in your arms and the heel is marker for the heel catcher and Achilles. Look down at Rome like you are the giant **Ogham**, a giant that escaped the flood, and you put the heel of your axe on the seven headed Satan and kill him in the name of St. Michael.

This is better than Revelations. We are holding our axes and we can take out seven cities or seven stars. Look down at the Roman dragon and say, "Hello dragon! I see you!" We will laugh about it later and the branch is from the axe head of Elisha which needs a branch attached it. The prophets saw it all, we say they "put the branch to their nose" and see the secrets of what attached to the Branch of Osiris, Baal, and Tammuzi.

I knew these gods when I saw the Pagan Temple of Osiris in

Bologna in 1997. Egypt and Christianity! Just like the Temple of Debod in Madrid, Spain where they harpoon the hippo. Now with the original resurrection of Ra and Osiris we have a sunset in Bologna. Put a circle around the cross and we go to Orion to find Jacob the Scorpio that stings us daily with his limping message. Ra kills the Serpent every day and Jacob brings him back to life. Jacob probably wrestled with the angel of Esau. We keep him alive and say that our savior Jesus approves of the Patriarchs when he found his father El Elyon and we changed it.

The Osiris Temple is round, and they have a procession of the Black Virgin (Isis) once a year. She walks by 666 archways like Mary. Also, Pompeii has a Temple to Isis where I felt a good vibration. Since Osiris is the phallus in the Book of the Dead, I imagined the plaque on the temple to fall into my hands and it became the Book of the Dead. I found the negative confession that **Nebuchadnezzar** would have said on his death bed in Babylon. I read about the forty-two gods in the body, the forty-two gods we confess to in the underworld on the way to see Osiris at the end of the tunnel. **"My heart is Osiris and my chest the Might One of Terror."** The neck is the divine goddess Isis who nursed all the fish of the Nile. Isis and Osiris were evangelist to teach farming and stop human sacrifice like Quetzalcoatl in Mexico.

CHAPTER 37

JEZEBELS

A ll the Book of the Dead taught me was to hold on to my phallus. The Ka or soul goes to Ra the sun and anybody who figured this out could have changed it. The Ka is at the right hand of Ra like Jesus is at the right hand of the Father. The lamb on the throne is us. If God is in heaven and Jesus and God are two different people where is the Holy Spirit? They all should have become one unless **Jesus is one of many Elohim.** In Italy they depict God as an old man. Not a powerful God like Bel Marduk who comes across the constellations with a net of stars and a Hammered-Out Bracelet (Psalms). Our God is weak and if that old man is Jehovah the Bible has more errors than Onan and Er.

This is so man-made I cannot believe that we replace all of history with the Bible. Seeing the art of Italy made me believe the church is a business. They hide the Gnostic books in their bookstores, but the art tells us everything. I see the Gnostic disciple St. John with his head on the chest of Jesus at the last supper on a stain glass window. St. Peter, the first Pope, is called "The Other Disciple" and he asks St. John to ask Jesus who is going to betray him. They race to the goal and John wins every time. He calls himself in the competition: "The Disciple Jesus Loved."

John beats him every time and Peter is crucified upside down as a political criminal and St. John is boiled in oil and it did not hurt him; he jumped out. Who would you rather be John or Peter? The end of St. John says: "If books were written about all of the miracles Jesus did the world would not have room to contain them." John 21:25. John's totem is also the Eagle and that is under the throne of Ezekiel. Peter does not have a totem or a gospel in the Bible and the Gnostic disciple beats him seven times in his book.

I would rather be the **Disciple Jesus Loves** than crucified on the cross of Satan like our first criminal Pope. This is in the Bible, but we read St. John and it is just a bunch of mumbo jumbo. It is no different than the other gospels, since God wrote the Bible supposedly, and for that matter the voice of Noah cursing Canaan is still God (Jesus) to us. We do not say, "St. Paul said" we say, "God said." The whole thing is given by God Jesus to Moses, and we blame all the evil of the Old Testament God on the New Testament God.

The things Jesus was against absorbed him and they give Jesus' credit for the Old Testament. We pray to him to get saved and then what? We keep the ten commandments the best we can. It is very simple that love is the fulfilling of the law. You won't sin against someone you love hopefully but we are still under the Old Testament. Jesus did not give a lot of commentary, but can we imagine what he would say about Jezebel? They force us to be racist and the Bible is set up that way.

"Canaanite" is thought to be bad, and the Bible wants to rid the holy land of them. We do not think this is supposed to be a Phoenician. The "ites" of the Bible are the ones we are against. We want the Jews to win with their miracle working God. This closes history when it is taken too seriously. If the Bible changed these names, we would see Africa come up. People think they know the Noah's ark story but not the part about Ham. Even on my tour last year of the Vatican Museum they said Ham was "teasing" Noah which is worse that Africa became the slave for a son teasing his father.

He sodomized Noah and cut off his dick is what they should say. But who wants to change slavery after all these years? An African America preacher could read Ham and not even know who Ham is. They try and hide these sore thumbs in the Bible from us. Jesus calls her dog in English and a puppy in Greek. They obviously twisted the

Bible to keep the Canaanite bad or a dog. The fact that she is a woman is the usual Monotheistic hate of woman. God has no wife, and he is always mad. Why does he care if I go to a hooker? Does he want me to suffer as well? All the other Gods have wives but even Mary Magdalene is changed from the wife of Jesus to a whore. They attack the woman and behind all this Adam and Eve is Inanna/Ishtar. **One of the gods who cried for us after the flood.** The love of the gods is still there they are just waiting for us to get over the fake Jesus we worship.

He is already inside of you, but the church sells salvation. The angry God of Moses is going to punish us and only Jesus can save us from hell. Do you think people take hell seriously. If we really thought, it was true we would be freaking out. It is so mean and cruel that I think the word eternity in flames is not relied upon. Everybody thinks they are going to heaven and the Sumerians believe we all go to one place. Think of what sin could put you in eternal hell. Tell me what it is. The church wants you to believe, obey, and pay. It is all a business. Angels and saints are just the emasculated gods.

We can't make sense of the universe with only one God. We believe he only appeared to the Jews. And nobody knows for sure if the story is true. I like to trace back the attributes of Christ to the pagan Gods. They have the same names and do the same miracles. The fact we do not know this is disturbing to me. I see the gods in the Bible and imagine them moving around. Even Jezebel and the window could be symbolic. Venus is space or a female Jesus ordered to die by the emasculated Jehu.

Jezebel is a Phoenician and so is her God is El. The son of El is Baal. When the pantheon saw Elijah descend from heaven he was after Jezebel. The story is so long and so many people are between Jezebel and Elijah. Finally, two or three of her eunuchs throw her through the window into the dung. Jehu could not do it, Elisha could not do it, and Elijah could not do it. We see as dung the woman Jezebel, her alphabet, freedom to fuck, and she chased Elijah. Jehovah wants to become Baal and the Bible confesses its own lies if you listen closely.

The calling fire from heaven is so stupid. One time and they kill the ministers of Baal whose God is associated with fire and lightning bolts. Baal is the Rider of the Clouds, and the Bible demonizes its own God. He is not God until he is Jewish, and all others are pigs or swine…Gentiles. What a fucking racist that is no matter what country I am from God calls me a pig unless I am Jewish. This is how all the problems start. The bad karma of the Bible follows us since we are brainwashed into being racist against the gods from other countries. All around the world they have gods, and the stories are brilliant. We miss out on this to worship an external Jesus but not the Sun.

The Sun, Ra, unites us all in something far deeper than Christianity. Building temples, statues, and monuments to the gods helps us understand history better. If the aliens analyzed Christianity or the Bible we would say, "We believe pre-marital sin and masturbation is a sin, but we do it anyway." No fear of fornicators burning in hell or instant execution for spanking the monkey. We don't die or see a curse, but we must keep it quiet in church or him with sin will throw stones. He may molest children, but he tells you God is mad at you for any kind of sex or orgasm.

To not experience an orgasm is what we believe Jesus wants. He has his law which does not even have the word "fornication" in it. Not in the ten commandments or the 613 commandments of the Torah… yet we teach our children fornicators burn in hell and pre-marital sex is what they say fornication means. 2,000 years of this law that we imagine and lie about what it says. We don't know the fake one or the real ones. People know Eve, the law, and the cross. The prophets are never quoted accurately, and they contain incredible information.

I rented Lives of the Prophets video from the library and saw a historical account of the prophets. Ezekiel eats his Torah and Isaiah walks around nude for three years. This put some humor on the breakfast table when we open the Bible and read Isaiah while he walks around on the television. Church people came by one day and we invited them in to watch it. They liked it but they did not laugh at the crazy nude old man going around cursing the women. He has Jezebel in his mind and wants to put more Queens into the dung.

CHAPTER 38

THE BIBLE AND THE DEVIL

This is what we sign up for and the whole idea of jealous Jehovah wanting 10% of your income is not like Zeus who encourages the worship of other gods. This is healthy and like Gnosis would make us smart. There is nothing wrong with Zeus and the other gods, and Gnostics who were all judged for sex. This is the only moral we have in America. We are hypocrites and everybody thinks they are going to heaven. We don't see the lies and the hypocrisy of the church. They tell us whatever they want, and they are only a business. They probably don't have a big charity unless it is something fake.

We have a God that is a man God, but we deny the man. We say Logos is Jesus only when it is each one of us. Gnostic gospels show the man side, so we lie and don't read them. The only thing that made the early Christians into Satanists is sex. Not even a commandment against orgy but they should wonder how great the love of Jesus was and how was that orgy? The fact of the matter is that love doesn't exist. I cannot touch you anymore. This was not because they lie and steal like the church. We forgive the church, but the Gnostic are Satanists for an orgy.

We could have kept their teachings and not had the Love Feast. Do a bake sale instead but don't lie about God to scare people into only having sex for babies. We lie to our kids who lie to their kids, and it is fulfilled the third commandment; don't take my name is vain...I will punish up to the third generation. If you live in America, your grandparents do this, and they lie about the polytheistic Indian. Your grandchildren will still think the Bible says masturbation is a sin when they look up onanism in the Dictionary. Both the Bible and Dictionary have an error.

We are not going to make any progress until we update our beliefs. Learn the Bible and move on to other books. Everything taken out of the Bible should be studied. We miss the Book of Wisdom by Solomon in the Apocrypha and the books of Enoch. Once Enoch ascended to see God, he was given 365,000 eyes to behold the glory of God. This is a Qabalistic experience, but we see the story continues. Giants, fallen angels, and the men are all missing so we can't see the connection to other religions. David and Samson killed giants so what about Thor?

We don't have the vocabulary to support the Bible. If I quote an Old Testament king, will you know his story? This gives freedom from sexual control. They tell people what to do and they listen. When you lust after a person and cannot have them is something I am used to in America. Barcelona, Amsterdam, Prague, Budapest and Lisbon are all different. I see her, I want her, and I fuck her. It is a paradise on earth, but Americans can't know each other that way. They never get laid, and some go without a kiss.

This is horrible to put on the young people. We have no explanations to give them about sex. Did Jesus preach marriage or condemn hookers? No, so we see everything was added to Jesus. Did he tell his disciples that he created the world? No, that comes later but many gods are said to have created the world. The Gnostics believe lesser spirits created the world. We have decorated Jesus to be an idol of forgiveness, but he brings hell with him to. Moses did not have hell, neither did Elijah, but the church created hell to scare us. How evil God is if that were true.

We have all felt pain. Imagine it never ending and burning. This makes anybody on Earth that wants to harm an unbeliever just. God does it to us for not believing in Him. We say other Christians are going to hell, but we don't believe it. Why aren't we worried about death if there is a hell? Hell is an invention of the Roman Catholic

Church! They use it to scare us into believing in Jesus Christ. Not Baal who is older than the Father of Jesus but the one limited to Adam. Nothing before Adam exists and the Christian claims the Bible is true and history the liar. A library of books is trying to plant seeds against the Bible. A Bible commentary and a Talmud would come in handy, but we don't see God through the eyes of other cultures.

This laziness is a trap. We feel comfortable with these lies and don't mind if other people suffer. To live without a free will won't even bother us. We hope the people making decisions about our bodies are smart. We give up the true teachings of Jesus to make room for Church Father Irenaeus. The anti sex is so strong we will burn in hell as lusty virgins. This seems to be the only sin we react to and in America it is permitted on television but not in church. What is one to think? Our favorite actors are going to hell. This is too hard to believe but we settle for this lesser God that relies on miracles that we don't see happen anymore.

The church father is dead but his curse lives on. We name anything Satan, and this is how the teachings we know started. They changed the Old Testament which was not theirs to change. Nobody refers to any of the important stories. The preacher can tell us anything we want, and it doesn't even matter if he quotes the Bible. We are sure they are telling the truth. They must be more educated than us? But what do our hearts say…is there really a hell…. are we supposed to wait for marriage for sex?

These questions go unanswered because people are so comfortable. The renaissance we would see loosens the grip of monotheism and gives a way out for the women of all countries. This treatment is not from God but from man. Man wants the woman, rib, to be his slave. The woman came out of Adam's side. This takes away the beauty of birth. The sacred vagina where the rest of us come from is attached to our mothers. It is so clear Moses passed on a white, racist, and sexist book. We obey the ten commandments which is to say Christ died in vain. The grace and the love did not last but 3,000 years later we judge each other by the law.

We don't even stop at the ten commandments. The whole Bible is full of things not to do. People imagine God is speaking to them. He speaks from the inside not the outside. Memorizing the teachings of Jesus in school would help us to get along. Forgiveness and do not judge are amongst the "commandments" of Jesus. He says, "Don't judge or you will be judged." People judge all the time and quote the Old Testament. Since we never quote the teachings of Jesus, we think the book is too big for us. And complicated, at times boring, and it has been changed.

The margins of the Bible show the editing of our body parts. The countries that are Africa have many names. The Queen of Sheba in the Song of Songs is like Isis to me. "Look at me and write your story." Isis says to the writers. Solomon got a taste of true love with an intellectual queen. She has something to offer, and their kiss is heaven and earth. This story is not read in church, but the Song of Song is read at weddings in Lebanon.

The Catholic Church does not recommend study of the Bible like I do. I believe ignorance is worse than sex. If an ignorant man flew the plane, it is worse than a pilot who has premarital sex. We know in our hearts sex or making love is a good thing. We miss opportunities to know our soul mates and lovers because of communication. Money opens doors that otherwise would never open. All these super models in Europe come with a price. Otherwise, we would never know them. In Barcelona there was a club with the hottest women on Earth. What an experience to have a sex dream on Earth. These days in America people are not getting laid at all. This is sad we believe so many of the devils lies.

CHAPTER 39

MY POINT OF VIEW

This is our decision to force the church on our children. I had a negative experience in the church. I realized it was all business. My ambition to succeed financially was gone. I would serve only the Lord Jesus and all these things would be added unto me. I figure God could get me a wife and a job. Later when I began to suffer, I could see the faces of the liars in church in a vision. They are all telling me God will make me rich and if I am virgin, I will get a beautiful wife. Now I feel a trick to get my money happened. They screwed up my entire life just to make some money. Now I take the Gnostic fork and stay away from the false teachings of the church.

When I come back from Europe nothing has changed back home. Nobody has any stories, and each day is pretty much the same. Traveling gets me out there and I meet people. Incredible things happen that would never happen back home. I find conversations at home quite boring since they have not traveled much. To see new things and explore what life is all about is important to me. My life was an experiment with God. I followed him with all my heart and studied the Bible every day. I should have gone into the ministry. Now with this religion background it is hard to get a job.

It is not funny all the abuses the church put us through. We were used for money, sex, and free work. Later when we are poor the church has no money for us. They risk judgement day for not taking care of the least of these. It seems the church knows the Bible is not true, but they collect 10% of our income. They dabble in the Old Testament and hope we don't find out it is not our true history. Do you feel comfortable leaving your children with these men? They have their wives, but they do children to.

For the rest of us that would like to see a Gnostic/Polytheistic revolution, imagine reversing 2,000 years of history. We would advance in knowledge and go back to making art that is a support for knowing God. In Italy the stained windows have secret messages. Think of St. Thomas, the twin of Jesus. After the death of Jesus people saw his twin and said he had resurrected. Regardless, all these miracles are standard to other religions. The stories overlap and connect.

To go without knowledge in general means we must learn things the hard way. We cannot gift a clean Bible to our children or explain to them more than the basic story of Jesus. After that the money goes right into the offering pot just because one believes. Once our attitude is changed toward the law, we keep it and then salvation applies. Faith without works is dead and we keep the commandments because we believe in Jesus. We are ignorant of what the commandments say, and we make up some that make life hard for all of us.

They stop every form of physical love imaginable. You are expected to be virgin until you are married no matter how old you are. This evil trick to stop us from loving each other supposedly comes from the Bible. We could have a beautiful book if we learned it. Now it says anything we want it to say. Even heaven and hell make more sense if the context were here on earth. Jesus says. "The kingdom of God is amongst you." People say they experienced hell on earth. If I do good or bad puts me somewhere. This is a more effective teaching them the idea that we will be punished in the afterlife. People do not react to that.

The ignorance and anti-Gnosis show the sincerity of the people. The Gnostic Gospels come up in Egypt wrapped in gazelle leather. We did not respond with joy that more knowledge of Jesus was available. It was a quiet episode. How many Christian preachers have studied the Gnostic Religion or read the Quran? This is sad we do not know these things and we trust anyway. Trusting is a form of laziness. I learned the Bible and prayer go together and I am very knowledgeable about the Bible.

We should say we are ignorant of other religions and not teach they are Satan. We are not under the first two commandments anymore so there is no God to pledge allegiance to. We can study the other gods and see pieces of the Bible everywhere. This is fun for me to compare Baal and Elijah. They both have their contributions, but Baal is better. The Phonetic thinking and alphabet come in handy to remember the Old Testament. Once we look behind a curtain or to the stars, we have a choice to honor the gods or dismiss them as idols.

If you don't have idols, you need the books about the gods. We see ancient aliens and astronauts leaving great monuments and mysteries. These are not explained by Jesus, and he really did not have any miracle knowledge about the world. He did not leave sacred numbers and they don't want a circle around the cross or Ra will appear in all his glory. The idol of Buddha is helpful for me to understand the bliss of meditation. If I read his book, I am enlightened. Jesus on the cross and the Bible is a contradiction. We imagine Jesus white and long hair when he returns. Would we know him otherwise?

Most American women don't know about the goddesses, but they know it is all the fault of Eve. Inanna, Ishtar, Anat, Aphrodite, and Venus are essential to their respective myths. We think the goddess is bad because of Christianity. They created their hateful criminal God for us to worship. Their book is our book. Isis and Osiris are gods in our body. Moses attacks them and takes credit for his God killing the Egyptians.

Egypt is the cradle of civilization. All these gods come out of the myths and tell their stories. Horus is the most like Jesus and Osiris and Quetzalcoatl are culture heroes. The man woman combination is as strong as Adam and Eve and Jesus and Mary Magdalene. The Song of Songs is like a song to Isis. It is the only healthy relationship in the Bible. They made Mary Magdalene a whore to take away her ministry and give it to upside down cross criminal St. Peter. The one Jesus said,

"Get behind me Satan." Now 2,000 years later we see our first Pope on the cross of Satan and the Gnostic disciple John boiled in oil and did not get hurt. The competition is in the book of John.

There is evidence of Gnosis in the Bible with seven competitions between the Disciple Jesus Loved and the Other Disciple. John enters on his own and a woman lets Peter in. Peter asks questions to John at the last supper. John is closer to Jesus in the Gnostic Gospels. We can turn to symbolism and understand all this better.

The symbols will then open the lost pagan religions that all had so much in common. To not worship the sun is the goal of the church. We are taught we are not all the same or equal. This would change for America if we thought the sun was Jewish. The universal religion that says we are all children of God despite our race is ideal. The Bible has its gibberish when dealing with other countries. They are having wars and we take their side and the brainwashing that all these countries are bad is just ignorance. We were taught wrong but there is no vision to fix it. Or learn it.

Teaching the trio of the Catholic Church that we called God's Word is the best. We can make an Exodus from Rome and create our own Vatican. We do not relate much to Italy and the history is a blur to most Christians. They don't recognize key historical figures. Once we learn the truth people will see God the way I see him. I have no guilt over masturbation or sex. If I look at a woman, it is a complement but not adultery. We can't imagine a smiling God or Jesus, and in Italy I have seen the old man that is God.

The Greek Gods have bodies we could admire and stories we could follow. Whatever the Bible says to stop the worship of the gods is in the commandments. I want so bad to be free, but Jesus and St. Paul did their best and nobody got it. Think Jesus is mad at you or thinking he will put you in hell is not good. These are ways we scare people, but most adults believe Noah's ark. If we studied and did what it said would be one thing. If I must explain fornication to the space alien, I am going to tell him it is a false word. My people don't understand it. The truth is they think it means pre-marital sex and they have sex and don't care. The church has fucked us that we are always guilty of lust under their rigid laws. The fact that we believe something not true for so many years alarms many. Some are lazy and go with the church which promises them love in the afterlife and no making love in this one.

Old men don't like it and church fathers are monsters. We listen and pass this crap on and on, but we don't talk about the Volcano at Pompeii. A Roman City destroyed after they killed Jesus. The second coming of Christ was Quetzalcoatl. Time changed with both, and they were both Venus. Now with a book of Revelations that is 16% correct we still wait and postpone telling people he may have already come.

These riches of history are ours and we are a big country hypnotized by a Roman Myth turned into history. It would be better as a myth since we would interact with the gods. As a history that we are not sure about I would guess most Americans think the Bible is accurate history. They don't seem to suspect them of lies even though the world was flat. They scare us with children's stories, and we never check the facts. There is so much more to Jesus than what is in the gospels. The fact that there is no curiosity makes me question America who claims to love Jesus and only him. They say he made the world, but they don't want to read his books. The knowledge might help you or somebody else.

The way it is now anybody claiming to read from the Bible and believes in Jesus is a preacher. The story of the Bible we don't know but the doctrines of the church we know. This is too much spoon feeding and not enough personal transformation. The Psalms and Proverbs minister to me and both David and Solomon express solutions to my needs. I need to know there is somebody there for me. I want family and friends to be on the same level as me. The way our beliefs are now stagnant. We don't apply any of Jesus teachings. By watching television, I question if we even know them. I only hear Jesus quoted by preachers.

CHAPTER 40

TODAYS BIBLE

The other countries have common language and things I wish translated into English. It seems in America we are friendly and afraid. We are a very trusting people and I notice people scamming each other a lot. We are very materialistic, and we are taught with advertising a certain product will bring us happiness. In Italy and other countries, I have been to the people just start talking to each other. Americans are very apologetic. They have a hard time getting to the point.

Americans to me are very restless and I think it is from being horny. We waste every day in chastity when God is not even mad about us having sex. The idea of love and what the fallen angels did to women shows even Samson got his eyes gouged out to forgive the giants and their parents the fallen angels and women. These stories were not talked about by Jesus and Jesus seemed to know the Torah but how deep did he go?

Today we have so many resources for understanding the Bible it is not like Jesus' day. The miracles all have alternative explanations. Walking on water could be a name for Hindu Vishnu: "He that is carried on the waters of unconsciousness." Jesus with Mary and Martha could be a Hindu teaching as well. The Celtic two birds in same nest; one is still and the other chirps. This is Krishna and Arjuna in the chariot and Mary and Martha working and praying at the feet of Jesus.

All these sacred symbols expand the Bible. They took out I think sixty-four books and I have read the Pseudo Pigraph which is better than the Bible. Satan talks in the Testament of Job and there is a lot of wisdom in those books. Sex blocks the way to everything just like Solomon's 700 wives. We don't study Solomon or know the highly esoteric language he used. Somebody who thinks about God giving Solomon a harem might figure out premarital sex is okay. They direct the attention to his father David who murders giants and circumcises them. He kills a man so he can sleep with his wife Bathsheba. He is like the Christian Alexander the Great. He kills Goliath with one stone.

Samson is a killing machine against the giants. He gathers them together in one arena and pulls the roof down on them. There is so much killing, and we let the Jews do the dirty work for us. The church hides the skeletons of the giants, or you will figure out fallen angels are sometimes "Descended Angels" and the church changed it so we won't think we come from outer space.

The miracles kill people, and we think any enemy of Jesus, the Dogs, is an enemy of ours. If I saw a Philistine die, we judge and say they are all evil. Moses ordered his own kind to kill each other for purification. Death was around him and the Death Angel knew to go to the house of the Egyptian (Ham). Moses is so incredibly racist, and he heard about El in a mountain just like Baal. He copied the so-called devils and fallen angels and made our religion. We are not under the law, but we are ignorant of this for 2,000 years. We still judge anybody different, yet we have shame before God.

Pick your country and go into a Christian church and see how powerful Christianity is. We take Gods name in vain, so we don't get laid. We lie about Sumerians and Babylon to hide the goddess. The order in which things come in is not important to the Christian. Gnosis is older than Catholicism and Jesus was not God until Emperor Constantine crowned him. We should say, **"Jesus is God since Constantine!"** He was man originally and his myth used to be Gnostic Solar Deity. **Gnostic Jesus smiles and his people have a Love Feast.**

Jesus in Italy is a theme of death. It is very heavy there. I have never heard of or seen a Virgin Mary smile. In Italy she is very sour, and the Italian women can be prostitutes if they want but they are still Catholic. The idea of freedom from this makes me think that love is why we are down here. Physical love is the enemy of every American. They can't control themselves, so they have sex and say sorry to their lying God. How pathetic that lusty Americans judge others and approve violence, permit rape, and encourage child abuse.

Without hookers we just must get it for free and that is a sin. America is a many layered cake of misunderstanding and lies. **I have been free since I learned Onan in college.** I have no guilt when I have sex and I thank God every time. People say I am not being a good boy but the preachers that sodomize the children will tell you, "Nobody in America has a free will." You are told what to do with your body and the people that enforce this on us are just gross.

Who else can we listen to, and isn't the Bible a little old? It does not even say what we think it says and man wrote it. This worship of the Bible that leaves out the Gnostic Gospels doesn't really want you to know what Jesus taught them. Even the miracle of loaves and fish could have been an orgy. The Gnostic teach Jesus is already in us and the real Jesus woke us up to this fact. The church has been selling lies and cheating you out of your money. What we have on Jesus is not much but the Disciple Jesus Loved has one pillar and the **Q Gospel** Matthew, Mark, and Luke the other pillar of Christ's throne.

The Old Testament is far more interesting to me than the New Testament. An experiment is happening with the I Am the I Am, or I Shall Be What I Shall Be of Moses. They recorded the miracle and the God that did it. Now we know if we follow the Torah what to expect. God punishes the Jews, and they say they did not obey the Torah. They hold to the teaching no matter what.

When times get tough it is a little mean to say God is punishing us. Job was punished by God and Satan, and he had not sinned. Job says, **"I know my redeemer lives."** Who is he talking about? **Melchizedek?** The book of Job uses different names for God. The four friends discuss with him what sin he deserved to be punished for. Job was an honest and generous man, but God tested him. This is better than being punished. If you love your children, you will support me in the belief that the church is no sex teacher. They often have sex with children instead of prostitutes. We need to grow up in America and stop this lie machine called the church. Every woman goes in is poisoned and shammed. She is not taught about Isis she is taught about Eve.

A bird's eye view sees these things differently. The "rib" birth of Eve puts all women down and they are supposed to be servants. This is so cowardly to hide behind the Bible. All of history is twisted by the Christians yet they want us to believe in the White Man's Religion. The karma is so bad we live under a curse. Nobody battles Satan and we wait for the end of times to finish the twenty-two books of Revelations.

What if we understood the Bible symbolically? Even the cross has symbolism and stories but the people on the cross are gods. India symbolically has the Ganges while we say Moses cursed the Nile. 320,000,000 gods lined up at the Ganges and Hercules and Osiris went there to build a temple. Alexander the Great who was called Amon Ra by the Egyptians is in a long line of polytheists. We are conditioned to hear the word, "Pagan" and think something bad.

Egyptian gods are often part animal, and they would scare the shit out of us in real life. If you read the stories and understand the symbols, they seem human, Maybe Moses was the bridge out of that country and God seemed more human. The little old man on the throne above the crucifix looks weak. The Roman Gods stand tall and proud, but we know only Abraham as our Father. Zeus is a better Father image and there is no gory sacrifice with his son.

CHAPTER 41

GREAT HARLOTS

To look and lust is a great example of how we all became adulterers. The sexual energy in all of us attracts us to other people but there is not much one can do about it. A man often scares a woman by being too aggressive yet women like persistent men. All the ugly men that could be with hookers are loosed on us. Why not put people where they belong? The comparison I make between sexual sins and violent sins is interesting. We cheer God on as he kills the bad people, but we don't like to talk about Jesus and Mary Magdalene having sex. St. Paul the celibate is our Christian Jupiter. The church has always been against sex, but we could live in a different world.

I am teaching how to escape the lies and keep your faith. The only thing between us and Gnosis is the Love Feast. No violence, stealing, and telling lies just physical love. What was it like to be there with the fresh pure love of Jesus? It had to spill out that the love went to a sexual level and today where are these churches? I have never been in an orgy, but I know the love of the church. We were so comfortable with each other we could have had an orgy. No judgment, forgiveness, and the Gnostic Jesus with his mother's heart in the sun, one circle around the cross and we go back to zodiac symbolically. Virgin Mary becomes Virgo maybe Jesus is Ophucious, the Serpent Bearer.

We could do so much better than we are doing interpreting the Bible. Once I read the Pseudo Pigraph the Bible did not impress me. I am also a big fan of the Apocrypha and other Biblical works. They all have the same characters and what happened to me after reading them was expansion. I would imagine the City of Seven Hills and the Dragon from above and other Italian cities started to stretch out. Italy and its churches have a pagan past. We surrender to our one love the Madonna. She did not have sex to make a child and although she is property, she is Queen of Heaven. She was exalted beyond the Bible's boundaries. Many think Madonna with child is Isis and Horus. She is "Virgin" or Virgo. This is the goal of Christian women; to be pure for their husbands. In the Bible we do not find a story in context that says we cannot have sex. All of this was added by the Roman Catholic Church and their upside-down teaching.

We have an idea of what the Bible is about, but we do not know it good enough to help others. The missing pages of sex and the suspicious circumcision is attached to our soul and the gods in our bodies. We go along being told what to do by those that claim to speak in God's name. We don't trust ourselves with our own prayers and study. An expert must read the sixty-six books to you. On our own we would have branched out and the teachings of Jesus would become proverbial by now.

Instead, we know a short story and find Jesus to be the hero that never kills the devil. Both are Sons of Gods and talk to God directly. If Jesus was daytime and the devil nighttime, we would think like the Egyptians. A circular study where the forces of darkness are defeated daily. We don't have any celebration for the defeat of the devil because we don't even have symbols or artwork of Michael the Arc Angel killing the devil. The date of his defeat is at the end of times. Very convenient for those making money off us. We could see in our lifetime a miracle if America will take the **Roman Exodus**.

The old ways we think, and the plagiarized Bible await us to open our minds. Those that taught us could be wrong about many things. We can escape the cruelty and the hell on earth. We say God is against sex and this lie hits the grandchildren and us. We can't stop lying in God's name because that is all we know. We barely study the Bible and don't know the representatives from the slave cultures. I have never heard the story of Jezebel in church because they don't want to teach Elijah and Elisha who are like John the Baptist and Jesus. They do miracles and fight an earthling from Phoenicia that has the purple history and the original alphabet.

The story of Jezebel shows how ugly the Bible is for the woman. The Bible does not say she was a beautiful queen. It does not recognize her being a Phoenician. She finishes in the dung with the Christian superheroes Abraham, Isaac, and Jacob posing for the story as two or three eunuchs of hers that threw her out the window. Why does the Bible not know if there are two or three? It is one or the other. The third eunuch is missing or wrestling with his angel. Jezebel in Hebrew means, "Chastity." So, Chastity hit the dung and was trampled by horses. Then the Bible wants us to believe she took money for sex. She was a Queen Whore and Phoenicians are the only culture that could take money for sex with no shame. The rest of the world is like us.

Everybody judges the woman and wants her to be the slave. Therefore, women do not get to express themselves and are generally closed. If she wants to do a man, she might wait for him to approach her. We have all the curses and none of the blessings. We say premarital sex is fornication and we go to the lake of fire for fornicating. Who decides where I spend eternity? Some old man in the Vatican whose ancestor was crucified upside down on a cross? We must work out are own salvation. Nobody can go to the gym for you and make you muscular. You must do it yourself.

Everyday pray, read the Bible, and write in a journal what you learned for 365 days. You accomplished more than going to church every day to hear myths taught as history. Our only link to God is Jesus but the fallen angels account for the gods that left heaven. All over the world we deny them. Jesus was against idolatry we believe and only the Bible is the good book they think. We eliminate the gods of the Indian in the land we live in. What does our ineffectual God do about pollution? The Great Spirit would help us, and the Great Spirit is not an idol. It is bizarre we are afraid of the God that fought for Israel in the Holocaust. If we saw the war through the eyes of the gods, we would see Mars and not the Jesus of Constantine.

We are denying the true God every day for this solar imposter of Jesus. Why don't we call the sun Ra? We are conditioned to think all ancient history worshiped idols. The Catholic Church has more art than a Phoenician. They make the image of God (Old Man) and Jesus (Bloody Sacrifice). Using idolatry to not study the older gods we have never heard of as they hide in the missing Baktuns of history.

The denial of being horny is a daily thing for me. I live in a land that will lock me up for paying for it unless I am an unprotected porn star. I cannot masturbate since I carry a Bible in one hand and a Dictionary in the other. Pre-marital sex is said to be fornication and we wonder why it is so hard to get our "Ribs" to have sex with us. We put them in the dung, we stone them, and put them in Babylonian Boxes. The hatred toward the woman Jezebel and Mary Magdalene is automatic that the **Great Harlot** would rise from the seas. It is as if we all agree a hooker is a bad person. She is the villain and the scape goat.

Another part of denial is that I want to have sex, but I cannot. My body is ready for many women, and I feel hot. However, since this is not going to happen, I think about a girlfriend or a wife to have regular sex with. My body tells me sex is good and my mind reminds me prostitution is illegal in America. I would be with a different woman every weekend. My mind knows we believe God said sex is bad unless you are married and making children. This hurts my body thinking that I will go to hell for having sex and jail for a prostitute. In America you suffer your whole life and are told you will be rewarded in heaven. This is the ultimate you get paid when you die. In the meantime, the church has sex with children and tells you that you will go to hell for having sex with your girlfriend.

It is scary how easy it is to trick us. We believe in things we have never seen and are told to do certain things and not do others. Since we are so ignorant of the Old Testament, we take it as our history book. All the flood and creation stories around the world are said to be false or Satanic. They all agree but we say the Bible is true and history is false. This is a crime against humanity, and we lose the American Indians religion to force the evil Christianity on them. Kill and say sorry, steal and say sorry, lie and say sorry and this replaced the Great Spirit.

All the legends attached to our soil and pyramids in our own backyard are also said to be evil. The lies that are necessary to keep the false god on our backs are many. We don't know these things about God, but we trust the Bible says them. What a sad country afraid to have sex but eager to take God's name in vain to make money. This sexless American life is a punishment and a laughter. While fornication is not a commandment, we go around the world as if it was one. Teaching people God is angry at pre-marital sex, and he hates masturbators. It is your decision to continue sacrificing your identity, gods you believe in, and history all for the fake Jesus.

They don't even read outside of the gospels about Jesus, yet they are the expert on everything. How the world was created and who lived and died to forgive our sins. We live a life of lies and cover ups to keep Americans emasculated and ignorant. To not acknowledge the Gnostic and their teaching because they had sex shows you that is what it is all about. Control people with psychology and guilt. I am not sure why historians have not found this. I know in my country the people have only one sin they react to and that is sex. Telling lies and stealing is forgiven and it is easy to set up scams in America. The only sin that gets any attention is sex.

I hate to live where somebody else drives my sex life. The push towards marriage and settling with the same person forever is next. This is the only choice not only is there no orgy there is no masturbating. How much has Jesus changed and what would it be like to see a Gnostic Love Feast? The fact is we still have a hard time determining what God said from what man said. The Maya has a prayer for the morning and evening where they call **Hunab Ku** God. The God loves them and has many children. We are all convinced that polytheism is bad, and we are still under the God of the ten commandments. Without the word fornication in the Torah, we lie about Moses and make a mockery of his law. We don't really study these things at all, or we would use the Talmud to interpret the Torah. We know so few saints and angels it is just a joke.

People share their personal experience with Jesus. They are ignorant of his history and astrology. All things are sin to them. Every new experience is judged as bad. Just a basic life denying gods and fallen angels are true. God in the Bible is so racist he almost hunts down sinners to put them in hell. In this century we still have not figured out the book of Revelations. We do not know what is true and we don't care. We assume the Bible has already been mastered and there is nothing new to learn. Americans know mythology from comic books. Don't we see Zeus or Baal as a more powerful and loving version of Jehovah?

The God of the Bible we believe in killed Onan personally. Remember the Jews don't believe Onan died for spilling his seed. The Roman Catholic Church wrote the lies we believe in, and we never doubt or question them since we are an emasculated country. They have the money and the power while we assume the position of our drunk hero Noah. The Father Son combo that started slavery is in the ninth chapter of the Bible. We say we read the Bible, yet we don't know why Noah is angry. They don't even have the guts to say Ham is Africa. Yet we are under the curse from the cursed and plagiarized Bible, and we have faith in Jesus. The creator of the world and omni potent God; there is no God but Jesus according to us.

He died in vain so we could worship Moses like all three monotheistic religions do. They agree on all the hatred, racism, and slavery but never said; "God is Love." Like the Gnostic disciple in the Bible St. John. We go without any tools to get any esoteric message from the Bible, and everybody has heard the same message so many times we think we learned it. Without being taught in school you are going to be a sucker for the church.

I have been to a church that said they would make us fishers of men and the whole sermon was about converting people. I did not learn anything new from the Bible and I felt the people were duped.

One thing about the love and the music makes me think the church is the best candidate to have a Gnostic Love Feast if pre-marital sex was not a sin. We all get laid, and the church teaches fornicators burn in a lake of fire for eternity. Would you like sexual pride and the free will the Italian women have to be prostitutes thanks to the Pope?

CHAPTER 42

SEX AND LIES

We are a horny people that can't have the sex we want when we want it. We are all poisoned for many generations with lies about God. He is mad at sex but not stealing and lying according to us. This must affect us. Americans brag about how many partners they have had, and they are always exaggerating. While the sky is bronze in judgment over America every time we lust or have premarital sex, we can be free with this book. Do you want to masturbate only for the rest of your life, or do you want to know somebody? I remember women from twenty years ago. We had sex and their memory lasted forever. Try having sex with many in a row and see what level of horny you get to.

I want Americans to be free of the Father of Lies but we need to have Michael the Arch Angel kill Satan and start over. Satan according to the Bible is the Serpent but the Gnostic who are before the Christian called the Serpent, Sophia for wisdom. Look at the exaggeration and lie of the Roman Catholic Church to take a talking serpent and make him Lord of the Underworld. Wisdom, Sophia, was at the right hand of God when he created the world the Proverbs tell us. Solomon mastered wisdom and we did not learn the secrets. We like David not Solomon and the church does not want us to learn how to do it without them.

The lost book of Wisdom in the Apocrypha is written by Solomon. How lazy our churches don't teach us this. They lie about history and don't even teach the Gnostic is before the Catholic. Jesus has only been

God since Constantine and we should call him Mars. Do you want your children to be taught about God from the Bible only? Everybody is a sinner and Satan is everywhere. It is taken for granted that the church is calling Osiris, the Lord of the Underworld, Satan the whole story must change. What if Christians can't enter the Boat of a Million Years and reject the beauty of Ra the Sun God? Satan would be the first resurrection and Jesus doesn't have a pyramid like Alexander the Great who the Egyptians called Amon Ra.

Jesus needs to make friends with the gods like Hercules and Baal. Jesus could be Baal if we speak in Phoenician. The angels and saints are asexual, and this is the sexless collection of gods we have in our Christian pantheon. The children cannot trust the ministers of the church. The gods show us how to behave and if you are so worried about sex think of the Gnostic Orgy. Love of God and the Gnostic beliefs which are better and make more sense than ours do.

To make friends with the gods we must understand what it means to be free of the first two commandments. Once we are free of the law, we are free of Moses. Since we judge each other by the ten commandments Jesus died in vain. The second you tell me the first commandment: "No God before me." That is under the law again and we are three thousand years strong obeying these commandments copied from the Book of the Dead. Next is idolatry and the image of Baal. All of this is fine since Jesus died and summed up the 613 commandments: "Love God with your heart mind and soul. And love your neighbor as yourself. This is the whole law and the prophets."

Once we realize we are not under the ten commandments anymore Jesus fills you with love and you keep the law anyway. The bitch is "idolatry." This cancels out every statue, god, artwork, pyramid, and even the stars turn off. It seems to me the Jews created a Torah based religion where they would study Moses and not have an idol. Legend says Father Abraham's father, Terah had an idol shop and Abraham burned it down. This is foreshadowing what Jehovah does when they commit the true "Fornication" of cheating on the husband Jehovah. That is what fornication means since you cannot have pre-marital sex with idols.

These two commandments are all you need. The Gnostics don't even have a concept of sin, but they respect the Jewish law. The Christians don't study the Talmud, yet they claim the Torah is part of the Word of God. God spoke it and man wrote it without making any mistakes according to the Christian who holds us hostage. Baal would free us, and he is probably Osiris and the Phoenician's traveled and learned a lot. The Bible is a copy of Canaanite stories but the Canaanite god, Phoenician El has a member longer than the seas.

With El and Baal I get a warm feeling and I love the poetry of the fertility gods and goddesses. In America we must trade in Eve for Lilith, Adams first wife, and stop teaching this 3,000-year chunk of history as all you need to know about everything. If we cared about people's needs, we would teach them Solomon's proverbs to make them wise. However, Solomon is sexual in the Song of Songs and with his 700 wives. Christians don't want to read about sex until they are married. The church will make you its slave and you have no choice but to go to church on Sunday. The Temple of Baal is out of business. No sex, no love, no orgy....and somebody stole our Satan. **Lotan** is Leviathan the phallus of Jehovah, a crocodile, and a hippo also racist in symbolism.

We imitate a racist God and wonder why everybody hates each other. Do you know who I hate? The people who make prostitution illegal. My life wasted in America each week...just look no touch. Brazil, Italy, France, Spain, Holland England, Mexico and many more have the smiling Jesus. In America he frowns on us for having sex. He wants you to know there is no God but him, but the original Gnostic stuff is Satanic according to Irenaeus who we agree with. So is Baal and every God that ever walked the face of the earth is an idol. All the planets, the days of week, unsolved mysteries, everything is Satan? What if we followed the books of the idols all around the world? Baal opens many great countries where he was worshiped, and his myth proves the Bible is a bunch of lies.

Elijah called fire from heaven one time and Baal does it every day. Baal has a pantheon and has sex with his harem, the Pleiades, while

Anat prays to El, God, on Mt Zaphon in modern Lebanon. Since Baal prays to El for his friends on earth would it not be better to examine who is the devil in the Bible. The Bible creates a devil about everything but Jesus. No religion, no matter how similar, is good. This is narrow thinking that we have about the one God with three religions and polytheism. The Greek and Roman Gods are heroes to me and in Italy I see the statues of Gods outside the churches.

If we had flayed saviors or Indian's that look like Jesus outside the church in America, we would see the contrast and competition. Hercules and Jesus across the street from each other in Italy is not a problem. They are proud of their history, and we should be to. With Christianity we must lie about the American Indian and Quetzalcoatl the winged or feathery serpent. We believe in a talking serpent called Satan but not a feathery serpent crucified on a cross with a cross in his hand. His city came up a hundred years after Jesus and Jesus said he would return soon.

Quetzalcoatl to the Aztec and Kukulkan to the Maya and maybe Virocha to the Inca covers our continent. Quetzalcoatl is on the centavo. Ironic to put a centavo in the offering. A combination of Jesus and the serpent in the garden of Eden and like Baal he has a pantheon he is not alone. If Quetzalcoatl was Jesus, he would have spread through our continent teaching people to sacrifice a flower not a person. This teaching is so miraculous that if he is not Jesus, he is a miracle.

If he had twelve disciples and walked on water or turned water to wine, we might believe it was Jesus. If Jesus came back in any form other than the white, would we recognize him? He would have to be in his thirties and look like the idol we know and love. Remember if you put a circle around the crucifix Jesus comes back as the Sun tomorrow and we go back to killing Satan daily. Are you waiting for the end of times for the devil to die? They cannot defeat him like the gods who earn their godship by talking an axe and killing a lion. Giants and fallen angels are contact with the original God. Before God was appearing in a whirlwind like Seth or Typhoon to check on Miriam while she was on her period.

We had stories of heroes and men from all over the world that deserve credit. Compare Jesus to Alexander the Great. And look at the backgrounds we are missing by hating the gods. We don't really hate gods in America we are just too lazy to read about them. And we are not too smart about heaven and hell. We don't present the Greek idea of the afterlife we tell them it's Jesus, the idol that says worship only me. The selfish, cheap culture that Christianity has produced is our fault for not reading.

Look at the story of Samson in Judges 13-16 and his relationship to the women in the story. His name means "Sunshine" in Hebrew, he kills a lion and finds honey in his belly, and Sunshine lay with the prostitute until midnight. The Philistines are Giants that are killed by David and Samson. Samson has a relationship with Delilah like Ra and Isis. Isis bit Ra with her beauty in the form of a serpent. Delilah means "She that weakens" and she is like a giant Isis.

Remember giants or Nephilim come from fallen angels having sex with the daughters of Cain. They were on the earth before the flood and after. They were known heroes and other mythologies have Thor and others fighting the giants. The fallen angel is a trick of the church. They changed the word descend to fall. No bad context of falling to have sex but this is the start of the lies. A god is a fallen angel and Jesus has no hero so the devil and Moses will torment us until the end of time. Right now, the world believes one way. They believe the Bible says sex is bad and they stole people and use the lie of hell on them.

What makes me mad and embarrassed is the gospels are so short. I have read the Divine Comedy in Italian and considered Dante my poet and prophet. He believes in the gods and the poets. I like to read it and imagine that Jupiter is Zeus and Baal, and every country has their place in this imagination of mine. The gospel you must memorize so you can communicate but in America the Christian is completely ignorant of the Old Testament and not so good on the new. I am teaching you the way out of the Bible is St, John-the Disciple Jesus loved. Even the current Pope can't stop John from beating him to the tomb. My disciple is St. John; he gave seven competitions with the first Pope before he went to the upside down cross. We have all these unread gospels, and all religions are Satanic besides Christianity.

Jesus is so mighty to the American and to me he is the liar I met when I was fifteen in church. As an adult I hear all the lies and I remember from the church days I was the only kid that read the Bible or knew anything. This is your whole life wasted making a fake God happy and obeying what you think are the teachings of Moses while calling the Jews who wrote it Satanist. We need the Talmud and other books to help us place ourselves in the Bible. Are we children of the national God of Israel Jehovah or his great son Jesus? No historical proof of anything and we are told to have faith or go to hell.

The Christian religion is so weak compared to polytheism. We don't have to deny Jesus or any other god. Do we believe Jesus is God and Jesus is our father? In the holy gothic Cathedral of Valencia in Spain I saw the Holy Grail. On the wall was a picture of a horned Jesus giving the commandments to Moses from the clouds. Once you understand we don't study the background of the Bible because the church wants us ignorant. People think we all come from the twelve tribes of Israel. Noah is Ziusudra and Ham never existed...these are the racist things that come up in the Bible right away, chapter nine, and they don't even raise a red flag that Jehovah does not love non-Jews. He kills them, drops the ceiling on giants, and other dirty tricks to kill them.

When Jehovah did nothing to help the Jews in the Holocaust, we should have made a new Bible. We ask where all the killing miracles happened like the Death Angel who knows to go only to the house of the black people or Egyptians. It is so frustrating that we do not know this. I hope this book goes around the world and changes Christianity. All the bad karma, curses, anti-woman, and the fear of hell are all solved when the Christian learns the Old Testament. The church doesn't respect the Bible like its art. They will tell us what to do. This has gone around the world.

Now we understand you don't have to go to church to be Christian; you don't have a choice. Somebody will hear my sex message and say they don't "believe" in the church. Right away the word "believe" comes up since he is Christian and doesn't know it. How many American women have been exposed to the pre-marital sex law? They think Jesus is against sex, so they are afraid to be sexy. Ironically in America if we don't like sex, we bring up the children who we are fucking royal with Christianity. A child will see it and there is no fun place in America for adult fun.

This makes me hate God for letting the lies of Satan over power America to the point our young people are virgins and have not been kissed. With all the evil that has happened to me in America I can't believe I have to be married which cost a lot of money. Or risk it with the prostitute and hope I don't go to jail or become a sex offender. Locked up with the rapist and pedophile because I give my body to a beautiful woman for a small amount of money. But it is okay for the church to fuck children and television showing pre-marital sex with no punishment. It is a very confusing situation for us and me. If I am wrong and the church is right, why does sex make me so happy? I feel so good and want it so bad, but I don't have a wife and it is a sin to touch myself according to the church. This has messed us up so bad nobody can get laid anymore. We were born with God angry at sex and our parents teach us the best they can.

CHAPTER 43

ATLANTIS AND MOSES

I defend you from the Bible since many people don't have the time to study it. I have dedicated my life to the Bible and living in Italy made me wise. I can enter the Bible through the seven mouths of the dragon in Rome. Move book to book with the Italy axe in my hand to slay Lotan. Which book do you want the Baal of the Bible to go to? We could see **Baal Hammon** in the **Song of Songs**. He is part of a pantheon, but Cesare destroyed his people. Black and white against each other is the race card. If I say a Canaanite is bad, people will believe me. If I say a Phoenician is bad, people that know better would correct me. If I refer to modern Phoenicia as Lebanon, we will never say they are bad. The Bible tricks you into being a racist. Even an African American pastor is ignorant of Ham. Nobody says that story is bad, and we have been using Noah for 3,000 years.

It is so obvious how all these names for the countries start with Egypt and then say the son Canaan is a slave to his brothers. No other flood story in the world makes the sons of Africa slaves. What kind of a relationship does an Egyptian American have with the Torah? He is killed and Moses does all kinds of evil to them while we cheer him on. To this day that is how it is. **Christ has killed every god in the world with the ten commandments, yet he can't seem to kill the devil.**

The devil or Satan means "adversary" and Satan tempts Jesus for forty days. If you are hungry do a miracle, they go back and forth with scripture. This could be internal and the devil a hungry stomach.

Satan should have tempted him with a big butt, big tits, and big hair woman or the women from Tijuana. Would Jesus have sex? If Satan tempted him with the sexy women of Barcelona, Prague, Budapest, Madrid, Lisbon, Seville, Alicante, Valencia, Milan, Rome, Athens, Santorini...and many other cities I have been tempted to spend money for sex. The 700 wives of Solomon could be done in a lifetime with women from all over the world, in America.

A job for every individual and we lift the Catholic ban on sex. I have explained the trio and we want to take this chance to grasp at knowledge. In my lifetime I have heard the sex and solo sex lies. How can we live with a Jesus that does not let us masturbate? Can you sleep at night knowing Jehovah made a personal appearance to kill Onan? Hair on the hands like Esau, blindness and craziness. The lies of the 60s and 70s doctors telling us whacking off has bad side effects.

Do we want to go down in history as a country built on scam religions? We have no pyramid in the Bible unless Quetzalcoatl is Jesus. With a whole continent that the Bible does not mention we have perfectly good Elohim wasted by the Christians. Their guy is everywhere, and mothers pass the curse of Eve on to their daughters. They don't teach them the Sumerians are the first civilization. They don't know Inanna or Ishtar, but they know the Virgin Mary who is always virgin. The stars make it all make sense why she is Virgo with the breadbasket of stars. Every night the net of Marduk, the stars he uses to subdue Tiamat, is cast over the earth and we don't know one fricken star.

The belt of Orion is the most obvious in the sky. It was the **Duat**, home of the gods, for the Egyptian. They line up with the pyramids at Giza. The whole sky tells a story but from the idol to the saint we are emasculated. We can't hold our own phallus and be proud of El. We only accept the Roman Catholic story. Why not pick up the pieces and expand the Bible so we can get something out of it?

Everything sexual will change the world. Solomons' proverbs come from a man who knew many women and he was wise about many things. Proverbs 5 is about adultery and there is another one about murder. If we wanted people to be faithful, we would teach this proverb. Once you see the risk to your business you will be faithful. Remember his father David had a harem. He committed adultery with Bathsheba, the mother of Solomon and Lemuel. Solomon knew how much his father was punished and wrote about it as a continuation.

If we did not block sex, we would be wise. All the mysteries of the ancient gods are hidden behind Jesus and what he said. We could read the Gnostic Gospels and not have Love Feast. Just don't teach God is mad at sex. To say you are going to hell for pre-marital sex is just ridiculous. An experience of love we are lucky to have, has been comprised by marriage and the church. American women are not really sluts, but they can't tell who they want to marry by looking at them. They don't have sex with just anybody; you must be a candidate for marriage. You don't have to marry them; you can drive the car before you buy it.

Jesus and Michael, the Arch Angel kill devils all the time. We do not acknowledge it in art, and we do not understand it in literature. Christ once and for all defeated the devil but he defeated the gods by attaching us to Moses. Once we hear the word "idol" we point our finger at art and demonize it and the people, this causes racism and not knowing where you come from or the things, I write about is obvious. Ham is Africa and he was a sexual bad guy like Lot with his daughters. They do not read the Song of Songs for sex but they like the black son butt fucking the white father. Just looking is even worse. Do you curse your children for seeing you nude? Or kill them for masturbating? Burn in hell for pre-marital sex and sex is love. If we love each other in an orgy, we do what Gnostics did. They were already free and did not have a concept of sin. We don't even know the Bible, but we use it to judge each other and condemn sex.

Sex is one thing that is interesting for me to discuss with my fellow Americans. In the country where the curse word is "fornication" we should ask people if they want to fornicate with us. I can't proposition with "make love" to a stranger but they won't like "Wanna fuck?" Do you want to fornicate with me is just a joke I am not being serious, but the word has to do with cheating of God only. Otherwise, it would be in the Torah which tells you not to have sex with your donkey or your neighbor's donkey. Do you think they forgot do not have sex unless you were married and then go "no comment" every time somebody gets laid in the Old Testament.

In context it is never bad, but we have Onan as the measuring stick. The lie of death for masturbation based on a man who pulled out and spilled on the ground. Prostitutes are everywhere in Canaan. The evil being done in the book of Genesis by the patriarchs is something you don't understand. We have Baal in this book so we can go back in time and worship him. Father Abraham is the Father Jesus spoke of and for this some say Isaac is Jesus, some say Jesus was Cain. He had to atone for Cain's sin. Noah is not true at all, and he is the pin that pulls everything together. Study Gilgamesh and you are free.

Introducing us to these lies young changes our lives forever. We believe God is angry and the voice of Noah is the cursing voice. Knowing this story is made up makes a huge difference. Jesus said, "In the days of Noah." And did not mention slavery or what the looking at nudity really means. This is so sick and twisted and we know what is right around the corner. We say this is God's word but what about the Sumerian story. We must be smarter than this. Now the Bible is above our heads and after reading this book the Bible will be under our feet.

The angry father image of Noah who had only three sons to repopulate the earth is our God. He gets his start and goes through the Torah creating havoc. Just because some law, we only know ten, is in there does not make it good. The Egyptian is saying a negative confession of what he has not done. Christianity is based on sin and say sorry. If we think we will meet Osiris and the forty-two gods in the afterlife, what kind of groveling do you expect to do? With Jesus you say sorry for my sins and in the Book of the Dead it matters what you do.

I have lived different times in **Lecce**, Italy's heel, and I am always heel catching with them in a good way. Since Italy is Catholic, I see the sad Jesus and Mary all over the place. Since the Gnostic Gospels and Love Feast are taken away, they should be sad. I am the only one to redeem Jesus from this misunderstood Old Testament. Remember the Gnostic respect the law but not the stories. They knew Noah was false and taught his wife burned the ark down three times. I have heard stories about animals walking backwards off the ark but Gilgamesh, the first poetry, is not known by many Americans. They would figure out Gilgamesh was 2/3 divine and 1/3 human. This messes up Jesus and Hercules was 50/50-man God.

The churches want to sell us Jesus so we cannot be divine. The woman is the secret to a man's divinity. We are sinners saved by grace but the 613 commandments which are unknown to us have grown stale for 3,000 years. We are still judging in God's name and when Jesus said, "Don't judge." We ignore it. If we followed the teachings of Jesus, we would have a heaven on earth. Forgiveness and no judgement for us who have a God that kills masturbators and tells their parents to tie them down.

Instead of masturbating do a hooker. Any time of the day it is available, and it is fun to go with a lot of women. This is what we would do free if we had the Gnostic orgy. We were free and then something happened. The church has been messing around with the scriptures until God is the devil. We are guilty because of Eve but judged in hell for our faith. This is man-made but why can't people see the lies of the church? We don't learn the Bible in school, so we are at the mercy of the church who knows and tells a small part of the story.

All the missing books and manuscripts are ignored, and I realize the Christians think they can replace them with their magic. They pick a verse out of context from the Bible and answer many questions with the same answer. Jesus is the answer to everything, but we do not know his teachings in the gospels or the Gnostic. How obvious it is the Bible has been tampered with to hide astrology. The book of Job has the constellations but that is another book I have never heard in church. They all threaten Jesus, and they don't want you to understand the dead Old Testament. I never hear a quote from the Old Testament that makes sense or is real. We need to study the Bible to get over the Bible.

The Bible is done yet Jesus is coming back soon after 2,000 years. If Quetzalcoatl was Jesus, it is interesting that time changed with both, and they are both Venus. Jesus and the pyramids could be what I think is a connection between Jesus and Osiris. Jesus is said to be copied from Egyptian Horus. They both walk on water and do the same miracles, but Osiris is the first resurrection.

When I saw the Pagan Temple of Osiris in Bologna, Italy it changed by life. I saw the sign and the Book of the Dead was opened to me. And the cradle of civilization will no longer be cursed after this book is accepted. If your heart and phallus are Osiris and Osiris is Orion; and a dragon that guards the Nile is Osiris, we see the Nile as the phallus of Ra. Ra jacks off with both hands to make the Nile flow. Think of Moses cursing it with bugs and frogs and all these plagues come on you. Good news! The volcano on Santorini, the Atlantis Plato wrote about, in 1500 B.C. erupted and caused the flood the Bible talks about and the plagues of the Nile!

Moses acted like his God was the volcano, but we know better now. We can visit the Atlantis Plato wrote about in Greece. I was there for seven days and visited the Chapel of Elijah on Mt. Illias. I did the Atlantis tour and published The Lords of the Poison with me on the cover of Atlantis. This changes the Old Testament but during my three weeks in Greece 2001 I went to Athens, Santorini, Ios, Mykonos, and on the way home after discovering Atlantis I passed Patmos and the boat stopped to let in a bunch of tourists on. They told me they had come from St, John's tomb and since I could not get off the boat, I asked them about it. They told me he recited the Book of Revelations on his death bed to a Greek interpreter and they believe it to be 16% accurate.

Now you have Onan for the Torah and Old Testament. Greece conquers the Old and New Testament in my three-week trip and The Lords of the Poison is the story of the pilgrimages I made to the dark virgin, Greece, and Barcelona. The church claims Revelations 12 is Guadalupe but who is the child in her arms? Juan Diego or Jesus? If he had wings, he would be a feathery serpent connecting heaven and earth. I go on pilgrimages to the Virgin Mary all over the world and I have made some incredible books: Nine Days to Healing a Spiritual Pilgrimage.

The Virgin Mary speaks to me and in the story of **Guadalupe** it is **Tonantizin** the Aztec Goddess. The story behind the story is Indian and Nine Days to Healing shows that the Guadalupe we know is based on a peyote hallucination of Maria Lucia when she was fourteen at the wedding with the Talking Eagle, Juan Diego. In Italy I received a new father and was free from Father Abraham. In Mexico and Montserrat, I am seeing the dark virgin and she is unraveling secrets to me. After I lost my mother, I gained Guadalupe/Tonantzin as a friend calling me Mikey to remind me, I am a feathered serpent and a saint. The diminutive in the Aztec makes one a Lord.

CHAPTER 44

THE ALTARS

This **tzin** would be a new cult with Guadalupe/Tonantzin. Together they have the power of the Catholic and the science of the Aztec. We should look at their creation stories and wonder how we got stuck with Noah. These other stories are true? What all these people write agrees. It goes with a sacred book.

How could we have world peace with the Bible and the church telling us everybody is a devil? The myths have heroes to kill the devil unlike Christianity who waits St. Michael. Jesus got rid of every god on earth but can't seem to kill a tiny little serpent in the Garden of Eden which the Gnostics call Sophia (Wisdom). Think of healthy Hercules and Baal .... they have sex they are a Satanist according to the church. We worry if these mighty gods whacked off or got laid is funny. I know mythology should be a part of everyone's life. Jesus was a Roman myth turned into history to control people.

Read what came first and then think of the Bible as music. We see the Gnostics are first, so Jesus went to them for a reason. Then the church father Irenaeus called them Satan for having sex and the rest is history. Aren't we curious to what the Gnostic Gospels say? More about Jesus! We should be excited since we love him so much. The true teachings wait for us like the father of the Prodigal Son. We come back to God, but we think we know the Bible and we don't. We start to impose the hatred on anything that moves, and the Bible is a purely racist book with a curse on those who do not understand it.

The church said, "If the Bible falls into the hands of the ignorant, they will take it literally and many cults will form." Are we ignorant that we think we know the whole Bible story or are we sitting on something we really don't care about? Some people do not like to read the Bible. It takes a lot of study. I used to believe in it when I was young, and I prayed and studied the Bible every day. Look now what we have in this book. A one-of-a-kind treasure to expose the lies we have been damaged by.

So many things on the forbidden list and we judge history to be a lie and the Bible we understand to be true. Polytheism/Gnosticism replaces the Old and New Testaments. We see what was going on around the world instead of just Israel and we learn something useful. The curse of sex is on us from the church. Even dancing for us was a sin.

The racism against the ancient cultures that invented the stories the Bible copied is bad. We are wiping out so many countries with Moses. He has the one mountain and one son we believe in. Now we have resources that could make us smart and experience sexual revolution. Imagine how happy Americans would be if they got laid all the time and men and women were equal. This is how it should be, and all these ancient cultures have something to teach us if we do not demonize them.

When I was a teenager, I took the Bible seriously and believed whatever they told me. After a while I realized they are always saying the same thing. They build up Jesus and give you a Bible that nobody produces anything meaningful out of. Jesus is the solution to everything, and the people use a special language. We say, "Praise the Lord." Quite a bit, and if we spoke Phoenician, it would be "Praise Baal."

This book works out many of the Bible errors and lies they have put in to hide sex. The child is the excuse, but America has turned into family only with no adult life. Everywhere I go but the bar is family style. In Europe they have clubs and dancing along with some of the hottest prostitutes in the world. If I was told I would have a woman more beautiful than the famous ones back home, I would have never believed you. Now in my life I have had the Budapest woman in Barcelona, and she is the most beautiful woman I have ever seen.

If we put these lies behind us and start loving each other the way Jesus said the world will change. We hold on to Eve for the curse but what about Mother Earth? It is not your fault if you are a woman. The serpent tempts everyone. Remember the serpent is Sophia to the Gnostics. With *Eros* at our side everything will be better. No more shame and talking God's name in vain just to cover sex. Why can't we say why we are against it? Why blame God and give everybody a messed-up view of the Lord?

More people would come to God if sex was not the first thing, they want you to give up. They will tell you not to make love to your girlfriend or boyfriend, but we are already past that in America. People never tell you they are not going to marry you and then we have these little relationships that end up with someone we did not choose. First lower your standards and go to the bar. Now you get one, but she was just there, or she was the only woman in the bar. There is no reason not to have sex but if you think it might end in marriage give it some time.

If sex was separated from marriage, it would be so fun to travel America and know women from the cities. We are all adults having sex all the time but let's not put it on God or the Bible now that we know better. St. Paul is a charming individual, but he became Jupiter, King of the Gods. Since he is a celibate, we have a bronze sky of judgment. In his writings he is so nice to consider that some men burn with lust. He tells them to marry but they married young, and the women were property.

Monotheism has done so much damage to the woman and yet with the Bible and Quran it all makes sense. The fact that we allow the goddess to be covered in shit like Jezebel is because Moses put Eve at fault for eating fruit when her male son became a murderer, Cain. The garden and its nudity could have many more meanings with symbolism; and Adam's first wife Lilith. She is also Venus so get in line to become a feathery serpent connecting heaven and earth. Venus is crowded with Jesus, Pharaoh, Quetzalcoatl and the women. We miss out on the goddess of beauty since we follow only the Bible.

This is futile to put down a woman calling her a slut or a whore. I am jealous of the power women have to get sex. Men must work so hard, and a woman could proposition many men and have a different lover every night. Men must lower their standards if they want to get laid at all and pay for dates. In America the number of women that use men for money is high. I have been out with gold diggers but when I was young, I did not want a girlfriend. I wanted many lovers. How to get this or get the quality I want? Without paying, communication is difficult, and the conversation is going to tend towards marriage.

I see why many Americans give up on sex. The pursuit of sex is so frustrating and expensive. How many nights out in Carlsbad looking for women and buying food and beer? We walk around and see that many are too young for us. Many are on dates, and some are ugly. We can go to Tijuana and take care of business as long as we don't run out of money. All these women that work the system young get more money doing this than by being attached to one man.

Money for everybody and once communication sets in a woman that likes me can offer me money instead of lunch and conversation. You could travel America and know our exotic women with sexy accents and large breasts. Do you really want her to be a virgin? How many is too many? Now to make things right with God we stop attaching his name to lies. We are so ignorant of the Bible; anybody can lead us. If they learn an Old Testament story and follow up with Jesus everybody comes to the altar.

CHAPTER 45

THE MARGINS

If we knew the prophets, we would hear God's voice as he speaks through them. There are solutions to today's problems once we understand the time the prophet lived in and how relevant their messages are today. We would be better off with a short story that sums it up. We would know the two commandments of Jesus which sum up all the law and prophets: "Love God with your heart, mind, and soul and love your neighbor as yourself." This would be the short story, but we have a whole book of law we have edited and added to. We eliminate sex and change body parts that can be changed back.

Moses was a certain kind of character, but he is no Jesus. Moses ordered his own people to kill each other when he left the mountain. We assume this is the only mountain where God speaks but there are other law-givers from the mountain. Elijah is a missing person in transfiguring the transfiguration. Jesus showed Peter: Moses, Elijah, and Jesus and Peter wanted to build three temples for them. Elijah crossed a river and did miracles, but Jesus says he is John the Baptist and John says, "I am not that prophet."

We have lived without all the saints and angels in America, and I don't see much art dedicated to them. We should return to the gods of the Native American and let John the Baptist and Elijah rest. He was beheaded and I ask if this is the way to make it even for Jezebel. A full circle came to keep the book consistent.

We have our decision to live in the lies of the Roman Catholic

Church and say Jesus is God like Constantine said. We ignore the Gnostic Gospels and say all religions are fake. If God was God, we could worship him in any form or color. With Jesus as God this slows God down since Jesus was a man-made God by Constantine. The Gnostic were made Satanists by Irenaeus. The god of the Maya is not Jewish and white so he must be bad or an idol we think. If Hunab Ku, the One Giver of Movement and Measure, loved us why do I say he is bad. We are racists like our God.

Quetzalcoatl made us from corn. He is even a creator God. But all over Mexico and America we find Guadalupe. **If we found Tonantzin, we would find Quetzalcoatl.** At this point Christianity has created so many devils and done so much brainwashing. We are under God, but we should say we are under Jesus. God can refer to several deities and names. Jesus is the one that attaches the Old Testament history of Moses to us and says this is your history to. Bad things happen to us, and we go forward anyway. Fucking up our children with the Christian virginity and heaven and hell is horrible. We are so ignorant we don't realize liars go to hell. We believe and practice one big lie.

History is large and fills in the missing blanks. There are so many spots in time where something significant happened that we are not aware of. In church they read very little of the Bible and usually change the subject. They stress the business side of making more converts. Trying to help people better their lives is not an issue. Collecting money and spreading the guilt is what they do.

If we had our own Vatican and our people kept track of all sacred history, we would expand. Get a true view of the world and why we are here. So far, they have cut off so many countries it is hard to make sense of the world using the Bible only. I feel sorry for my country that we are sexually frustrated and trying to use each other so much. I have lived in different countries and found many treasures I want to bring back to America.

We struggle so hard to maintain this facade that we are all happy. We need help from outside and it will probably not come from our country. Don't you think our system is a little outdated? We can connect all religions and calendars through the constellations on the stars of the Tilma. We know where she goes in the Bible thanks to my pilgrimage and book Nine Days to Healing a Spiritual Pilgrimage. The story we have is so short and we all assume we know it. Aren't you scared of going to hell if the Christian religion is true?

We serve every day and miss the point of action. The planets or gods revolve and circle Ra. They line up with every Astrology and the Bible. The book of Job has constellations in it that we can attach to the Egyptian or Maya. Every symbol in the Bible can be illuminated and history will go back to Phoenician El and Baal. We should make statues of Baal and read his tablets. They tell a story that spread everywhere, and the Phoenicians invented the alphabet. With polytheism we can embrace the saints and angles of monotheism if they don't call the gods fallen angels.

The fallen angel and Nephilim create the explanation for mythology. The mythology of every country should be known before studying the Bible. I can see where they copied stories or felt guilty for lying. If one reads Baal and then the story of Jezebel and Elijah, we see how many clues to this mystery are in the story. Elijah can't even kill the daughter of Baal, so he anoints Elisha to anoint Jehu, to tell her own people to kill her. Baal is so many other gods around the world and we don't even see the connection between Buddha and Christ.

This brainwashing and lazy bones Jones attitude will keep us under the curse for another 3,000 years. I have already done the research. I have been to Atlantis and back and read about Homer in the Divine Comedy. It all makes sense to me, but the challenge is to explain our own beliefs. We take them for granted and disobey them all the time. We believe Jesus says it is a sin to look at a woman. In real life I hear men groan when they see a beautiful woman. They fantasize and that is it. Remember no onanism! So, the American male must be horny, and therefore we have so many sexual deviants and child molesters.

They can't get hookers, so they go after us and our kids. The government does not want us to have free will over our money or our bodies. We are told what to do and they have ruined our lives. Yet they preach fornicators will burn for eternity. And they judge us if we pay for sex. I am an adult, and my cock has been working just fine without any help from the government. The average American woman sells her free will for a hot dog. In Italy and Mexico, the women are clean. They won't put you in jail for giving her money. We are consenting adults missing a heaven of earth.

All my sexy travels taught me a lot about this and taking God's name in vain; to enforce the Catholic sex rules is something we are never going to be free of without this book. We are such hypocrites that non-Christian television is all about pre-marital sex. They insinuate it or show the clean aftermath and no punishment goes with the sin known as fornication. We do not fear hell but we teach it to our children so they will accept Jesus. One thing leads to another, and the Jesus people want 10% of our income. Look how great the church has become. There is a church on every corner. The problem is American women go in as whores and come out as virgins. They don't want to have sex anymore. They think every man is raping them and put up a fuss about sex.

The government lets us have pre-marital sex if it is free. What about a man born blind or an ugly man? They can have a super model hooker love them or they can masturbate themselves to death. We are so cruel to take the hooker away from the horny man who now looks to see if hair has grown on his hands from jacking off. We don't even allow a manual release, let alone a hooker, but people on television are having pre-marital sex which you think is fornication. Change the channel to Christian television and all those sexy channels are sin.

If hell is true, why are we not warning people about it. Ra kills the serpent daily, but we do not celebrate the sun. The sun is also an idol and a foreign religion to Christians. The idea of Osiris coming to stop cannibalism, and with his wife Isis teach them farming. Then he becomes the first resurrection. Then stays three days in the constellation of the Southern Cross and is reborn. Jesus is a parody of sun worship, and he is coming back tomorrow. We think he will come back at the end of the world based on what old St. John recited to a Greek interpreter on his death bed on the island of Patmos. Our whole future depends on a tiny book copied from the book of Daniel.

The condition the Bible is in compared to what is used to has to do with the editing. They almost put some crazy stuff in the book of Mark. Men had to edit the Bible for sex and the Hippo ('Bohemoth) in the book of Job has his penis turned into his tail. An adult can read the unedited Bible to their children, and they will be fine. When you know your phallus in the Book of the Dead is Osiris, we don't take for granted the lie of the Hippo. His tail is not a Cedar of Lebanon. His phallus is. God has even humor, but we edit for the children, so they don't know what a dick is. Are we going to tell them later in life about Osiris or his son Hours? We depend on Jehovah to kill the Egyptians with the Red Sea, plagues, and curses? This is totally racist and a lie. We depend on lies since we are too lazy to read the Book of the Dead or see the miracle Horus/Jesus did.

We mess up people's lives with the curse and we refuse to study Moses. He has oral tradition and a much more enlightened book. We go with the evil against Egypt and act like they were bad people. The fact that there is no pyramid in the Bible is also interesting that we don't look up to the belt of Orion and see Giza. We are comfortable teaching our children the racists lie of the Bible and all the hatred God had for Esau. He let his boy Jacob rob him the way we are robbed of our hooker bucks. Whether you are prostitute making money with physical love or the customer who is saving money from sexless dinner dates.

People never think if we were all hookers, we would all have a price. If you have chemistry with them marry them and maybe, they have talents you don't know about. In theory there is nothing wrong with it but more than that to me is the feeling of freedom I have in Europe. America is such a blister that I look at a crowd of women and know they have been poisoned by Christianity, but they still want me to buy them dinner. You are never going to get anybody good like this. There are lots of soul mates for everybody but what are we doing now? Having sex with our boyfriend or girlfriend so we don't feel slutty. The goddess celebrates her sexuality, and the gods approve. This is normal and should have never stopped. Now we are outside heaven's gate with the virgins and the whoremongers. The Bible judges us and we consider it our only source. How does your pastor know the Quran is not true? Did he read it? Can he teach it? This would make me want to go to church if information was given out. The churches I have been to hide behind Jesus and make stuff up to promote the church. Since they tell women I have dated they are going to hell for sex, I get to hear all the lies. Venereal disease and other disasters come upon the women.

Men think they have an advantage with Adam and Eve. She is his serpent, and he is sinful. The woman is controlled by Adam since she was created from his rib according to the story. We are in an age of experimentation. This book does not say we have to have an orgy like the Gnostic, but we should know the whole picture. We think Jesus is automatic. He gave us the tools, but we must do things for ourselves. My life was an experiment with the ministry. I figured I would learn the Bible better than anybody. Now I see it as a revelation waiting to happen.

Once we are knowledgeable about the Bible and not just its stories, we have a foundation to learn all history and religions. We have left too much out for the Bible to be true. Why did they take out the books of Enoch? He talks about fallen angeles and gives them names. We should build temples to the angel/gods and sell books there. This way we, everybody, can learn it from art. The Catholic Church gives us the last supper and the artist puts it to music. Once we see how far the twelve disciples are from the twelve months or twelve zodiac signs don't hook up, we understand the sneaky Bible. The New Testament copied names and stories and looks highly suspicious. I would hesitate to call the Bible the Word of God after understanding Joseph and Jesus are so similar or Judah and Judas. They have so much in common we see they have copied the characters of Moses and teach it as literal history.

We block out certain books that would interfere with the Bible lies. The Bible is a raped book written by evil men that we would never tolerate in America. Baal or Quetzalcoatl are foreign sounding names unlike Jesus and Mary. We must get over insisting on this English interpretation. If I say Lord or Feathered Serpent, we accept Lord, but the Serpent is phallic, and we are systematically against Osiris and the penis. This is the serpent in our own bodies. An evil kundalini coiled up ready to strike as the devil's advocate asking Eve: "Did the Lord really say?" This is our own adversary not Satan. The Gnostics called her Sophia (Greek for wisdom). Notice she is female and at the right hand of God in the Proverbs. Now we have the angry, lonely, old man on the throne with his crucified son. The story of Abraham (Father) and Isaac (Laughter); is complete. An old man in the sky with no wife. No Mother Nature or female deity; just the trinity and the book of men that hated their women.

This is the only book we are supposed to follow, and we can't understand it. We just keep telling the story of Jesus without learning any of his vital lessons that would change the world if applied. Forgiveness, don't judge, …these should be the commandments. Imagine if we did not judge. We change other people's lives by forcing Christianity down the throats of Americans who have no background in their school to save them from racist miracles and lies. The books of Greece and Egypt are in every good bookstore, but do we get the history behind the Bible? The Atlantis, that Plato wrote about (see The Lords of the Poison) turns the book of Genesis and Exodus upside down. Zeus caused it with the volcano on Santorini and the flood and the plagues are accounted for by loving mother nature.

Even on judgement day it says the Lord thunders and we expect to see Jesus on the throne. I imagine Baal riding the lightening and doing all the work. Baal did not make promises like Jehovah, but his story is classic and should be read before reading the Bible. Since we are blind with greed, we put Jesus and virginity on everyone when they are born. There is no Gnostic or Polytheistic church or idol with a temple. Shrine temple prostitutes and temple for every type of person. A collection of Temples to Feathered Serpent but modern English and anti-Babel languages; better ask about the Phoenician God who we call Jesus.

The names must be English for us to think they are good and there are so many stories of the saints. When I am in Italy, I like to know the saint of the city. It makes for good conversation, and I learn of new miracles I never heard of. In Egypt a priest does the same with the god of the city. It is easier to keep track of the gods than the angels. In Revelations they ascend from heaven, but they do not have names. Since the devil is also a son of God, we see too much activity for the monotheist to make sense of.

It is easier just to use the gods and see what they had in common. To go on emasculated and ignorant is an option for those that have not read this book. Once you know the true story of Onan and his broken duty to his brother it all makes sense. We know the kind of lie they tell and how they do it. If God is not going to kill us for masturbating it makes sense looking is not adultery. Jesus is just swallowed up in the Old Testament. His useful teachings are never even quoted, and we tell the whole Bible story just to get to him.

Jezebel and Babylon are way out of context in Revelations. Revelations calls Rome, Babylon for many chapters. They explain a spiritual Babylon, but it is really Rome. When Jezebel was Queen, she took Naboth's Vineyard for her husband Ahab King of Israel. Elijah comes down to punish and it is so cruel. What she did with his vineyard was not a sin, she was Queen. Her demise and continued hatred for her is seen in Revelations. Old Men don't understand queen prostitutes and they should not make decisions for us.

The finishing of Israel's Queen is an obvious set up. When the Bible tells lies the author expresses guilt. Knowing this is the end of the woman, to die in the dung. Jehu's men turned the Temple of Baal into a urinal. They see the image of Baal and see what the storm God looks like. All these things would be so good for us to understand better a Phoenician and a Canaanite. The Bible twists the other countries and hides the fact that the Bible authors borrowed from the ancients. The fact that nothing goes together makes the Bible weak. It has only itself to turn to since it is considered by many to be the complete word of God. The other gods we must pretend do not exist since they throw off the man God story.

All these things existed before Jesus, and we are all the product of a fake religion. The things the Bible supposedly says are going to happen have already happened. Jesus says, "I come quickly." And it has been over 2,000 years. If he has already come back and we do not investigate it, what kind of love do we have for Jesus? If he has more teachings, why do we not embrace them? They could change the world, but I am showing you how the Bible has been changed.

They want one God with heaven and hell to motivate us. Why do they take away sex from us? For control they tell us what to do and keep us feeling guilty. Look how long the crucifixion is in the gospels. They are working guilt for Eve's sin, and we feel guilty for lusting. In my own body I know this to not be true. If sex is for babies only, why am I attracted to so many women? I feel it is my body and then I read in paper what the church expects of us, and I feel the contradiction. Whoremongers and virgins appear on either side of heaven's gate. The anger of God is hot, and Jezebel is thrown into a bed with her lovers.

The basic Christian story seems to say God punishes only sex. Think of how we are punished by the lies of Constantine and the church. They use us and have power, but I teach the Bible. Once one knows the hot spots, they can see the gods of history smiling at them. They wait for us to come back and know love. All our celestial parents are turned into monsters by the church. We would be better off with a book on symbolism then a book about the Bible. Let's see what is on the other side. If the other countries did not know God, then why did they copy them.

To contain what is false according to the church shows how powerful they are. They will stunt your growth, keep you a virgin, and consider the woman to be lower than a dog. The Bible in Greek says puppies but in English it translates dogs. This bad treatment of women and suppression of their many gifts causes us to sin. The man will never find the goddess in his woman treating her like property. Real love comes to us in the Song of Songs, but we edit it as well.

A child reading that in the Bible is all you are afraid of. Change the body parts back and see if this grim Bible can hold up. We discover

Osiris and El, who has a member longer than the seas. We need these more powerful gods to look up to. The Old Man on the throne we see in the Catholic art is what we know. If a name sounds foreign, we think the person is evil. Daniel, Mathew, and John are cool but what about the ones we are trained to hear as a Satan. The church has created so many Satan's, yet they believe in one God.

The history we would learn with the true story of Jesus would change the world. We pass through life ignorant of so many things. We accept heaven as a universal destination for ourselves and hell for the less fortunate. Who is a man who deserves to burn in hell? What crime is so bad we must burn for eternity? The church made these things up and we don't follow what Jesus said about these things.

The gospels are so small, yet we do not know any lessons by heart. They should be proverbial by now. How many people have laid hands on you and prayed for you when you are down? How many times has a Bible verse helped you? Only one kind of person can be a part of it. The emasculated hate the bright morning star. It reveals who is who and Isis bring back Osiris from the dead. We miss on all these crucial dynamics, and we assume the church studies them.

Certain books are not found in Christian bookstores. Christianity is strong but the secular is weak, and nobody reads the Book of the Dead like a Bible. We ignore history and consider knowledge in general to be unimportant. We talk about Jesus as a story, but we never use his wisdom. It is all magic and you don't have to do anything, is what they think, but I question the before and after of a person who was bound for hell and now is going to heaven. I don't see much change or love. The small message that controls the world is Jesus. They lie and tell you he does not want you to have sex. They put everything on him and ignore the upside down cross of St. Peter.

The Bible just sits on the table like a potato. It can't ward off evil or stop the devil but if you study it yourself it is different than having the story told to you. They make the whole Bible the story of Jesus and they add to what he said. The racism and sexism are still there, and this is what has fucked up the world. Our priorities are stupid and what matters is the faulty beliefs. We only know one way to do things and the only monotheistic God we have ever heard of is Jesus.

In Sumerian and Egypt, they had monotheistic religions before the Bible. The idea of all information being given to one God and that God is Jesus. What a short story to ruin all other religions with; nothing left but the gory crucifixion for artwork and a dove for peace. The animals, gods, stars, constellations, and calendars all connect through the other religions, and they all say the same thing. The Bible has borrowed titles for Christ from the pagan deities. The church must keep track of this somehow. We need to connect the idols to their books for a perfect religion that does not need to lie about history or scare children with hell.

The saints and angels are emasculated gods, but we can still honor them in polytheism. The only thing that changes is sex. Therefore, the Bible was edited for piety. They pulled the gods out of us and put them in the margins of the Bible. A foot becomes a phallus and a navel a vagina. If we use sexy words from the Bible on our lovers, do we have to be married to them? It is hard to believe we allow this to mess up everyone's mind in America. Believe in Jesus or go to hell and once you believe no more sex. This is no way to celebrate life …living like a monk. We chose to have sex or not and if somebody else chooses who would that be. If you pay for sex, they will lock you up, but it is okay to do it free. Hookers use condoms and porn stars don't. I can't understand why I cannot go to many hookers if I want to. I am single and I have the money. Why do I have to date food whores that think they are dammed for sex? A hooker is pure physical love and although you might not like it personally, **I don't think the John, or the hooker deserve jail when pre-marital sex is a sin for the rest of the world.**

We could not be any more hypocritical to judge a man for loving and paying; two good things that would make us rich. We are pretending to be pure and virgin each time we have a partner. The double standard is in place, but men are the biggest losers. When a woman gets her freedom from this ancient way of thinking it is good for all of us. We are afraid of sex since we have heard the lies. Threats of what will happen to you and how sex displeases the Lord. The measure of the feminine is Mary Magdalene. If she plays a part in the resurrection she is like Isis. We cannot ignore all the Egyptian stuff because some of the theories still affect us today.

CHAPTER 46

ALIENS WITH EYES

Old Testament prophets are not very well understood. The Old Testament is a big question mark. If we cannot handle the small Bible what if we had the unedited version. I think the preachers get off easy. The Bible is so small anybody could learn it. The guilt of Jesus and hope of heaven does not do anything for us on earth. Giving everybody in the world a job with their body is a start. Men are forced to take whatever they can get. The stress, money, emotional loneliness and dating are a pain in the ass. When I am horny, I just want a hooker. I do not want to be in a relationship.

What if I just broke up with my long-term girlfriend and I am in pain? If I take a few hundred dollars to Mexico, I can replace my ex's sexual image with the prostitute. It takes the power away from women and is the only way to get laid. Everything besides money is a shot at marriage. The money to the hooker is like a mini marriage for an hour. Honesty the whole way and no jealousy over other partners.

Everybody loves everybody and it is not mandatory to participate. From the orgy to the more severe God, we have invented is the measure of a curse. You are not supposed to even masturbate but originally the Gnostic had a Love Feast. We have made a long trip and picked up a lot of liars along the way. Now we can't even pick up at church unless we are getting married. Let me tell you what happens in real life. Both partners wait too long to come together. Waiting for marriage may take a long time.

If all churches had orgies, imagine how fun it would be to travel. If the orgy was done in the love of Jesus, it would be different then a regular orgy. What if you loved everybody involved. You only did certain things to certain people. It is hard to imagine strangers in America hooking up in church, but we will never know what it was like. Most people won't have an orgy in their lifetime. The point is people have pre-marital sex in the Bible. David and Solomon have harems. Now we have the severe teachings from the death penalty God invented by the lies of the Roman Catholic Church. We die for it, we are punished in hell for it, and we still trust in the curse of Eve to make us automatic sinners. Nobody is perfect.

How hard it is to get sex these days is mind boggling. In the 80s and 90s I watched people having sex in clubs and San Francisco was the easiest city to get laid in. I was a bouncer for three years and did a different beautiful woman every night. This was the 90s, so things were different. Now women are materialistic and frigid. They are hot but they don't do much with it. The amount of time my friends and I have spent chasing women is absurd. We could have had sex with a different hooker every day or pay the tabs and restaurants, bars, and movies. Our life and my life are wasted. I could feel young and choose whoever I want. She will be from different countries and speak many languages. The American woman is just a food whore because she does not want to go to jail.

How much the country controls us? First, they scare us with this cheeky God that is not even true but somehow, he gets rid of Osiris. I see the Budapest woman with legs like pillars, breast like melons, and a bubble heart shaped butt. I am supposed to get her for free and burn in hell according to America. If I pay her $120 and lick her pussy and butt, give her a climax in the 69, and then coming in elephant? When I saw her face in missionary I went to heaven. I saw angels without wings sitting on couches watching me. I could see around me, and heaven looked like the Qabalistic books I read.

I am supposed to tell her, "Sorry my country does not let me pay you …I will have to take you to an expensive dinner you don't want."

To think of eating with her is not making me happy. The love magic between me and the Budapest woman was an answer to prayer and a miracle. She is the most beautiful woman I have ever seen.

This experience happened in Barcelona where they have tons of brothels and clubs. In America I am going to have that experience? Every day I see attractive women in Carlsbad, but I can't do anything about it. What we would be experiencing without the lies and curses of the Roman Catholic Church is unfathomable. If Americans are horny and get laid a lot imagine how much better if Jesus blessed, you with love. Money doesn't change anything. We need a place for the rapist and pedophile to go to besides our loved ones. What are they supposed to do if even whacking off is considered a sin? We let the frustration build and build but we are not capable of waiting for marriage.

In America people often have fake relationships to justify their love. They want a boyfriend not a booty call. Women must remember since we can't love whores, we must go to you for a good deal. No more high heels, thongs, sexy make up, and big hair just a regular woman who can't pay you the complement of having sex with you until she gets a few meals. Being a food whore is better than going to jail but everything your pussy produces your mouth eats. Old rich men can get laid every day and prostitutes usually love old men. They love the money, and you are a part of that appreciation.

With masturbation we have a release and sex with ourselves. Our bodies don't lie but the church does. Do you believe you were meant to be with only one lover? This ruins people's life and America stops the party and lets us drink beer and look for women. Why not do eight in a row rich guy? Try and do that without paying. It is my money and I want to use it the way I want. If I want to spend $120 on the Budapest woman in Barcelona that is my choice not yours. This little crusade America is on to emasculate people has backfired. The adults, not the children, believe Noah's ark and see nothing wrong with slavery.

The trail of evil that goes through the Bible is celebrated when it happens to Esau not Jacob. He is hated and Jacob steals his birth right. The evil nature of Jacob the Patriarch is forgivable to the Christian. He steals, lies, and wrestles an angel. We know him for his ladder, and I believe the ladder had eyes with angels on every rung. Maybe it goes up to a UFO and he was receiving messages from the stone he lay his head on. We can change to UFO and alien or pagan and polytheist when we see Ezekiel's vision of the gods. Marduk and the others are underneath, the living creatures, the throne darting back and forth. They come from the North like King Cyrus the Persian.

The ladder of eyes or Ezekiel's wheel intersecting a wheel full of eyes is symbolic of life and intelligence. Aliens interfering in history and Jacob's minister writing about it! Killing Egypt and all of Africa, putting every island into the hands of Satan and his liars, and the words Satan, sinner, and saint all come out to describe the cosmic battle between Seth and Horus. Jesus shares names and tiles with pagan Gods like Dionysius and Attis who are before him. Jesus has only the Bible to support him and he can't stand on his own without heaven and hell. All other heavens are false, and all other hells are false. Only the Christian one is true, and we have Inanna saving us in Sumerian from the afterlife where everyone goes to the same place. Dusty and dry put pleasant and Inanna still saves you when you die. She like Jesus, Osiris, and Quetzalcoatl are the bright morning star.

The woman saves you when you are the hero. Isis putting her body on the dead body of Osiris rose him from the dead and she gave him a phallus of gold. This is where our Ka or soul is, and it is seated at the right hand of Ra like Jesus sits next to God in your place. You are like the others under the upside down cross of St. Peter. The other disciple asks the disciple Jesus loves what Jesus said. Peter the first Pope and John the Gnostic have a competition in the book of John. It says seven times the disciple that Jesus loved, and the other disciple and the disciple Jesus loved has the true teachings.

We look at the gospels and don't know the synoptic gospels are Matthew, Mark, Luke, they are all from Mark, Peters disciple. John is the beloved and the Gnostic so there are two pillars of Christ's throne not four. Marduk appearing under the throne of Ezekiel is really Baal. The four evangelists have their totems: Ox, Lion, Man, and Eagle. These come from the living creatures in Ezekiel's vision. When Ezekiel had these visions the evangelists where not even born so I favor the gods under the throne of God and are they all aliens?

An alien and a god are the same thing. We have descended angels turned to fallen angels for lusting after women. This is two strikes from the Roman Catholic Church. They hide the alien or God as a fallen angel and change the meaning of history. This hides the history they don't want us to know about. The second strike is punishing the descended angels for lusting with their eyes. Samson lost his eyes and was killed with the giants. He atoned for the sin of the **Nephilim**. The force of Jesus is even in the Old Testament, but Samson came first. The falling angel is the work of the Roman Catholic Church to explain the holes in history the Bible leaves with the three-year ministry of Jesus.

If Jesus did not talk about it, we certainly don't learn on our own. What if Jesus was questioned about Atlantis or the Native American? We look at the Old Testament as our history book. This is sad I used to think we all came from the twelve tribes of Israel. The myth becomes history to control the people. We read in complete ignorance this false and meaningless document that holds the gods in hell. Everybody is in hell, and everybody is Satan according to the church. When do you think Michael the Arc Angel will slay the devil?

If Jesus played the devil, it would make sense. Both a Satan and Jesus are numbered with the sons of the gods. They have an arena with other gods. The gods all connect through the goddess. One big happy family that we miss out on by being monotheist. We know so little about the Quran and the Talmud, but we assume Moses is the chief. Not all three agree on Jesus and Mohamed but they agree on Moses. Moses did all the dirty work and gave us a book too hard to understand. He is the hero that talks to God on the mountain and comes down angry and hateful.

Moses never said the word fornication, the Gnostics have orgies, and St. Paul said his celibacy was not for everybody. The Bible never said the evil we say it does. It puts you in hell for loving somebody physically. These are the days to spend fantasizing that this book reaches the world. I imagine all these faraway places and the change it makes to every Bible in the world. We become the Bible, but we must study the idols. They are the one trick that makes every religion seem wrong, yet the church decorates Italy with the savior. He is never happy and is never seen smiling. Italy is all about death and preserving art. It is dark spiritually and the art is in the Bible, but the Bible lies and calls Rome Babylon for many pages. This is where my three-week trip to Greece in 2001 makes sense of the God of Moses and old St. John on his death bed telling Revelations to a Greek interpreter. The volcano on Santorini blew the first two books of the Bible out of the water. The volcano on Santorini, the Atlantis Plato wrote of, caused the flood the Bible talks about and the plagues on the Nile. Moses is gone with a three-week trip and Revelations is hardly accurate.

We trust our spiritual leaders to know the Bible and they are business only. Just like the Bible hero Jacob we are busy stealing others energy and living in a world that is doomed according to our own book. The whole Christian story goes on until the end of times. This is very convenient, waiting around for Jesus to return on a white horse. In other faiths they have calendars and they do not consider other faiths bad. We could be looking at the end of an age and the rider of the white horse is Vishnu. 2012 A.D. was the end of the Mayan calendar, and we barely felt the end of the age and the end of the Baktun of the Transformation of Matter. Guadalupe shows Revelations 12 to be December 9, 1531, A.D. when the Spanish came to America. The constellations of the Tilma of Guadalupe mark that time in the heavens and tell the story of the dragons in the sky. We are so far behind in all of this, and the fault is Christianity for demonizing everything.

CHAPTER 47

LIES OF THE CHURCH

The scriptural contribution of Revelations 12 is incredible. We see where we are in the Bible and after the **Baktun of the Hidden Seed**, where Juan Diego appears is the **Nican Mopohua**. The voice of Guadalupe/Tonantzin is heard in the 218 lines of the Nican Mopohua; talking to Juan Diego, the Talking Eagle. The serpent is still Quetzalcoatl, but we are going to have a Talking Eagle for the talking serpent of Eden. Sophia to the Gnostic and Satan to the Catholic is the talking serpent. What if Juan Diego speaks in the Bible? We would hear the voice of the child in Revelations 12.

This Bible could be made in America by writing over history. We need a starting place that agrees with the pagans and polytheist. The Great Spirit and the Holy Spirit are one and the stories of the Great Spirit are better and happened on our land. What do you think they are telling lies about to keep you paying them? The church will not feed you, but they take your money. They don't seem to know all the Bible and they go against the teachings of Jesus. If we understood the laws that Jesus laid out for us the world would be a perfect place. We mix the ten commandments of Moses, and he comes back to haunt us with his God who speaks in the whirlwind like Egyptian Seth and Greek Typhoon.

This God of Moses is worried about women on their period and most of the good stuff is buried. He questions Job from the whirlwind like a beast. The church is the enemy for changing the Bible and not telling us how. The Gnostic teach you are born saved, and Jesus wakes you up. Jesus is in you at birth like Krishna in the Rig Veda.

All these sacred body parts we are missing are traded for a bunch of stories that rely on miracles to be true. Unfortunately, our Bible is far from Atlantis. I think if we give Jehovah credit for the volcano that went off in Santorini (Thira); He could be a powerful God in the pantheon. He curses the Egyptians at the bottom of the Red Sea and steals the commandments from the Book of the Dead. The "Thou shall not" is "I have not" in the negative confession to the forty-two gods in the underworld. **Nebuchadnezzar said a negative confession on his death bed**. It shows more integrity to have not done something than to do it and say sorry like a Christian. They don't fear taking Gods name in vain and they do not fear the wrath of God upon even the grandchildren.

We can't explain sex to our children, and we must lie about every god that is not Jewish. Without the gods to help us and the fertility gods, we cannot explain a love story about the first woman Inanna. Ishtar does it for money in Babylon and she is considered Inanna by the Babylonians and Sumerian King Gilgamesh is their hero. This is so awesome I wish I could be with other people that believe in the gods. What power did they feel when they all believed in Bel Marduk and space travel. Dragons are defeated and heroes are crowned king, but it is not like King David who relied on the racist miracles of Jehovah.

They will end the Gentile world rule the prophets say, and we celebrate our own demise. To be Christian in America you need to play dumb and act ignorant when it comes to many things. The Native American have a culture that was destroyed by the Catholic. We are Christian so we figure it is a sin to read the real stories of our country. Their God was not good enough for even the Mexican to worship Quetzalcoatl. I sent my book Nine Days to Healing a Spiritual Pilgrimage to Tepeyac and they ignored it. Every Mexican would know the true Guadalupe/Tonantzin if they read it, but this knowledge is stored for a wiser more intelligent generation.

People today seem less intelligent, and I am used to living in

Europe where there is great interest in my books. Americans are not curious. They know what they need to know, and they just get by. Their whole country believes in a God that kills masturbators but other than that you are doing fine. They force us to worship the hateful God of Revelations that throws Jezebel into a bed with her lovers. Virgins and whoremongers get their rewards. The virgin gets no sex and the whoremonger makes beautiful love to photo models and goes to heaven early.

Americans can't fit into the New Jerusalem, but we count on this divine city to set us up for eternal church. What if hell was a place they had beer, marijuana, and prostitutes. Rivers of beer and women in the beer, no seventy-two wives just orgy with the Gnostic Jesus, no more marriage…ejaculate as much as you want. Fornication goes away with adultery and marriage. These are the things that we have learned. We are all waiting to have sex until marriage to please God, but the Bible never said these things. We must remember the church lied to us not God.

CHAPTER 48

RETURN TO THE GODS

Our bodies don't lie to us when they crave sex. Are we to believe the Egyptian Procreation Only Theory? After you are married, you are only supposed to have sex to make babies. All else is lie and sin working together to enslave the ignorant. In America it is hard to have a conversation about this because they are so ignorant of the Bible. Many don't know America is a Christian country. We do not study or pray yet we love secondhand information. The lies they told us in church we believed when we were young. Every week a new story and more breaking us down to brainwash.

The word Babylon triggers different reactions. We are programed to think everybody the Jews meet is evil. They worship a false god. If we studied these cultures and talked about them, we would learn the story of the gods. To not know this and just live the ignorant Christian way is a waste. We can all know the true story and figure out if Jesus even existed. They are all questionable and we choose to worship this nasty horrible God of Abraham, Isaac, and Jacob. Jacob is a thief and a liar, and he wrestles with the angel for the name Israel. Names to the polytheistic Indian had great meaning. Their gods are on the pagan list of the Roman Catholic Church who recognizes the patriarchs as the first monotheists even though the first monotheist was a Sumerian. We lie about Gilgamesh and Sumerians to keep the Christian religion true. There can't be more than one God, or we are worshiping pagan gods and the planets.

Jacob means heel catcher or deceiver and he deceived his red hairy twin brother Esau and stole his birthright. What heel catcher brings up is Orion and Scorpio. The home of the Gods was stung and deceived. It did something with astrology we don't know about. Heel catcher, deceiver, and liar get the name Israel, or he who fights with God. Jacob is the most popular male name in America, and I have sweet and delicious Jacob Mango poetry books for sale. To look at the Patriarchs as real people and then worship them makes us evil. The whole Christian religion is so weak. They are not under any law, and they are ignorant of the four words for love in the Greek. God is love but they don't interpret love killed the Egyptians or the Philistines. Death was good and there is the Death Angel to go to the homes of the Egyptians. The Bible is so racist only one race is chosen, and their man Jesus is the stone that became bigger than the world.

Since Christianity is a cult in America they can make up and say anything they want. It is all based on faith, so they get you to believe and then tell you what to do. They tell you that you are not under the law and then they start to judge you. Not just anybody can understand the Bible, but anybody can memorize a few stories and start a church. It is so obvious the church is based on lies and false history, but we hold onto the racist father of Jesus.

All the cultures and gods that closed to us I have seen in Italy and Greece. The gods don't die, people just don't study their stories. We think we will avoid hell by believing in Jesus so there is no reason to study. Christianity makes us ignorant and lazy since we never study the other side of the Bible to see what the gods are doing.

In America we don't feel strange about the gods of the Native American. Moses calls it an idol and we obey even though the New Testament frees us. This is so suspicious how we side with Jesus and Mary after seeing what happened. The god of the wind is a personification of an element. In Nine Days to Healing I describe the Aztec gods and their calendars. It all fits in with Revelations 12 and the Stars of the Tilma of Guadalupe/Tonantzin/Maria Lucia.

With this knowledge we have only the remaining ten chapters of

Revelations left, and I think it ended in 2012 A.D. The significant end of the whole Mayan calendar was not celebrated but Chicken Little made a lot of money setting dates for the end of the world. This stuff is either true or false and in America we believe a big lie about Jesus that leads to several little lies. We don't even look at the Indian for guidance since the whole world is bad thanks to our white Adam and his slave Eve. Everybody is a masturbator or lusts, and we call them pagans. Every culture that expresses physical love is sinful and false and Satanic. We put the word Satan on everybody but Jesus. That is why if you don't worship Jesus and give money to the church you are a Satanist.

Satan means "Adversary" and we each have one. **The talking serpent is the penis and Osiris is the Dragon of the Nile.** Santorini cursed it and Moses took credit for it and said the volcano was his God. All lies and nobody really does anything but receive racist miracles. The reason we are not more fucked up from following Abraham, Isaac, and Jacob is we don't read, and we listen to liars. They don't know better. They figure we should not have sex until we are married and the whole world changed. Christianity went all over the world and brought this poison that stops us from loving each other. I love Jesus, my mom, and pizza…the word love in English is like using the word "'like." Eros is the oldest God and Osiris is older than the Bible let alone the New Testament.

These areas of history that are blacked out by the church remain a mystery. I love to trace the progress of God from Phoenician to Roman. We had a good God and we changed him to fit human psychology. To believe in hell is to believe in the church. Hell was used on the three Hebrew children, and they did not bow. We bow to the church and never question what they do with their powerful white God. This book opens our eyes to the errors of the Bible, and we can see why it is bad to ascribe all this evil to God. Remember you don't like sex, so you bring God into it. Now the women in church are ruined, they are brainwashed. Now they feel guilty for having sex and it creates confusion. We must ask why our bodies are telling us lies. We want sex but we can't have it. What would it be like if we abandoned the evil sex teachings of the Roman Catholic Church or never had them in the first place?

Jesus has been in my fifty-four years a lot of brainwashing. Everything they say would work even if there was no God. I am asking us to take the name "God" from every religion and piece it together. What I am really after is a sexual revival and return to the gods. We must stop teaching these huge pieces of history are false when they threaten Christianity. The Bible has enough crap in it to stop up all the toilets from here to Africa. We have believed and lived so many lies in the name of Jesus and we can't even keep track of history.

People with stunted growth in America walking around with their ten commandments. We don't even know what a Nephilim is or why Enoch got 365,000 eyes when he saw God. Space travel is too hard to see, and we blacken out all the planets in the name of Jesus even though 2,000 years ago he said he was the Bright Morning Star (Venus). We have no Bible astrology for the twelve disciples and the stars and constellations talk to us every day, but we are busy with our New Testament hybrids and plagiarisms we call the only word of God or Jesus.

This ignorance of the gods and their legends leaves us with the history to study. Would you not like to know what a people was all about based on their gods. Every country had them and the cross is on the world. We all believe in one of the three monotheistic Gods. Moses is the only thing we can agree on, but Christians call Jews Satanists because they don't believe. They called the Gnostics Satanists, and they are the original followers of the Way. So, Jesus has the power to make every God, people, and religion Satanism. The Christians are not accurate with this, but the people are ignorant, so they get away with it. They can point a gun at any god but Christ and make them into a devil.

Since the Greek and Roman Gods are sexual, we understand why the church hides sex and the origins of Christ. You believe every religion is Satanic except for Christianity. This gives the Vatican great power over the world. Revelations describes Italy but calls her Babylon. This is the lie that is hard to believe we have not discovered Italy in the Bible. We figure they are talking about Iraq. If we miss the teachings of this book, we will not get another opportunity to learn the true story of Onan and be free from the Bible.

This wicked maze, the Bible, made me smart by exercising my brain to keep track of so many characters. To study one book is to study them all. Reference from one point to another and then keep track of it. We need books about the Bible to understand the Bible. Comparing Old Testament parallels to Baal we see the first cave walls that produced what is now God should be included in the Bible. Moses did not go there so none of the three monotheistic religions can believe.

Historians and scientist can stand up to the church with this book. They have the guilty face of Jesus looking at us like it was our fault he had to go to the cross. But this is the only God we know, Jesus. God is a devil without Jesus all our faith is based on one man. If the Maya have prayers to God, why do they have to say Jesus. Quetzalcoatl is the Jesus of the West, but we do not recognize him even on the centavo. This is the darkening of the whole American continent with the lie Jesus is God.

If Jesus is God, why does he imitate the teachings and miracles of Horus? Why would he deceive or make a man, Jacob, into a nation, Israel? There are patterns to the lies in the Bible and I can feel the guilt of Judah in the voice of David. They do bad things and in false humility confess their sins. These stories are all happening before the church. They tell us the Old Testament is our history. Every God is false of every country but Jesus.

This narrow view on our history has changed us. Had we forked Gnostic we would have all the information in the world but since we chose the narrow path, we have Gods turned into fallen angels and a male Trinity. To say anybody but men wrote the Bible is wrong. We worship a lesser God so we can keep our lies. We have modified God so many times and now we practically say Jesus wrote the Bible.

CHAPTER 49

THE GOD IN THE WHIRLWIND

All the guilt and frustration we feel trying to honor the wishes of God from the edited Bible is bad. We give money to the church, that is in there. We get a basic love story that does not work until we understand it. I never hear the teachings of Jesus used on television to solve a problem. This is because we don't know it. The peace and new age that this book can provide solves issues using the true teaching of Jesus. The miracles are what mess us up because history has not provided us with these kinds of religious miracles.

The war showed that the promises in the Old Testament are not valid. We still follow but we are in the greatest age of darkness spiritually. We don't have the language, gods, saints, or even a Phoenician alphabet to tell the story of the Father going to the cross or Tau. Saints are connected to miracles, and they go with a city like an Egyptian God. Saying everything is taboo or bad or sinful is just laziness. We should read about Rome, Greece, Persia, and Babylon. The Tree of Life is Nebuchadnezzar and Daniel who was given the name Belteshazzar like Bel or Baal. The whole message of the King putting the three children into the fire furnace is hell. A Son of God appeared in the fire.

Sons of God including Satan (in the book of Job) approach his throne. Why are there more than one Sons of God? I thought Jesus was the only begotten Son of God. If there are more, we turn back to the Gods and find the true story and where the Bible copied all its stories.

Choose between monotheism and polytheism and think of where it is going to get us. In monotheism we have three groups with the ten commandments. They are not agreeing with each other on much. The Muslims says Jesus was a prophet. What if he was not God? A good man but not powerful enough to be God. Jesus the magician is pen on paper and maybe it is not true. Hindu Gods do these things all the time but that does not make them God.

The boom was lowered on us a long time ago and we as a people have not escaped the curse. With the curse everything goes bad, and the enemies of Israel are always a type of idol worshiper with the true stories Jehovah borrowed from. We see a book can be more powerful than an idol. Nobody can understand the Bible, but they hear a couple of good stories and think they know it all. It comes down to psychology. They tell you what you want to hear and ask for your money. It is all business, and they are never going to feed you like the Bible says. They don't respect the Bible or study it very much. Now we have a chance to escape the brutal lies we have been believing for 2.000 years.

We say sex is a sin, but I see people do horrible things and say they are good since they are virgins. They lie and steal all the time but making love to a stranger is a big sin. We know it is a sin and brag about how many we have. My friends lie all the time about the women they have been with. We are never going to get together without money since that is the only way to communicate. Not compliments only, to get someone in bed, it is not enough. If somebody compliments you compliment them back. It is not the same as money.

In a brothel you choose, for money, who you want to have sex with. It is romantic, out of 30 women I chose the one I liked, she also says yes to me. "I must not be too ugly"' says a man rejected by countless women. Wasted money at the restaurant for a chance at sex? Go pick somebody good and taste the fountain of youth.

If prostitution was legal in all of America, I would stay young. Matching the energy of a hooker keeps me young and works muscles I did not know I had. Getting it when I want, and as many times as money will allow. Many women in a row keep by abbs ripped yet I see all these women at the gym working on a machine. The muscles that sex works and the love energy it creates makes people feel they are in love sometimes. This charge of physical love is hard to come by, yet we have variety as the spice of life.

Condoms are provided by the hooker since she has the money to buy them. Since it is about business, jealousy disappears. When you get your new lover, you release the old one and it only lasts for the time you pay. If you want more pay more or do your wild fantasy with a discreet businesswoman who has sex with you.

Families without planned parenthood take over America. They must be supported and since they can't be whores, they work the system. The money could be spent differently and getting them invested gives them more to lose. Every sexual act, including solo sex, has a dark cloud of Seth over it. If my book is not read, we are in sexual trouble. Think of all the beautiful people that you would have made love to. They wanted you but they did not tell you. There is no communication. What would happen if I walked up to a woman and said: "I want to have sex with you." Or "I want to fuck you?" That would be offensive because she thinks that I think that she is a slut. This works better on the more beautiful ones who are sure of themselves. Ugly women get more men since everybody's self-esteem is so low. If 200 hookers loved, you how would you feel about yourself? If you sit for years without sex and get old, ugly, and frustrated you are better off getting hookers. If you are ugly or even if you have a bad personality; it does not matter. The Proverbs says, "The prostitute reduces you to a loaf of bread." And this is okay with me since it is just business. After I feel her and want her again but there are others.

A proposition to a woman can be an insult and a compliment. They may worry they sent out a slutty signal that they probably did not. Many claim getting laid is just a numbers game. In the 90s I propositioned women in the gym and the beach....it worked. Now at my age I would not dream of doing that even at the gym I am afraid to say "Hello" or even smile at most of the women. America took away the money and the free will and they stopped the party. They travel to the ends of the Earth to make people believe in Noah's Ark. A false history taken all over the world to stop people from having sex.

Your sex life and mine is ruined already unless we had been with one American goddess after another. Honor Ishtar for a change and check your Virgin with Jehovah the national God of Israel. The church says this is your Father not Baal. This confuses the alphabet of Jezebel, the Great Harlot of Revelations, the Phoenician Queen of Israel. We think a Queen had sex for money, so she deserves to die. Elijah is practically invented to kill her.

On the side of Phoenician Jezebel is the boat that saved history. The only culture to not frown on prostitution is later remembered by the Phoenician Queen turned into dung. This is where Venus is and every woman. John the Baptist is not Elijah according to him but according to Jesus he is. The head of John the Baptist on a platter to atone for the sins of Jehu and his men.

Jehu kills the ministers of Baal and superhuman Elijah comes down with a whirlwind and chariot. Seth and Apollo are forgotten, and we worship the Egyptian Satan. Look in the Book of Job for who talks from the whirlwind. We have a broken piece of the puzzle. We eliminated books, idols, art, statutes, countries, cultures all for the Lord Jesus Christ. Baal resurrects in the whirlwind and causes it to rain. Mot the moon is his brother and God of infertility. They connect all religions like Bel Marduk in Babylon. This connects to aliens and planets that the gods when they were with us provided us with much knowledge and wisdom.

The Christians only read certain parts of the Bible. I have never heard Solomon quoted in church. They hide from the link to esoteric secrets and the Song of Songs. A new Adam and Eve could be Solomon and Sheba. White and black like a Yin Yang, and sweet wine of sex and love in what the Christians could call God's voice. The Native American and the Greek could be blessed, but we do not even tolerate a kiss from the serpent Sophia. We should go back to the works that are closer to Jesus' time instead of the most recent.

It was a lie a long time ago and not many Americans are going to know who Constantine is or what he did to us. Once they streamlined Jesus and Moses, they took the ten commandments and the cross to the world. They taught us God killed Onan for masturbating and premarital sex is a sin. If you really think pre-marital sex is a sin stop watching television. Can you conceive that we all believe the God of the Bible is against sex? If we did not tell this, lie in God's name we would not have 2,000 years of punishment stored up for our grandchildren.

We have many times in history where a ruler told his people a lie and disaster came out of it. In God's name or the Aztec Sun God wants human hearts. The teaching and the action are two different punishments. The teaching goes on to all the generations that believe the lie and get punished. The action is a one-time thing where people suffered. If we don't take God's name in vain, we don't get punished. If America was given a test on whether pre-marital sex is a sin in the Bible most people would say yes. This fake religion makes you live like a judgmental hypocrite all your life and then you die in sin. Not knowing if God forgave you for having premarital sex.

This is a horrible thing that no matter what church you walk into they are against sex when the original Christians had an orgy. We are so far from the real teachings of Jesus yet Gnostic books are available. This horrible guilt and shame we put upon sex makes men lie to women and women get hurt and quit having sex. If he gave her money, there would be no need to lie about tomorrow and a possible future. A man has two heads, and one is his penis. The woman can control a man through his ego and can avoid the lies of the penis. The penis says things to me like, "I want her! Get her, I don't care what it takes." Next thing I know I am searching for a woman that wants to go to dinner instead of doing eight hookers in row for the same price.

Berlin, Milan, Barcelona, Lisbon, London, Brussels, Antwerp, Amsterdam, Rome, Naples, Lecce, Seville, Paris, Nice, Monte Carlo…. and many more …are the cities where I have known beautiful women. After these trips returning to America was so hard for me. I like being a slut better than some woman's property. I take my vision for the American male who needs to make up for lost time. We have a lot of growing up to do and Christianity needs to be muffled. No more teachings on sex, adultery, fornication, and onanism…get rid of Noah for God's sake…Zuisudra is the real name; and the Babylonians call him Unatapshin. America could use these teachings since it has been 2,000 years of ignorant Christianity.

CHAPTER 50

THE BIBLE IS JESUS

A ll this brainwashing and stimulus is religious psychology. We have a story of Jesus which takes up the whole Bible. Everything outside the Bible is considered false by the church. What they are doing to us by taking away our history and identity is hard to explain to the space alien. I would have to tell him we believe pre-marital sex is a sin in the Bible, but we do it anyway. We keep spreading these lies and guilt to reach the whole world with Jesus. The only acceptable book about him is the Bible.

How could all these other teachings be false? Especially the ones that came earlier than Constantine. We could have investigated every teaching in the world on Jesus and made our own Bible. As it is we need to do more than just believe. Study is a word that I find hard to apply to the people I have known when we talk about the Bible. They know a story or two, but they are not familiar with my stories from the Old Testament.

We cannot blame those above us if they are ignorant to. We need to fork back to Gnostic and follow the roots of it to Alchemy. If we are free from the Bible, we can erect temples to the gods including the Native American. We demonize these cultures in ignorance and the church plays the devil card to keep us ignorant and obedient. A return to what was once true for the whole world is good for us. It is not evil we are just too lazy to study it.

Do we think the Maya are wrong about their religion and sciences?

Baal could be Chac or Tlaloc at Teotihuacan for the Aztec and the Feathered Serpent. They all connect, and the Christian has the three wise men for the belt of Orion. We need to be above the Bible and understand books like Job. Job has the constellations, and he has seven daughters. He is a man from the East, and he says, **"I know my Redeemer lives."**

Symbolism connects all cultures, and the symbols seem to have the same meaning. If we drop the race card against Ham and study his religion; books will be read everywhere, and we can finally know for sure what is true about Ham and Jesus. The magic of Africa is put in Benjamin's silver cup, and he somehow disconnects the moon. If we had the **Popul Vuh** of the Maya to read, we find the Sun and Moon are the hero twins. They pass all the test in Xibalba. With the belief in the Popul Vuh we look up at the Moon-Hunaphu and the Sun-Xbalanche and find another story written in the stars. The Popul Vuh is a good replacement for the Bible. It is on our ground and the Sun and Moon can change names and stories in every mythology. Baal and Mot are a good one, they battle, and Mot is the God of Infertility and Baal makes in rain. They fight and have a story that can be seen in the stars.

Do we really believe all these pagans and polytheists are wrong and their books are lies? This is what the church has been telling us and we listen like children to the God who hates us for sex. This cruel invention of man that is based on copies of what he would later call the devil. I mean Jesus Christ…Peter the first Pope is on the cross of Satan…what more can I say. The signals are there but these dark riddles of hell and salvation have always been there. The book of Daniel is what Revelations is copied from. The model of the furnace is hell, but the Bible does not say Ishtar. The sexy whore of Babylon is connected to space travel. The Gods have information we need to know about.

We cannot go on with the monotheistic way unless we combine the three. They all hate women and have a male Trinity; but we do not need to worship the Roman Catholic Church anymore. With this book there is a way out for you and me to reunite sexually with God and each other. This seems to be the only moral we have in America. Sex is used to sell merchandise and products and we all fantasize about being with the beautiful women on television. With prostitution one can find their perfect match sexually and then take it from there.

Have you seen a person you wanted to have sex with but could not figure out how to approach them? In a brothel the tables are turned, and the women go after the men. If this were reversed and women could go where they have hot men ready for sex, they could celebrate with their friends and get laid by someone good. The idea of we permit sex only if it is free is so stupid. All the lost money and opportunities to have sex we miss in our lifetime. Maybe some would have bought a house with **the gift God gave them.**

Other countries have no problems and I have seen it everywhere. We lack in adult fun in America and the people are so superficial. It would be good for us to exchange love and what if a slut does more than a prostitute? Are we going to take away her free will and put her in jail? The person that says sex is a sin, but I do it anyway, and don't fear hell, is going to judge me for paying? If sex is only for making babies tell couples in love to get rid of the joy of sex. These people have not helped the world or offered much, and we study their fake history. Don't you want to be free and see what love would be like in the world if we **Exodus Rome.**

To read the Bible and study the Bible is two different things. To keep track of names I use a pen and paper since the stories are long and detailed. I would love to be free from this God that puts all this pressure on us in this life to avoid hell. We wonder everyday what will happen when we die, and most Americans think they are going to heaven. The idea of a single soul entering the fire of hell for eternity is so cruel. He did not believe in Jesus and keep the law. Now he is gone in the flames forever. It is better to never be born and **we should stop having children if it is true.**

The punishments and lies that rulers make up to keep you in line are believed to be fact. With symbolism and some story telling we can make the Bible say anything, but we do not look very deep. The Bible is much too long for an American to understand but they think they know it all. Some of us go to heaven and some go to hell. We walk around not worried at all about this. When someone dies do we worry that they have gone to hell. The Christian religion is so obviously made up. They scare you with hell and then invent Jesus again with all the scriptural emphasis on the cross. All four gospels have the same ending and most of the Catholic art I saw in Italy was the crucifixion.

They don't even want us to interpret the story to receive healing. They scare us with hell and then we imagine heaven to be eternal church. If we studied the Osirian religion and the Book of the Dead, we would see the Bible unraveling us. The divinity we had from birth is stripped from us. We are no good sinners, and we are corruptible. This is how people act and we blame Eve, a woman, for sin. The negative confession of the Egyptian and Nebuchadnezzar shows integrity. When we die, we think it is how they say it in church. We go to the clouds and play harps with the angels.

The art of the Catholic Church has blinded us to the true meanings behind the scriptures. Something temporary became something eternal. If the artist conveys a message, it is not noticed by everybody. The last supper has many tricks to it and messages in Italy. Seeing John next to Jesus makes me proud to be Gnostic. I don't have to listen to St. Peter he is getting secondhand information anyway. They had to disconnect us from God so they could charge us for the attachment. We are sinners and the myth becomes history. I feel sorry for people that believe in Adam and Eve. The story doesn't get any better and we read about the wickedness before the flood.

As a god or a goddess, we stand tall, have beautiful bodies, and we are slave to nobody. Even if an American has never been to church it will still affect them. The woman you want has been to church and has given up pre-marital sex. This will frustrate you and the lie of St. Peter's upside-down cross is not even questioned. He understood the opposite of what Jesus taught and became the first Pope. I understand Mary Magdalene was the wife of Jesus and they had a son. The church would have to give the ministry to Jesus' wife after his death. To get rid of Mary Magdalene they turned her into a whore. Yet people that believe she is a whore believe in putting prostitutes in prison. How would Jesus, who hung out with prostitutes, feel about his wife being in jail for taking money?

We got rid of the whore and got the cross of Satan to start our uptight, ignorant, judgmental religion. What would it be like if we did not call everybody Satan for two thousand years? Here is another one that gets me. The phrase Born Again Christian comes from the book of John and Jesus uses a double word in the Greek that can mean Born Again or Born from Above. Since he uses the same word twice, we interpret what he said to Nicodemus: You don't enter your mother again you are Born from Above. My brother learned this in Bible school, and you don't enter your mother again like Nicodemus. You are born from above and I am a Born from Above Christian.

The Christians applied the misunderstanding of Nicodemus to their own name. They are supposedly taught by the Holy Spirit who is also God, and they make mistakes in his name and cripple us. We are slaves to the old ways and do not look for anything new. I notice religions are mysterious and often must make up stories. The Bible is bad, but we don't know it is bad since we are brainwashed. Anybody can read the Bible and start a church. It is not too hard and with many resources anybody can make a sermon.

Talk good about Jesus and tell the congregation that he loves them. The money is in the bowl and business as usual. They contradict logic, themselves, and the Bible and the message of money is always clear. To have no choice but the church is sad because I desire closeness with God. I cannot sit in many churches and listen to them lie. With this book we have an opportunity to establish a relationship with God in our own land and stop telling lies about history and the Native Americans.

The resources that we forfeit for Jesus' religion is incredible. All these advanced societies had pantheons of gods. We have angels and saints that are emasculated like an American. We miss out on life, but we don't know it. We think things must be a certain way. Jesus is a parody of Sun God worship, but we don't worship the sun. We only worship Jesus one way and we use only one book: the Bible.

CHAPTER 51

THE WATCHERS ARE WATCHING

S ex is a simple thing to me, and I imagine being in heaven with the Watchers. We look down on earthlings having sex. When I was with the Budapest woman in Barcelona I looked into her eyes while I made love to her, and the bed lifted to heaven; I saw the peripherals of heaven and the gods sitting on couches watching us. If I stopped looking at her face the bed would have come down. I could not see above me, but I saw the sides. This experience with the most beautiful and perfect woman I have ever seen. She is the best memory I have. I see her like light around me, years later, and I try and remember her beautiful face. She reminds me experience is important to me and now I know what it is like to be with the goddess, Ishtar.

Babylon has the only Venus that took money for sex. Inanna (Sumerian) was free, and Ishtar (Babylon) got money for her virginity on an altar that lays you out on the universe. A buff, handsome friend of Nebuchadnezzar wears stag horns while he has sex with you, and you are given a purse of money. The man illuminates the forty-two gods and goddess in the body: eyes like Hathor above Nut. Your eyes are like the sun above the water. This incredible experience we miss out on since every god to ever walk the earth is a joke to us except for Jesus.

With Jesus I am amazed at how small the gospels are, yet nobody quotes anything from the gospels because they have never learned the stories. We cannot heal each other or help each other, and I never hear Jesus quoted in context to make his teachings understandable. "When you are praying at the altar and remember you have offended your brother, leave your gift at the altar and go to him." This teaches a lesson in priorities. Your brother is more important and comes first. The altar is to remember God and your brother. "As you have done to the least of these you have done unto me." Jesus spoke about judgement day, and we never quote it. If I ask an American what is Jesus going to say to you on judgement day, what are the chances he will say, "The least of these." Loving your enemy can make them your friend. First God than people are the cross. "Love God with your heart mind and soul and love your neighbor as yourself." This sums up all the Torah and Prophets.

If we understood the stories and their esoteric meanings, we could easily link religions through symbolism. What have we been missing out on with the gods? Why don't we fear they will come back instead of Jesus? We call them all devils even though we are completely ignorant of everything but Christianity. The brainwashing has made us racist, and we find only one sad executable image of Jesus. Not so much healing and the miracles but the cross; this is the image we know as God. When the Catholic Church puts the old man in the clouds above the crucifixion, we could photograph their artwork and have a picture of God. This shows how mentally impoverished we are thinking these are the only forms God takes.

It seems when we hear the part about all other religions being wrong, we would smell a rat. They make the only way and ask for a tithe. This looks like a business invented out of thin air. We don't require proof since we have faith. Faith that the altered Bible is true is not enough. We have had so many signs to get off this old ride. They are going to guilt you and sell you forgiveness. Then you start talking to Jesus who was already inside of you. The stealing of our superpowers and the killing of physical love.

The 3,000-year-old Bible fits in the Mayan calendar. We are missing 800 years, the Baktun of Star Planting and Baktun of the Pyramid. The Bible leaves these things out but why did Jesus not know about them. He looks very human, and I don't think doing miracles that nobody saw makes you God. Jesus did not give us numbers like Pacal Votan did (13,55,66) or refer to something that a man would not have known. Like other parts of the world and his evaluation of what would become the Old Testament. He seems to know nothing outside of a small circle.

History does not support Jesus if nobody heard of him, and the story is only true in its origins with the Sun. Ra the Egyptian is the Sun in the Book of the Dead and Xbalanche is the Sun in the Popul Vuh. All the good stories would be the sun and moon and they connect. When Jesus was the Solar Gnostic God, we could all relate to him. Once Jesus was attached to Moses and Noah the racism begins. Doesn't it sound better that all of humanity worships the Sun as a common ancestor than a story that claims we are all Jewish?

The Sun pulls the tiki off the island and gives it books. How could they all be bad? The gross sacrifices are in the Bible and even God gets involved. First animals and then a human who would be worshiped as God. Since this is all we know it sounds good to us. If we knew the creation stories of all countries, we would not get on Noah's ark or partake in Ham's slavery. Jesus is attached to these evil books that think people are considered good by faith and not works. Therefore, Christian's sin against one another and say sorry to God. If we thought, we would be judged by our works people would stop sinning.

Sexual sin, even the thought of it is something we believe Jesus introduced. The word fornication is not even in the Torah, but we are fucked in 2023A.D. believing it is one of the ten commandments. If is funny to think the ancients had more freedom than us and we do not fear the lie since we do not understand the damage it has caused. A religion based on control wants your money. In America it is all but forced on you. Tell a child he will go to hell if he does not worship Jesus. This is the weak God we worship, the old man in the clouds and his son on a stick.

The people can't place history together, but they believe the Old

Testament is for all of us. I don't like how monotheism has played a role in my life. Everyone in America is an expert in their own minds but they are not a wise people. They cannot help me with my problems and the people live a sexual death to please the jealous God they call Christ. Thomas the twin of Jesus is probably what the resurrection was all about. They saw his twin and thought it was him. We take this bundle of racist lies and call it the word of God.

The lazy people are gold to the church. The hypocrites can tell the story of Jesus, but they do not interpret his teachings. It is not even modern and much of it does not make sense. One book changes the world and makes the gods evil. We are so sure of Jesus and his idol that we cast away the wisdom of the ancients and put another soldier in Satan's army. The rapture is going to levitate us to the sky to meet Jesus. This could be interpreted many ways, but the Bible doesn't talk much about the afterlife. We know heaven, hell, and purgatory.

The book burning to the Bible cancels out ancient wisdom and keeps us in the dark. We can't answer hard questions and it turns into a joke. We say God is responsible for racists murders and lies while the devil or the serpent tempts Eve with an apple from the forbidden tree. The devil and God or Jesus don't work well together in Christianity. Therefore, the church doesn't teach the book of Job. It has other names for God and Sons of Gods coming before the throne with Satan with them. In the Testament of Job, Satan has dialogue with Job and disguises himself as a beggar and goes to Job's house with four doors. You hear the devil talk and see what he does but in Christianity we are a clogged toilet waiting for Michael the Arch Angel to kill the devil.

The devil is sort of killed at the end of the world to keep the whole lie afloat. They are charging for merchandise you get after you are dead. Only then will we know if it is true. The church tells us the most obvious lies and we don't get them. The American government cannot help you since they believe the lies to. We go on and on with Christianity cursing our own gardens of sex and the world will not see the Gnostic Orgy of Jesus.

To see the transformation of the world, that the trio explained is better than ignorance. If God freed us to have pre-marital sex it would be a celebration or an orgy. The fact Gnostics had orgies and we practice and teach to our children the lie that pre-marital sex is a sin shows the difference. The real Jesus caused an orgy what did America produce? We say the wife of Christ is a whore and put her in jail for sex for money. Now the rapist is free and can't spend his money on a whore. He rapes you the victim for free and saves his money for Amsterdam and Rio. America controls us and our bodies and they are Nazi Christians fucking up our lives.

To see the sexual revival and the restoration of God to books besides the Holy Bible is my goal. I want the whole world to read this book, and even though we are having pre-marital sex all over the world, we think it is a sin according to the altered Bible. Even St. Paul frees us to have sex and go to the house of the idol, Baal. Everybody is having an orgy except for these fuckers in the Bible. They are like Satan to me and if I must see them in heaven maybe I will go for Nirvana instead. Paul says, "We all know an idol is nothing." This is our excuse to condemn ancient polytheistic religions which all connect. They have so much in common they have to be true, and we are brainwashed to think they are bad.

CHAPTER 52

A PILGRIMAGE OF PEACE

We go on in life waiting for things to happen to us or people to decide for us. We are hypocritical about sex and the Bible but that does not free us either way. If the church is right, we go to hell and if I am right, we go to heaven on earth. If we are wasting away horny and frustrated it is because we took the church too seriously. They just want to control you and sex is the main tradition. They want to build their empire and enslave their people. We are always guilty of lust, so we repent. The body goes one way and the mind another. Listen to your body and what it wants. Is that all false or made up? God made us horny and there is nothing wrong with sex. The fact we don't love each other in this lifetime is a tragedy. Imagine America celebrating sex and not just Hollywood. We would not be afraid of the phallus, and we would read all Bibles to see what really happened. How much is true and how much a lie? They have scrambled us sexually and we go from the orgy to masturbation being a sin.

These things hold us down and make my life crappy in America. The women are entitled and don't really care about the men. They get free food and put out when they want to. It is a very mechanical experience. Traveling showed me all kinds of women from around the world. I solved curiosities and lived a heaven on earth; but now I know stuff. We are so backwards and as we aged people believe God said it is a sin to have pre-marital sex. This stops the orgy and starts the dominion of Satan.

Not having a free will when it comes to your body, mind, and money doesn't bother America. The reason is because we are Christian and ignorant of the Bible and history. So much time has passed we have accumulated a great amount of information. Now we should look at the books they took out of the Bible. Why did they choose them and how are we supposed to know who Enoch is?

These Old Testament characters keep growing and the disciples of the New Testament are hard to keep track of. The number twelve for the tribes of Israel and the disciples stops its numeric symbolism at the months of the year. They don't want us to read the zodiac or find our way back to the stars.

Put a circle around the cross and Dionysius returns to his throne. Baal has sex with the seven stars all called his wives while Anat is his consort like Osiris and Isis. All the fertility gods united, and we start building temples and statues with the help of the Mason and Grand Master Architect. Look at Park Guell in Barcelona! Copy it and we learn Alchemy from a park that is also Catholic with a Masonic Cross on the Closed Chapel. Secret language for everything and a learning lesson for the American's who are against the gods because they associate them with art and idols.

Antonio Gaudi's influence and art followed me on my five-month visit to Barcelona. On La Ramblas, the biggest metropolitan street in Europe, I would see streetlamps with Gaudi's dragons on it. I imagine Antonio Gaudi and Eusebi Guell dressed in black tuxedo's holding champagne glasses. A toast to the Grand Master Architect and the Mushroom Pavilion, everywhere I walk in Park Guell I find masonic symbols and alchemy. This park takes eight hours to walk through, and it is wise to get a tour book.

Delphi, Greece went down in a tidal wave 1500 B.C. and Park Guell came up to shower us in symbolism. Atlantis (Thira) or Santorini also went down in 1500 B.C., but Apollo is present in Greece and in Spain. Apollo went into Delphi in the form of a dolphin and killed the Serpent Python and replaced him as the protector of the waters. At the Cosmic Temple to the Sun and Moon in Park Guell there is the Tripod with the Philosophers Stone in it. The first of the four platforms have the horned bronzed serpent and on the second is **Gaudi** as a **Salamander** which replaces the dolphin at Delphi.

This park transformed me into a Catholic, Mason, Alchemist.... and my brain returns to Park Guell for inspiration. I did a tattoo on my right tricep of Esuebi Guell to remember the park. He has a seven-prong crown and a black tuxedo; he is carrying a bag of mushrooms. The lessons I learned at Park Guell are many. The house of labor is on the walls and a lazy boy gets a lesson from the Grand Master Architect. The park tells a story and seems enchanted; eighty-eight pillars serve as tubes for rain that is stored in the belly of the beast. Eighty-eight pillars are for the eighty-eight constellations and Serpens Caput is the serpentine bench held up high in the sky by the eighty-eight hallow pillars. On the serpentine bench is writing from the black Virgin Mary of Catalan: "Oh country rich in treasure, do you serve me, her eyes, her forehead, jealousy be gone."

Barcelona also has the *Sagrada Familia* church, and it has a young Jesus working with a hammer...I also tattooed this on my right forearm. I collected holy relics on my body and published poetry, fiction, and photography. These relics have important legends that should be included in the Bible. I went to the *Santa Faz* (The Veil of St. Veronica) in Alicante, Spain and I bought books about the legends. These stories inspired me and helped me create the cult and book called The Lords of the Poison (lulu.com).

Finding the deeper and oldest of the legends of Jesus put things into perspective for me. The Santa Faz did miracles, but the miracles have explanations. They drove off locust with fire and when the Santa Faz was taken out of the monastery the men worked harder. The inspiration it gave them must be incredible. Instead of the Santa Faz magically making the locust disappear it provided the inspiration. It must have been a magical march with the Santa Faz held high in procession.

We could access greater understanding of miracles and legends of Jesus by thinking outside of the box. We know only the Bible and every other sign of Jesus is Satan. We don't think of Satan and Jesus as brothers, but it makes more sense. The Christian calls everything he doesn't understand Satan. If we studied Baal, we would be better off. The ugly hatred towards the woman we have is disgusting. The people that believe in the false Jesus think he hated his own mother.

The hatred and repression of sexual expression comes from the Judeo-Christian tradition. We are too modern to hate our females, but we believe and teach that God hates them. This is where it is so obvious the Bible was written for men. The female half of us is Eve and Lilith and we consider the feminine to be bad like Jezebel. Omeotl, the God of Duality to the Aztec, is male and female. When Omeotl divides the god becomes the Lord and Lady of Our Sustenance.

This is a better way to think about male and female then the rib story of the Bible. The man is hurting his balanced half by eliminating the goddess and denying the Virgin. We all need the word Virgin in the name to know what the church represents. They are going to lie to you and tell you fornication means pre-marital sex. This along with the trio represses us. We must believe other lies to stay in line with the church doctrines and dogmas.

Look at all the world religions given to Satan by the Catholic Church. They could easily say Christ is Vishnu or Krishna. We compare his stories to Horus, but all the Sons of God went out and got crucified or boiled in oil. They have stories that are outside of the Bible, but the Bible is only a steppingstone to knowing God. We must believe the myth of Moses to get God started but America does not believe in or accept as true Baal and Anat. The gods and goddesses before Moses being Sumerians and Babylonians; all are false according to us as we follow ignorantly a code of racism.

Moses blocks history at the Nile like a Satanic chess game. The Nile is the phallus of Ra and Osiris is the dragon of the Nile. It all makes sense in the Book of the Dead and other legends. The Boat of a Million Years is headed by Thoth, then Osiris, Isis as a couple behind Thoth and Seth and Nephthys behind them. Forty-two negative confessions will get you to Osiris. The Christian will be saying sorry of his sins, but he can't escape Karma. Just like King David was forgiven for his adultery of Bathsheba and murder of her husband. His son died and he experienced untold grief. Absalom slept with David's harem on the roof of the tent. David was forgiven and punished just like the rest of us.

If the Egyptian story is true, we are in big trouble thinking Jesus has prepared the way to the sun. If he was questioned about the Egyptian religion, what would he say? Twelve dumb fishermen are his only students besides the tax collectors and prostitutes. We judge sex by what our parents taught us. Later we think our father is God and he is mad at you for masturbating. Since we miss out on the Gnostic Orgy and believe it is a sin to even touch ourselves. The Bible was changed and that does not bother you. Nobody puts it back together like me. I have studied this stuff since I was a teenager and did spiritual pilgrimages to Europe and Mexico.

CHAPTER 53

MODERN JESUS

The thing we look at now is the Book of Revelations chapter 12. This fight in the stars is between the Dragon and the Virgin with child. This is 1531 A.D. December 9, 10:20am in the morning. Guadalupe is from the 12th Baktun of the Maya, **The Baktun of the Hidden Seed**, and 2012. A.D.; is the end of the Mayan calendar, **The Baktun of the Transformation of Matter.** So, 500 years from Revelations 12 to 22; we have now need to read the stars and return to where we came from.

The idea of Aliens making us and returning to see us or supervise life on Earth makes sense. One God doing everything is a little hard to imagine and we see Jesus as the only God for 2,000 years. It is hard to imagine Jesus making us, but Quetzalcoatl made us from corn. It is hard to see in Catholic art Jesus as the Creator. He was stuck onto the Old Testament and everything else is Satan to us.

To not use masonry, alchemy, astrology, astronomy, science, and common-sense messes us up. We would refer to the Bible by memory if we really studied it in school. Nobody would use the Bible to take advantage of the young people who find Father Abraham. A red calf full of blood and Satanic rituals performed on woman is in Leviticus. They examine your privy member and see if you are acceptable. The Bible is so gross we have an Old Man in the clouds waiting for us? This is the only way to God?

The Gnostic concept is different, and Jesus was their solar deity.

The Gnostics believed all matter was evil and Jesus smiled above the cross because he was separated from matter. The Gnostic concepts all make sense. Why would somebody who claims to love Jesus not read about him outside of the Bible? Extra wisdom and more information led to this salvation through knowledge. We forfeit the wisdom for the church and their Bible still charges you 10% of your income.

We need to understand our relationship to the "Trio" and taking God's name in vain and provoking the punishment of assigning his name to lies. The children believe them, and our grandparents believed them. Masturbation makes us go blind and they grow hair on their hands. These are the kind of lies we are stuck with until the Trio goes away with ignorance and knowledge in battle. We must want to be smarter as American's when it comes to Revelations. We wait for the world to end, and it is just a war we are reading about. The many fake things of the Roman Catholic Church have blocked our history. As an American do you feel you understand Cowboys and Indians? We bring Jesus and Mary to the Indian. Jesus has the second commandment which kills the gods by turning them into fallen angels that lusted after the daughters of Cain.

The gods are in books and oral traditions. We see the god of the wind and he is an idol, but there are so many idols in the world that we do not know about or study. We risk angering the Elohim and we live in the age of God's continual punishment for taking his name in vain. All the truth that would have helped and healed us is hidden behind Jesus and the idol. We say Jesus is the only one and call a sea of gods fake and this cancels out the history and poetry of important countries.

Another option is to honor Elijah and the Talmud. If we have only the Old Testament, we are free. Once St. Paul is misunderstood, we say God preaches against sex. Just by getting rid of that teaching won't do it. There is something deeper than the God we know but we must be polytheistic to understand it. We miss all the power of the gods; and the pyramids sit there with the sinners. They are not in the Bible so we only can associate it with the Mason's Cross that has the symbol and Apollo.

We don't get the gods and they are even the days of the week. We believe in the twelve fishermen of Jesus but not Draco or Hydra. We are brainwashed by the church to believe these things. When it comes to Jesus, I must say he is never quoted by a character that knew the Bible better. We hear "Camel in the eye of the needle." And "All things are possible with love (God)." If we said to each other "Jesus said all things are possible with love." We would find the thread of the forgiveness and healing not to mention miracles.

Since we interpret miracles, that no one saw, as the proof Jesus was God, we would know him by these miracles. If Quetzalcoatl turned water to wine and walked on water, we would think he was Jesus. Time changed with both important figures. The study of Gnosis frees us from the Bible. The difference in the teaching is big. We are born with Jesus already in us or the church and its sinners' prayer. The Holy Spirit enters us, and we speak in tongues. The idea of time changing is more significant than a few symbolic miracles.

People go around with these ideas of the Roman Catholic Church. They feel guilty when they lust and have a hedge around them that stops them from having sex. The people would be free from the monstrous teachings of the church. They want to scare you, so they change the God of the Bible. At first Jesus was a man and the church touched up the story and turned the wife of Jesus, Mary Magdalene into a prostitute.

The male sided Bible and church keep us spiritually off balance. We end up with Noah, the Sodomite, and his hot son Ham. The woman is a rib and if she does not yell during a rape she is put to death. A woman was traded like a mule, and we think this male sided story brings us closer together? You cannot get closer than an orgy or a Love Feast. Now death for onanism and hell for fornication, this is the modern Jesus we believe in.

CHAPTER 54

SEX MESSIAH

The ideas of the Roman Catholic Church led us to a dead end
sexually. I do not believe they are closed minded to it. Does Mary
have to be a Virgo in Bethlehem and does Venus align the gods? The
other Mary, Magdalene, was turned to into a whore by the church.
America thinks the church has made progress, but it has gotten worse.
We think God said sex is bad and he did not. Solomon was given
riches and many wives by a Genii that was God. Today we have layer
of layer of lies of the Roman Catholic Church and their unscientific
interpretation of the Bible.

Even the Hippo, Bohemoth of Job, was edited for piety, his dick
became his little tail. Since Noah and Ham is Horus and Seth imagine
Seth butt fucking you in hell. Look over your shoulder and see his
snout. Personification of night and darkness; called Ham in the Bible,
the stories are stolen from Egypt and Babylon. Greece and Rome have
the answers. In Italy I see a statute of a god outside the church. In the
church is the only one we believe in, and his only book is the Bible.

These words are sacred and provide the only way out of culture
shaped by monotheism. We miss out on the wisdom of the Gods
(Elohim); and pyramids on either side of the world that tell a story of
man and God. We are so brainwashed, and guilt stricken we associate
symbols like a crucifix without the circle with pain and misery. I
have never seen Jesus or Mary smile in Roman Catholic artwork. The
other side of the smile is knowledge and sex. We put a circle around

the crucifix and study the Gnostic Gospels. The history of Native American comes back to us when the Holy Spirit is also known as the Great Spirit.

Polytheism pulls all these things together. We get our history back, pyramids to Quetzalcoatl, sacred calendars, and most of all every ancient culture Gods. Elohim do not have to be Jewish, but we curse ourselves until we realize Jesus called his disciples Elohim (Judges). We are the Shinning and God is the Shine.

Attach to polytheistic and pagan cultures and embrace stories older than Moses. We teach a brief history of the world with our plagiarized Bible's and the funny thing is people believe. The Bible has so many stories, but Jesus is the main message. We know him as the Lord and Savior but Baal and others, who in some images even look like Jesus, have his story and he is pieced together by pagan gods that we stopped honoring a long time ago.

We need to study the Egyptian and the forty-two gods in the body. Isis is the neck and Osiris is the phallus. We cheer the Lord of the Underworld for stopping cannibalism and Quetzalcoatl for teaching against human sacrifice, these Avatars, come into the world. Our penis is Osiris and our chest the Might One of Terror. In judgement one says a negative confession to forty-two gods lining the tunnel to the Throne of Osiris.

I trust Thoth more than I trust Moses and the bird broken by Abraham is the lifeless God of Writing and Universal Intelligence. The Ibis, sacred to Thoth, nose points to Isis and they all look at her and are in love. Only in America we don't appreciate our own Moon and Venus. Venus is the planet that lines it all up. Aphrodite to the Greek…. the goddess is in every culture! We miss out on this and take the bite of the white snake of Moses. **We thank the devil daily with our actions.** Children all over the world get Seth as a father. Midnight only and the dark story of Noah and his son Ham has cursed the world. It is a plug that stopped the sunlight which is healthy for a book we don't understand.

Now take actions to secure your own fertility. Learn the stories of the idols and we are free. No more will the Christian call us Satan like they did with the Gnostics. This is too much power for any one organization. I don't believe the average American is going to hell for sex, but they think Jesus and the Bible say it is bad. This is the block our children have with God: They get horny, and God disappears. The non-sexual Catholic artwork makes us guilty, and this is what the old men want. They want you to be like them and while this book is for America it is for the entire world. We have all drunk the sex teachings of the church and have shame for onanism.

This old thinking is at its worst ever. Television shows sex all the time but nobody is punished. If we read the edited Bible, we can come up with all kinds of stuff. They have you at Adam and Eve, that is the hook that catches the sinful fish and forgives them for breaking the ten commandments. Are we going to grow up and stop taking God's name in vain and just lie or get educated? The Gnostic Gospels are not that well known, and this shows we really don't want Jesus anyway. He stops the party and sex. If he was still the Gnostic Solar Deity, we would have sacred Gnostic artwork. Jesus would have changed the world and he still can.

The Gnostic concepts are more realistic, and they connect to other information that is forbidden fruit to the shit soiled Christian. They want Jezebel and go underage to molest children, but they don't risk whacking off. The death penalty, and we say these are the teachings of God. Man has written all the Bible copying sacred art. The stairways to heaven were many and Jacob's ladder stopped the fertility gods. The Bible is one big war against Baal or 'Lord.'

Jesus comes to take Baal's place and gets married to his miraculous virgin mother. The church is against sex, and they interpret the Bible for you. If we find the Gnostic Fork, we go back to pre-Constantine days and see what really happened. The Gnostic teach Noah's wife burned the ark down, three times. Maybe they saw slavery as bad. Now an African American trace his lineage back to Ham. The embarrassing and disgusting story of sex between a bad drunk parent and his son. Now the children come out already slaves: Egypt to Ethiopia. It is sort of hidden and why chose the name of a meat for Ham?

It sounds almost sexual, but this story is not in the **Enuma Elish.** Sumerian and Babylonian accounts don't have slavery, but they have Ishtar. It is a shame sex workers in America don't study the goddess. You get treated better. The whole Mother Earth thing does not fly with the Christian. Venus to Ishtar is sexy and might get their attention. Another bright morning star to go along with Jesus.

The white male at first thinks Christianity is to his benefit. He gets a woman for a slave and a Hamite. Later we see the Egyptians cursed us with the story of Moses. Moses is the single peg that holds the three monotheistic religions together. The law is even respected by Gnostics, and I think that is how we should be. Introduce a bigger Bible instead of one edited for piety. God was sexy at one time and the Roman Catholic Church changed that. Now God is an angry old man with no wife.

These teachings don't apply to us anymore and we need symbols and other cultures. Some of this information is new and we can update our Bible with Baal. Remember he has a pantheon, and the gods are real. We go through life Jewish instead of Phoenician and rely on the Old Testament for our history. This puts all of us at a disadvantage learning the lazy Christian values at a young age. We never would have come up with this stuff on our own. It was to be passed down like the curse.

Why do we even believe we are cursed? Ask Moses, Adam, Eve, and the Serpent (Gnostic Sophia) to bring the answer. What was "Wisdom" is now Satan and he could have been Quetzalcoatl (the Feathered Serpent). Osiris is the Dragon of the Nile and he all falls under this Sophia/Serpent dilemma. How can you fight your enemy if you don't know who they are? We accept non-Jewish wisdom to be Satanic, but the Serpent in the Garden of Eden has to do with the phallus.

All these saving powers transmitted by the pagan gods is incredible. Forty-two gods in the body and the buttocks are the guardians of the eye of Horus. Each part of us connects but we have cursed Egyptian knowledge and called polytheists pagans. It is so much healthier to be a polytheist. One man decides for you and that mentally impoverished individual worships an old man on a throne.

God goes back to Phoenician El, and we understand the history of the Bible. The Gods are silent like the Elohim. Angels and Gods go together in polytheism, and we worship the Goddess. The ancient cultures had so much in common. It is wrong to judge them. We go without this basic math that the constellations and alphabets all line up. We don't see Jesus in the stars because we only see him in the Bible.

This book may cause a revolution around the world for polytheism since monotheism has ruined so many lives in the name of Jesus. How can we escape these laws that won't go away? Jesus gave us the answers, but we worship him as an idol. We know he is white like the men in the Bible. Egypt is known as the black land, for magic. We need green Osiris and Isis to enter the divine couple before the divine God (El) like Baal and Anat.

This pantheon of Baal is not seen in the Bible but if all the Phoenician Gods were in the story of Jezebel, she would be a Goddess. How did she pray to Baal and what tablets we read with the Biblical story of Elijah? The Phoenician God El is the starting point, and they did not know what came before El, but it is older than God in the Bible.

All this butchering of the Bible to have sex bad and enslave the women has blocked us from discovering the God within. Gnosis (Knowledge) and Sophia (Wisdom) are soul mates, but we call Sophia Satan or the Serpent in the Garden of Eden. Christians in America know the miracles of Moses and Jesus but not Elijah and Elisha. The Old Testament in too complicated for the average American to wrap his head around.

CHAPTER 55

THE BIBLE AND THE BODY

T he law of our bodies we no longer need to deny. Everything we believed about the Bible is false. If the Solar Jesus was sexual, why do we judge each other? We apply a double standard to men and women if they have many lovers. The woman is kept in check with the Bible lies and she stops loving the male. I ask the American men if their sisters and mothers are worth more than farm animals? Ironically the Trinity: Father, Son, and Holy Spirit is male. If the Holy Spirit was female, it would all make sense.

The net result of treating women like property is men won't get laid. We don't have hookers; we need the food whore, and she is waiting across the dinner table wondering if the man is Mister Right. Does this seem to be what Jesus wanted when he himself hung out with hookers? We sit today with no freedom for premarital sex, masturbation, and looking. This is sad we are not up to date with the Bible and new discoveries. Denying the gods is scary to me and that is why I don't trust white, sexist, and racists books. Can we worship Jesus without the Bible, or could we put the crucifix in the middle of the Sun?

These sexual teachings of the Roman Catholic Church are old and ornery. They have gone all over the world. Jesus is associated with no sex and so is the Bible. The Bible does not say or suggest we cannot have sex. Even the church gets paid when a couple gets married. They are collecting money and giving you a license to have sex. Do we believe this from the Gospels? The Bible and the Roman Catholic Church have different views on sex. The Song of Songs celebrates the sexual love between King Solomon and Queen Sheba. God is not against sex, and he wired us to be horny.

As it sits now, we cannot have premarital sex, masturbate, and looking and lusting is also forbidden. The gods now must disappear, so we don't get their point of view on Jesus. Just to hide sex we fuck up the Bible which starts with white Noah and black Ham having sex, a father son combination. The love of Jesus and Mary Magdalene must have been incredible, but they had to sacrifice her to for the love of the demon. The monotheistic demon scared people with hell, asks for money, and tells people he loves them. All kinds of healthy behavior are stifled. We deny Zeus and Baal who are better father figures than Jesus. All of this is tied up with the Roman Catholic Church.

Sex is the one thread that if you pull on will straighten out the Bible and expose its inconsistencies. They hide our body parts and the meanings changed. Since Osiris is our phallus and Isis the neck we are circumcised and emasculated. The Dragon of the Nile and God of the Underworld is between our legs. The editing of the Bible makes it read like a children story with Noah and the animals. We are missing the countries and Ham is curious. This divine slavery makes sense when we see it from the Jewish perspective. The Christian sees it secondhand and learns to judge and fall for the clever Bible racism.

Egypt is the cradle of civilization, and the gods get going there. Anybody exposed to the story of Horus could have brought the Egyptian Jesus to us. We would expand. The Bible shrunk and they want to match the church, while we should be taught history. The Gods in the body, the Boat of a Million Years, and Thoth are important to know before we trade the sun in for a man that was called God by Constantine. The sun is a necessary symbol. Jesus is the Sun God to the Gnostics. We lose all this doctrine because of sex.

To keep the no sex lies going they hide important parts of the Bible from us. They can't change the no premarital sex. Try and explain the story of Samson or Absalom. The New Testament switch is St. Paul.

Jesus did not talk about pre martial sex, but St. Paul was a celibate Jupiter that said there are two paths. He is not even judgmental, but we use his words "fornication" to enslave countless souls.

Now we wait the end of the world for Jesus to come back and get our rewards in the afterlife. We pay the church to spiritually emasculate us. The love stops and turns into hatred, jealousy, and anger. A woman who just got laid walks the streets of North Beach with a smile on her face and a dance in her walk. If we had sex all the time, we would be happy like her. San Francisco is a very sexual city with a lot of single people living there. They are more European and open to prostitution.

We are so clogged up in America by this false doctrine of the church. We do not acknowledge the teachings of the Indians. The feathery serpent connecting heaven and Earth is Quetzalcoatl. We go to the pyramid of Jesus and Quetzalcoatl. The twin serpents connecting us to our own land. We have everything in the back yard we just must connect Jesus Christ with Topiltzin Quetzalcoatl.

The calendars and alphabets will lead us to Baal, who was worshiped by many countries. Once we connect them, we see how much more powerful history is than the Bible. The brotherhood of the gods could even include lonely celibate Jehovah. He announces the birth of a new god in Babylon; Israel and history......here we are at the ladder to heaven and no constellations. If we transform the Bible with the Book of Job and the Tilma of Guadalupe/Tonantzin we see time and she has the dragons, Draco and Hydra. See Nine Days to Healing a Spiritual Pilgrimage for more on the Stars of the Tilma.

The Gods would connect and if we want to know about the law, we read the Talmud. It says when the Messiah returns, we will eat the Leviathan (Lotan - Phoenician); and we already have with this book. The Leviathan is a sea monster with 365 eyes down its spine. Jehovah plays with Leviathan for three hours a day. The rest of the day is spent praying his mercy will overcome his wrath.

Solomon asked for wisdom to rule the kingdom and he got that and riches and women. The teachings of Melchizedek are like Job and Solomon. It is a more elevated literature that one can depend on. Melchizedek is eternal and the Gnostic believe he is Jesus. We don't know this part of the book of Genesis very well. Our Father of Monotheism is Abraham and his son Laugher tied up.

Ezekiel does a comic street theatre, and he ties himself up with a rope to imitate Laugher or Isaac. This sacrifice is complete with Christ, but it took a long time and a lot of animals to get it done. Ezekiel has the Father figure of Nebuchadnezzar and Baal. All these great kings are hidden by the prophets. Ezekiel means El or God will strengthen. He was a priest that got exiled to Babylon and he sees God on a throne with the gods underneath it. An image of Elohim under the throne or spaceship and Cyrus the Messiah (Isaiah) on the throne or in the cockpit.

All these wonders of the world are lied about in Christianity since they don't want to change their story. They don't research the Gnostic and they consider Irenaeus a God. It all goes back to him and the church making devils of the early Christians. We could be Gnostic and not have sex to get the truth back. What is more important this book getting us all laid or being restored to Gnosis and the God within? Even Jesus was thirty before he received the Holy Spirit and started doing miracles

Nothing connects to the stars but the three wise men. Eastern Job has the oldest names for Elohim; Elowah. The Leviathan and Bohemoth get transformed in Revelations. The battle Baal has with Mot (his dead brother the Moon) and Yom (The Serpent that swallows Baal). Since tablets and other writings have come up recently, we see Baal differently. The Bible leaves out Alexander the Great and other phenomenon that would challenge their lies about Jesus. With Baal we have a compassionate God that will hear our prayers. Fertility and all kinds of religious symbolism would come alive. I want to see a sexual renaissance in America. I want to be the one to free the planet from the lies about sex.

What will happen and what temples we should build? Bring back the lost Bible and make sense of it. This book frees a person sexually, but it imparts the truth as well. We will never find a book like this. We have our interest in mind and our own divinity and afterlife to look forward to. The Native American and their prophecies will come to us, but they won't be an idol this time. I have read the Bible many times and I understand how people lose track of things. After deep study I don't believe God wrote the Bible. There is nothing miraculous about it. Copied literature from the pagans we don't believe in.

The Bible is tainted with Ham. His Gods are going to be disrespected. This shows how not only is the art in Italy all white people, but the Bible is a white man's book. By calling the son of Noah Ham takes us far from Africa. Modern people living in America will want to acknowledge a better flood story. The Bible is the evilest book ever written. Its superstars are criminals, and it claims to be based on the lie of Jacob. The kings of the other countries have Gods that are covered up.

Jonah comes out of the whale to scare the king who worshiped Dagan, a merman. This is a joke that the great king was scarred by Jonah but the fish with Jonah's body halfway out is Dagan. The king thought he saw his own god and threw his crown down. Each prophet has certain gods that we fail to acknowledge. The church changed the gods into saints. This connection to the white man makes the heroes fertile with bullshit and more anti sex.

This book is our hope at a worldwide celebration of sexual freedom. Since we can't stop lusting, we can't stop sinning. This is the control the church has on us. Without the weapon of sex, we won't be sinners and can start working on other bad behavior. We worry about the tiniest things, yet sex is such a big deal to an American. You are probably Christian and do not know it, but society takes charge. Some women think of a prostitute as a poor woman. This makes it an insult to their job if you call them a whore. A man bringing you sex for money is a beautiful thing. We make it bad, but God did not.

The Freedom is to be with God even if you lust or God forbid commit adultery. This separation from God over a sin that is not a sin is what we have now. We are guilty and we do not want to offend anybody with a proposition. Prostitution is the money maker that could put the body into magic mode. Sex can earn me money and prostitution save us money.

This book covers the pagan elements of the Bible and gives us a background to understand what is really happening in all these stories. As the planets revolve Jesus went around with his disciples. We could connect all these ancient books and beliefs. Now let's look forward to our sexual revolution. If we have as much sex as we do thinking it is a sin in the Bible, imagine it was not a sin and sacred prostitution changes the world. All the war and power-hungry people could make love not war.

Otherwise, we are continually disobedient and can't reach God. We always lust and this is considered adultery. Lovers will never know each other. Our Christian culture frowns on physical love and we suffer. The days pass and nothing happens while we wait for our partners. In countries with prostitution, they do not have problems. America seems a little immature about sex and Jesus. This book gives us a bird's eye view of our religion. It helps make clear what we believe.

CHAPTER 56

DOGS AND PUPPIES

When the black gods turned white, they killed all the black gods. Is this not what we do today when we decide whose side God is on? We specialize in racism and people are so used to it in America. We think green Osiris is evil for being Egyptian. The legends of the Bible gods can express themselves like Baal with a Pantheon. All his friends are family and compassionate El (God) is on his throne in Mt. Zaphon.

Now imagine Elijah interacting with his God. If Anat where there or the Phoenicians (Canaanites) had their purple empire remembered, we would have stories of peace. The Bible is stories of war and God participating and helping criminals steal. Our first Pope was crucified on an upside down on a cross as a political criminal. And the church is just after money and keeping us guilty for sex.

These are all the frowning saints and anti-sex art. Outside the churches in Italy are often statues of gods. We accept the gods are idols and wave our second commandment at them. Satan is a serpent in the garden, so Sophia (Wisdom) became the devil and Gnostics are called Satanists. Gnosis means knowledge so the Christians called Wisdom and Knowledge the Devil and Satanists. Doesn't it seem reasonable we would open our minds.

We should be aware the curse is around the world. Pagans and polytheist are replaced with Noah and Moses. It should raise a curiosity that all the saints and angels are white. Demons are often dark or red and horned. The realm of hell that we go to has to do with our actions which come from our beliefs. Jesus said on judgement day he would ask about the least of these. "When did we see you hungry and not feed you?" Jesus says, "As you have done unto the least of these you have done unto me."

With this book we are free from the sexual curses and lies of the Bible. We can stand on our own and read the Gnostic Gospels and study more about Jesus than just the gospels. Polytheism prepares the way for study and the sciences. We can explain things better now than ever before.

Look at the statues of Jesus and consider do we idolize him? This shows nothing bad happened and the church has been making idols for centuries. We know our history and the many saints through Catholic art. If we had the gods back and the Native American beliefs polytheism could break the evil spell of the curse.

Also, Dagon (Dagan) the god of the giants is part of the curse. We assume in Christianity all other beliefs are false. This ignorance of history scars us and gives us reason to believe only on a superficial level. One person goes to hell and the other to heaven based on faith in Christ. I suggest there is no hell since Jesus spoke of Gahanna; the valley they cremated dead bodies in. It would be normal to say, "Let's put Grandma in hell" when she died. This is only destruction of the body. Who would be so cruel as to keep somebody alive in the fire for not believing in them?

Belief is a tricky thing: "Have Faith!" Could mean many things but the question is, "Faith in what? "All of the idols take us to God, but we need their stories. Don't take the Bible for granted but explore it with the knowledge in this book and see the Song of Songs sexually! "Intelligence is reading between the lines." (Alessandro, Bologna). Solomon and Sheba are equals and they are in their own garden. This is as close to the goddess it gets and there are songs to Ishtar and Isis like the Song of Songs.

Imagine the conversations they had in the Kebra Negast. He is sexual so why is he not being punished. The life of Solomon is very interesting to me, and I have always been curious about going to Ethiopia. We must take a bird's eye view on the Bible and see where it hides the kings of the other countries it later calls gods. The Hebrew word for Gods, Elohim, is used by Jesus of the disciples when he called them in English, "Judges." The Gnostic idea of connection to God is deeper than the Constantine Christians who call Jesus God and live by his standards. And reflect his glory only but not the Gnostic sun.

Christianity is just a lifestyle forced on us. The real love of Jesus produced sex and later it was all put together in the time of Constantine. We should not say Jesus is God anymore. We should say, "Jesus is God since Constantine crowned him king." The face of Apollo on the giant statue outside Constantine's Arc is replaced with Constantine. He is our king more than Jesus and we are intellectually weak for not reading the Bible or some other book.

I recommend my first book Nine Days to Healing a Spiritual Pilgrimage and the Nican Mopohua for short reads. The stars of the Tilma of Guadalupe show us the sky at Tepeyac 1531 A.D. when the Spanish came to America. The Nican Mopohua is 218 lines of dialogue between the Virgin Mary of Guadalupe (Tonantzin) and Juan Diego the Talking Eagle. This would be a perfect size for us to study while the Bible is too hard. Keeping track of all the lies is too hard and that is what this book is all about.

The Popul Vuh (The book of the Mayan community) is more interesting to me than the Bible. Once we are familiar with the stories of the Hero Twins (The Sun and Moon) we see all mythology differently. The Bible is a wise book, but we should turn in our Torah's. The hatred toward Isis and then the imitation of her has left us a breadbasket in Virgo. We only know virgin but if we say slut or whore that is to control a woman sexually. This all comes out of man's insecurity with his own sexuality.

We take the hatred out on our ribs and deny them the honor of coming out of a glorious vulva. The man is the mother and the god of the garden. Little Adam controls the world, and it is his wife Eve's fault we are sinners. When you think there are only ten commandments that is not much of an accomplishment. If Love fulfills the law, there is no more Torah and the flood story; we don't know there are 613 commandments so we can't do or not do them!

Since they don't mind ignorance of Talmud and other books used to interpret the Torah, we get screwed. They pass the $3 story of Jesus to us, and the flames of hell turn on. Am I a dog or a puppy? Guadalupe/Tonantizin gives her tzin to Juan Diego and he becomes Juanito Diegito; Juantzin Diegotzin. The tzin is the diminutive and in Aztec the diminutive makes you a Lord. Since the true story of Juan Diego and his wife Maria Lucia is hidden at the place of peyote at Tepeyac (The Peanut Tree; see Nine Days to Healing a Spiritual Pilgrimage). The peyote makes Tonantzin appear at Tepeyac if you go alone.

What Juan Diego (the child in Revelations 12 and first Saint of the Americas) saw was his dead wife Maria Lucia at age fourteen. It was their wedding he saw and then Guadalupe comes into the picture. In the Aztec wedding vows when a man says to a woman "I do." She says, "Buy me a house." You think American women would want to learn this but if you are happy with dinner. Ha ha. Anyway, this is the part of the Nican Mopohua where Guadalupe says, "Build me a house at Tepeyac; tent shaped with seven doors."

The wonderland of Tepeyac is to connect the gods with the Virgin Mary. She knows them but she is not allowed to talk about them. As for me I saw the great clock at Tepeyac; El Carillion, and it has a video cartoon of the Nican Mopohua. This set me up for Tepeyac and I saw a vision of Juan Diego in the Old Basilica.

The stars of the Tilma is my greatest contribution so far. A book marker for Revelations 12 (1531 A.D. 10:20am December 9) And the story of Revelations told in the stars. Draco and Hydra are both on her starry mantel. Leo is pointed toward Virgo and her feet are on the stars of Orion. This positioning gives us ten remaining chapters of Revelations.

Now with hell as our only reasonable motivator we rely on the unseen miracles of Jesus written about him in a story. We know no other God and the Buddha is an idol to the Christian who has the same teaching. The idol of El and the story of El are two different things. They are trying to keep the pagan countries out of our intellectual reach. We think as Christians and interpret things by the only known language that keeps us babbling in Babylon. The fact we haven't figured out Rome is the Babylon that the books of Revelations refer to; the City on Seven Hills, is disgusting. A tiny book like Revelations I can put my Guadalupe book marker in chapter 12 and finish off the Bible.

To be funny I take my Bible and tie it up like Isaac. Before I pull the knife out and stab the dragon's heart, I remember the Greeks sacrifice laugher to Venus. Since I believe in Phoenician El and Baal, I sacrifice the tied-up Bible to Anat. She tells me to stab the heart of the devil and I put the knife in deep. The axe head of Elisha comes up from the deep and the serpent stabs me with laugher.

It's all a joke Satan is a talking serpent and Balaam is a talking donkey. We must raise Jesus to a new level artistically. In Italy it is almost all crucifixes and humble celibate saints. Do we want to live like saints and nuns? In America the people would love to hook up but look at what the church has done to us. We dry up sexually and don't drink from the knowledge of the Gnostics. I believe them because they were first and initially Jesus was a man. The fact Irenaeus calls them Satanist or having orgies show us what we think Satan is. A horny devil not a murderer like God. God in the Bible tempts Eve with a tree. He is the tempter not Eve.

Now we know where the brainwashing comes in with the Bible. Matthew is a good name for a child Beelzebub is not. If we see El and Baal switch places of popularity, is it not the same with Jehovah and Jesus? Baal is Jesus personified and he prays for us. I am always running into a myth of Baal, and he was God up until the men of Jehu killed the ministers of Baal and turned Baal's temple into a urinal.

If we get inside the boot of Italy through Revelations chapters 12 and 22, I will drive us there. Look at the urinal of their God and their Queen Jezebel. We are brainwashed to be racist like the 2,000-year-old dog that Guadalupe/Tonantzin could call doggy or puppy. We saw Jezebel is a woman in the dung, but it is okay since Jehovah does not like Phoenicians (Canaanites). Since we are racist and think she was a whore she is the bad girl. A queen that took money for sex…. they are just bashing her for making an idol of Baal.

When the rain comes down it could be Baal in the Pleiades, making love to his seven wives. Ra kills the serpent daily and we wait for Jesus to kill it at the end of the world. Polytheism is good for me. I have all the saints and angels to, and Jesus is a friend like Abraham was a friend of God. We should all straighten out the relationship of our own fathers by calling Abraham a friend. This is what the Virgin Mary taught me in Bologna. I found my Father but not the one Jesus spoke of.

Now I am on top of the world holding this book instead of the Bible. All the sexual lies the church used to sidetrack me from my career has ruined my life. "Jesus will give you a model wife if you stay virgin." They speak. The whole world believes our God, Jesus is against pre-marital sex. Centuries of talking God's name in vain and bringing his punishment on the world. If you are a man, one day you will see her and want to fuck her. Too bad she was told she would burn in hells eternal flames for pre-marital sex. Now you go pay her and both end up in jail.

America puts sex offenders into three main categories I would like to compare: The John and the Prostitute, rapist, and child molesters. Since the rapist must do your mom, daughter, and sister how do you know he won't do you? America is afraid to let us have our free will. They want to control us. If the rapist and the pedophile do the prostitute our families are not the free whores. Remember he can't pay for it unless he films it with a porn star. Then pre-marital sex is a sin again. So, you put the prostitute in jail where she can't help turn a child molester or protect us from the rapist. What do you expect the rapist, pedophile, and John to do? Whack off? That is a death penalty according to the bullshit Bible and the error in the dictionary.

We must see the irony of one fornicator putting another fornicator in jail. They both had pre-marital sex but one paid with money, so we use our tax money to lock him in a cage and make it hard to get a job when he gets out. Since I have seen prostitution all over Europe, I notice they do not have the whole country lining up. Often, I am the only man in the place and prostitution does not cause chaos.

In Amsterdam a man can travel to his destination. Sample a woman from every country. This heaven on Earth we don't get in America. We are teaching the Bible says sex before marriage is a sin. What do you expect Earth to be like while we assign God's name to the lie of sex? It is only for control, but they have changed the world. We should stop teaching sex in churches period. It is none of their business and since they make pedophilia their business I must come to the rescue with a hot hooker.

All the men stirred up in America cannot get a release and we do not have normal relationships with women. If God kills us for masturbating, we might as well pay a super model for sex. We are very brainwashed in America about sex, and we don't know who to believe. They are so ignorant of the Bible we suffer. People could be healed by Psalms, Proverbs, and Prayer. The awesome works in the Old Testament, excluding the Torah, are great stories.

What we have taken on is the lies of the Roman Catholic Church and called them the only word of God. We don't even know Elohim (Gods) created the world in the Bible. The ancient city of Eridu was a city to the Anunnaki who created the Gods. We are so distorted in history I can't believe historians have not nailed it on the head like I do.

I can explain the Catholic miracles but look at how dark the world gets with the evil shadow of St. Peter. He never understood Jesus and was told: "Get behind me Satan." By Jesus who later leaves Gnosis in the book of John. The seven competitions between Peter and John are called The Other Disciple and the Disciple Jesus Loves. John always beats him, and St John is the Gnostic disciple. Matthew, Mark, and Luke all come from Mark, Peter's disciple. So, it is Gnosis verse Irenaeus since he is the one that fought the Gnostics.

This is a way out for us, and I have mentioned the Book of

Revelations is not accurate or inspired from God. It is created from Daniel just as Jesus and Judas were created from Joseph and Judah. The white men of the Bible at the last supper; whose head is on the chest of Jesus? John and the Other Disciple says to the Disciple That Jesus Loved, 'Ask him who is going to betray him?" John put his head on Jesus' chest and said, "Lord who is going to betray you?"

CHAPTER 57

FEATHERED SERPENT

Quetzalcoatl is a twin or precious serpent associated with Jesus and St Thomas (Twin). Tezcatlipoca is Quetzalcoatl's dark twin. He has an obsidian mirror on the back of his head and one on his foot. He saves Aztec Noah (Tata) from the flood and the two brothers united are Ometeol - Lord of Duality.

The Aztec Quetzalcoatl spread to the Maya and Inca right after the time of Jesus. I see Quetzalcoatl as a mix of the serpent in the garden of Eden and Jesus. Time changes with both the Feathered Serpent and Jesus and their religions spread about the same time. Jesus said he would come back soon and 2000 years or even 2000 more years is not soon.

It is easier to tie the knot with Jesus and Quetzalcoatl with Venus. They are both the Bright Morning Star! In Nine Days to Healing a Spiritual Pilgrimage I go with Julio with the Slippery Shoes to Teotihuacan and Tepeyac. I tell Julio the story of the Holy Grail of Valencia in Spain (see The Lords of The Poison). Near the grail on the wall is a horned Jesus giving the commandments to Moses from the clouds. On the wall is an engraving of the grail with a serpent poking his head out of it. Next to the grail with the serpent is a pistol handle with a crucifix coming out of it.

Julio and I joke and act like we are using our pistols on each other. At **Teotihuacan** I met an evil vendor trying to sell us an obsidian stone for $80 he stole from the gift store. We pointed our imaginary pistols with crucifixes at him. I said to him in Spanish, "Why does **Tezcatlipoca** have an obsidian mirror on the back on his head and one on his foot?" The evil vendor said to me, "Why?" I said to him, "If you look at the back of his head you will see yourself as Quetzalcoatl and if you look at his foot you will see yourself in the grave." The vendor ran away from me flapping his arms when I told him about a sweet riddle from Samson's belly.

We ignore all this technology, and the stories aren't half bad. The constellations tell their stories, and the Gods are real. We carry the customs of the ancients in a superstition. What we define as pleasing to God has a lot to with our sexuality. The church controls us too much and we don't have a choice. This one Bible we believe tells us we cannot study Zeus or Baal.

We have a jealous God who wants ten percent of our income to believe in Jesus and make converts for his business. Now we are all dumb because of so many years listening to the Christian prophets speak for God. We have a long list on sins and laws, but we lack the internal love and compassion.

These culture heroes mark time and the advancement of civilization. We are in a dark age, and we can only see the light when it is pointed directly at our faces. The old tales of the Bible are mostly miracles to us. Somebody kept track of sacred history and we say it is the Word of God instead of the words of God. All this pagan stuff has to do with the real Elohim that went all over the world. Yet we believe only one, the Lord Jesus Christ. All others are devils and false gods.

This calendar and woman Israel (Guadalupe/Tonantzin) from Revelations 12 puts us on the mark. We know when Revelations 12 happened and there are only ten chapters to go. The end of the world is a convenient lie since the church has your money. We will be paid back in heaven and God will bestow on us material gifts. We drag the dead weight of history behind us attaching Jesus to the commandment of no idols or graven images.

The church ignores this, and it has no reason not to since Paul said, "We all know an idol is nothing." When we say pagans worshiped idols, we exclude them immediately, yet Jesus was pieced together out of many of these Pagan Saviors. The whole picture is what I am trying to provide. Seeing Jesus or Jehovah in a pantheon shows us our saviors from other cultures. The riches this book provides us intellectually is overwhelming.

The main commandment we must deal with is idolatry. Protestants don't believe in the image of Jesus, but they use it anyway. We would not know him if he did not look like his image. We are already brainwashed by the church to know only one God and that God was born a man. He was not even born with the Holy Spirit. He got baptized at the age of 30 and the Holy Spirit came upon him as a dove. Then he started doing miracles!

The Gnostic teach we were born with Jesus in us, and he came to wake us up spiritually. The book has been closed for many years and we use the Bible less and less. To think one can, learn the Bible the way they teach it is absurd. They don't even read an entire passage; instead, they make a whole sermon with one verse.

The whole world was one way, polytheistic, and now we only believe in Jesus. His book is supposed to explain the creation of the world. After Jesus dies, they say he created the world, and we think we have this big powerful God from the Old Testament. The prophets talk about the great kings of other countries and especially Ezekiel gets a glimpse at the gods.

We could all be feathery serpents connecting heaven and earth. Astrology is the name of the game and excepting these advanced civilizations as genius. We exclude them and never think the gods or aliens might get angry with us. We call them demons and the Spanish burned expensive manuscripts.

CHAPTER 58

ART SPEAKS

To show how powerful art is let's look at Italy. St. Paul gave Italy the freedom to make art and they stored our history for us. Milan, Venice, Bologna, Florence, Rome, Naples, and Lecce are the seven cities I call the seven heads of Hydra. Water is everywhere and out of the primordial deep comes an axe head with a branch attached to it. The city of seven hills is not Babylon it is Rome. This is the true secret. At St. Marks in Venice, we see the five-foot Ham and the nine-foot-tall Noah. Noah is pointing to Africa and tells him to go. Abraham sent Ishmael away but now Ham is a continent.

Look at the boat driver in Venice and tell him you need a photo of the lion St. Mark. One of the Babylonian deities under the throne of Ezekiel, Nergal, was changed into St, Mark. Many gods are saints even with the Aztec (Nine Days to Healing a Spiritual Pilgrimage). The axe head points towards Baal Hammon and Tanit in Sisley. Also St. Cecilia plays music for Tanit in Ibiza and the seven headed dragon heard of it.

All the world is animated by these gods. When it rains or there is lightening mythology plays a role. The Bible is studied as if it were history. We do not interpret its symbols or see the original myths it was based on as being important. The art of Italy shows we believe in very human saints and whatever looks different is a devil. The gods are considered devils even if they fight the devils. If we went by English names the myths would tell a story like Samson and Delilah.

The hidden giants and fallen angels of the Bible are not talked about in the New Testament. We have a short story with a big piece of history attached. Everybody divides but we still believe the Bible is against sex. This is the only thing they all have in common. We are worried in the Bible about the tribe of Judah lining up with Jesus. Many kings have stories, but we could have studied gods instead. Get a collection of deities from all cultures and get their wisdom.

Osiris was against cannibalism and Quetzalcoatl was against human sacrifice. What did Jesus teach us about love and the law? It seems Jesus returns in avatars, but we do not recognize him or read much. Anybody can learn the lesson and teach it. Where are we with world history? We don't even know it enough to refute the Bible.

The forbidden fruit of sex has us tied up from the beginning. The Catholic Church is above the Bible. They make decisions with their Vatican experts. To see the whole world sad sexually is because we could not develop or reach our potential. To hide sex, they lie about God and take his name in vain. Isn't it hard to believe all religions are wrong but Christianity? If remnants of Jesus and his characteristics are in other cultures, he probably visited them to.

The white names in the Bible are the only acceptable ones to the Christian. We see Babylonian gods and the four disciples in one vision. The gods often look scary, but they are not supposed to be. Even Death is a God that consumes everything. Dagan is a god beyond time, and he is exalted above the Sun. We can't keep explaining away the gods by saying they are fake. There is a whole world of polytheism and history for us to experience.

The gods take us on a journey and help us explore people before us. There are a lot of lumps in history and things we cover up. The job of telling a lie about history is hard but the Bible is no match to a good book on symbolism. Pagan rituals will come up and they will have lessons and stories. We piece together another people the Bible speaks ill of. Idolatry has been going on for hundreds of years. The saints look similar and celibate. To hide sex, we must cover the gods in case they had sex or masturbated.

This white man's celibate journey through life is manifest in

America. We killed the Indians and say they worshiped devils. Pagan is so much more powerful than monotheism since the gods, aliens, and constellations connect. Jesus is a rigid story of virgin births and miracles. We are sinners and Jesus was baptized by John the Baptist. This Elijah and Elisha story confuses many that the Old Testament contains the miracles and everything. They just kept pulling out of the book of Genesis until they had the Bible.

The Bible is capped off with Revelations and we wait for this prophecy to come true. The books of the Bible are no match for my Phoenician alphabet. The ox to the tau is the father to the cross. On the way the twenty-two letters of the Phoenician alphabet tell stories and create names for cities. We must examine everything with the "curse" on it and study the origins of the well-known Bible stories.

EPILOGUE

Now I know more about sex than I ever did before writing this book. The whole world sits still and waits for this message. We are embarrassed and ashamed of sex since the whole world believes in Jesus. We take the slanted road and to keep sex a sin we sacrifice world history and the gods. It is time to grow up mentally and get intellectual background.

We are acting as if our parents are as God. People tell me what God thinks and it is their own father talking. Even if you read the Bible a million times an American is not going to know or care who Father Abraham is. Everything is Jesus in the Bible, and we forgive the sins of the evil Bible heroes.

The Bible is a horrible racist book that brought us Ham and Noah. Americans read the flood story and skip Noah's drunken nudity and slavery on his son Ham. What an evil man Noah must have been. We model ourselves after the well-known Bible character for faith. History is a lie at this point, so you must decide before we curse Ham.

The slavery is impossible to believe Jesus approved but a Canaanite dog told me a story in Bologna. "The puppy is Greek and the dog English." The children of Ham become slaves again. With this book Ham is free and Noah is judged. I declare Africa free in the name of Jesus. Now we go over it again. The whole story added up to "Be nice to people." And "Don't have sex." The party is over in America, and we are going to hell for our own beliefs. No sex on earth and no sex in heaven.

The value of this book is tremendous. It gives us our history back and explains better the mystery of God. I love the Roman Catholic Church and I thank them, but I cannot follow the Other Disciple or bow to his upside-down cross. The fact you tell my country we will burn in hell for premarital sex makes us all hypocrites before God. We believe sex is bad for everybody and we try and do it anyway. Not afraid of hell, are you? We are transformed into monsters that don't get any money for our bodies. We can't touch each other or make each other happy according to the Demon God America worships called Jesus. My teaching and belief are Gnostic, so I do not have to follow the Bible with a blind man guiding me. What we believe is good is evil on so many levels. Christianity has not really produced much, and they just want your money. Go for help or tell them you have a need and see how little they help you.

This is my experience with the church, and I have suffered. I want others to be free from suffering though my books on emotional healing and pilgrimage. The Americans need to travel with their eyes open. I bring back huge souvenirs: Parks, Cathedrals, Temples, Lost Cities, The Atlantis that Plato wrote about, and other sacred places. My books take the reader on a sacred voyage.

This book ministers to everyone on Earth. We all have the curse of Eve, but that curse is our choice. We don't have to believe Moses or his commandments. He copied everything and wrote about himself. As bad as he is he is not as bad as the seven headed dragon of today. In the day of Moses, we could masturbate, have sex, and look at women. It is not until the Roman Catholic Church changed the Bible that all this evil Satan stuff comes out.

I see the heel dipped in honey and it is the heel of the heel catcher and Achilles. What more can I do but deliver my own country Italy to America. We are too afraid to go after the seven headed dragon, so I caught him in the head with an axe. I punch his heart hard and kicked his fucking ass. The devil is dead, and I have the axe of Italy to present to my country America. If I am Michael, I am Michael the Arc Angel.

Printed in the United States
by Baker & Taylor Publisher Services